Profession

XSLT

The Ultimate Guide to Transforming Web Data

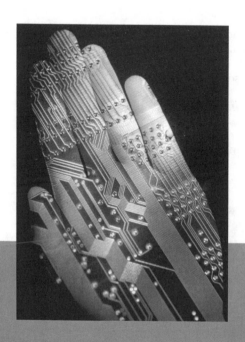

Johan Hjelm

Peter Stark

Wiley Computer Publishing

John Wiley & Sons, Inc.

NEW YORK · CHICHESTER · WEINHEIM · BRISBANE · SINGAPORE · TORONTO

Publisher: Robert Ipsen
Editor: Carol A. Long
Assistant Editor: Adaobi Obi
Managing Editor: Angela Smith
Associate New Media Editor: Brian Snapp
Text Design & Composition: D&G Limited, LLC

Library of Congress Cataloging-in-Publication Data:

Hjelm, Johan.
    XSLT: professional developer's guide / Johan Hjelm, Peter Stark.
        p. cm. — (Professional developer's guide series)
    Includes bibliographical references and index.
    ISBN 0-471-40603-1 (pbk. : alk. paper)
        1. XSLT (Computer program language) I. Stark, Peter, 1972– II. Title. III. Series.

    QA76.73.X58 H54 2001
    005.7'2—dc21

                                                            2001045450

Printed in the United States of America.

10 9 8 7 6 5 4 3 2 1

Professional Developer's Guide Series

Other titles in the series:

Contents

PREFACE

It seems that new programming languages are appearing everyday, but few are as useful as XSLT, which, strictly speaking, is not a programming language, but a transformation language. The reason is that XSLT is designed to take XML input and turn it into other text formats. As the world of XML continues to grow, so does the use and usefulness of XSLT. Whatever use you can imagine for XML, there is a corresponding application of XSLT.

By foregoing many of the features of traditional programming languages, XSLT trades off versatility for powerfulness. You will not write HTML browsers in XSLT (although people have written parsers for different XML applications). On the other hand, you do not have to worry about memory management. That is taken care of by the program that executes the XSLT transformation.

XSLT is not a scripting language. It is more like a batch process description language. But it does not matter when you use it. Transformations are really simple to create. Even nonprogrammers can do it.

XSLT really shines when it is used to create a device-independent representation of a Web site. Write once, show many is an actual reality. We try to show you how in Chapter 8, and try to go through as many other interesting functions as possible in the rest of the book. Showing how to do it is the simplest way of teaching programming, and we have tried to give as many examples as we could in this book.

Who Is This Book for?

The reader of this book is probably a programmer, working with scripting languages like PERL or JavaScript. You want to widen your horizons and understand how your company can use XSLT in its Web sites and services. Or you may be a consultant and interested in finding out how you can enhance your customers' sites. After reading this book, you should be able to use the most frequent functions of XSLT, and experiment with more advanced ways of applying it.

What Is on the CD?

On the CD that comes with this book are all the code examples. There are also several XSLT processors, a couple of XSLT editors and tools, and some other useful things. These are either freeware or trial versions.

CHAPTER 1

An XML-Based Web

T he *World Wide Web* (WWW) contains a massive amount of information. Most information on the Web is marked up in *Hypertext Markup Language* (HTML), which enables Web browsers to display the information. But there are surveys that indicate that 70 percent of all HTML markup has errors. With the HTML markup the information is divided up into headers, paragraphs, lists, links, and other structural elements that we consider to make up a document. The browsers use the markup to present the document according to its internal rules about how headers, paragraphs, lists, and links look like. What is missing in this model is information about what kind of information is contained inside the headers and paragraphs of the document. All the HTML markup tells us is that the following text is a paragraph, not whether it is an address, a receipt, or a fragment from a best-selling novel. Here is a typical HTML paragraph:

```
<p>John Wiley & Sons, Inc. </p>
<p>www.wiley.com/compbooks/</p>
```

The <p> elements don't indicate what kind of information they contain. The browser presents them as any other paragraphs. The fact that they actually represent a name and a Web address is not available to the browser, or to the user who is viewing the document. Consider what we can do with XML:

```
<address>
<name>John Wiley & Sons, Inc.</name>
<www> www.wiley.com/compbooks/</www>
</address>
```

We defined our own elements that represent the kind of information we want to describe, instead of just saying where in the document structure it fits in. This is the power of XML over plain HTML.

Most content on the Web–in terms of pages, if not in number of servers—comes from databases, and is presented as HTML only as a convenience. Since a database is a structured format, using XML as an intermediary format to the presentation comes naturally. This is especially true if the information is going to be used in several different presentations.

Now that we have used XML to indicate what kind of information the document contains, how does the browser know how to present our markup? All browsers know how to present HTML markup. Browsers don't know how to present the <address> element that we just invented.

There are two ways:

1. Use Cascading Style Sheets (CSS). In the style sheet, you declare how each element should be presented (for instance, <address> should be 40 points Times Roman Bold). The style sheet for the document can be stored in a separate file, and used for other documents that contain the same elements. A characteristic of CSS is that the style rules never change the actual markup. Style rules are added as a layer above the markup.
2. Use XSLT to transform the markup into something that is known to all browsers; for example, HTML.

The following example is part of a language for describing mobile telephones, expressed in XML:

```
<phone>
     <manufacturer>Ericsson</manufacturer>
<model>R320</model>
     <network>GSM 900</network>
</phone>
```

The meaning of these element names is not defined by XML but is declared separately in a document called the *Document Type Description* (DTD) or an XML schema (which is another type of document).

Both of these tell which data types the elements can be, in which order they should come, which elements can be contained in other elements, and so on. The author of the document can define a DTD, or he or she can use a predefined DTD.

A DTD (or a schema) enables you to declare what an element name should mean, but it has to be done within a set of rules. The benefit of XML is that it represents an agreement about what an element is and where the < and > should go and a few other things such as how to find out the character encoding of the document. It does not sound like much, and in fact, it is not very much: The XML specification is very brief. But it is what it takes to make two computers on the Web read the same document without protests. When the XML processor reads the XML document, it passes up the element names and their content to an application that understands their meaning (or at least can present the information on a screen or on paper).

Before XML, there was no common agreement on how to mark up information. The markup (the elements and the attributes) adds information to the data (what is inside the elements). With XML, the Web has a universal data format that can represent everything from documents to the primitives of a communication protocol.

XML is, despite claims that you might sometimes see, not intended to represent all types of information. Not all data can be represented as an XML tree, either, because not all data has the required structure. It is quite possible to represent an image as XML. (There is nothing that says that the content of elements has to be text, although the element names have to be.) But given the success of XML on the Web, the simple tree structure with elements and attributes seems to be capable of describing most types of data. We will look more at XML in Chapter 2, "XML Technologies: XML, XHTML, and WML."

The Web and its infrastructure are full of XML documents, and they are proliferating because XML enables authors of DTDs to create their own applications. An XML application is nothing but a way to describe an information set. Descriptions can be quite varied, depending on who creates them—and the same situation applies to XML markup. A mobile phone can be classified by its network and manufacturer, as we did previously. But in an inventory application, the main thing might not be the manufacturer but instead the package. It might be classified by the battery duration or by any other attribute that it might have. What the XML elements describe might depend on what the author perceives as important at the moment.

The Case for Transformations

With so much data on the Web expressed as XML, there will be a repeated need to change XML documents and not just the trivial cases described previously. There is a need to change the structure, to change the names of the nodes, and to insert or remove content. There are a number of reasons for these needs:

- To present documents that are represented in an in-house XML document type in a browser that can not handle that specific markup language.

- To present the information in a Web browser, a *Wireless Access Protocol* (WAP) browser, or as plain text, the private format of the XML document must first be changed into HTML, *Wireless Markup Language* (WML), or plain text. The process of transforming the XML documents into the language that the presentation device supports is called styling.

- To upgrade XML documents to a newer document type with richer functionality. A Web author who was on the cutting edge in 1998 and created Web services for mobile phones will have lots of useless WML 1.0 documents lying around and will want to upgrade to a new WML version that is supported by at least one mobile phone on the Web.

- To support the multiple XML-based schema languages. Most developers need to use one but still want to be able to change their schemas into a different schema language.

These use cases are common and will be more common in the near future. Today, most users are using PCs to browse the Web, but in Japan, 30 million subscribers are using mobile telephones with the iMode system, which uses a special version of HTML. In Europe and in the rest of Asia, manufacturers have released mobile phones using WML, which is an XML application, to present data. Market figures point to a prolific use of mobile phones with Internet access (to the tune of several hundred million dollars in the next few years). It will not be long before mobile phones have overtaken the PC as the default Web browsing device. Television sets are also becoming Web enabled, as well as more exotic equipment such as microwave ovens and refrigerators having Internet access. And DoCoMo (the company behind iMode) as well as WAP Forum (the organization creating WML) have decided that future versions of their systems will be based on XHTML.

With Web-enabled mobile phones and TVs, there is an increased need for tools that style the same XML document for different types of presentations. And there will be an increasing number of applications where the result is not presentation but input to another program. XML has not only established itself as the default data format of the Web, but it has also established itself as the favorite format for data exchange (for instance, between different database applications). Where there once was one document type, HTML, there are now many document types. The number of markup languages on the Web increases. More languages mean more versions and variants to keep track of—and transform between.

Enter XSLT

If you have a document in an XML format and want to transform it into other XML formats, you need some way of describing how the original format is similar and different from the format into which you want to transform the document. The XSLT language is used to express rules for how an XML document should be changed, transformed, renamed, and filtered. Each rule identifies a set of nodes from the source XML document and then describes which rules should be applied to those nodes; for example, move this element here, change the name of that element, add this text, and so on. The rules are contained in a document called the transformation sheet (or style sheet), a name that has historic origins. We use transformation sheet and style sheet interchangeably in this book.

The transformation sheet, together with the original document, is the input to an XSLT processor, which generates the output document. The result of a transformation does not have to be an XML document, however. It can be plain text, HTML, or any other data types that can be described in XSLT. As long as they have a structure and that structure can be transformed into some other structure, you can use XSLT to transform the document.

For simple transformations, XSLT is simple—and a transformation sheet can be written by hand in a text editor such as EMACS or Windows Notepad. For complicated transformations, an XSLT authoring tool is recommended. XSLT performs much the same functions as other scripting languages, like PERL and ECMAscript (that used to be called Javascript). It is, however, designed especially to process XML. While it is a full-fledged programming language and has been used to write advanced software, it is optimized to transform content from XML to other formats.

Again, consider the following XML document that can then be outputted from a database (a serialization of a relational database table where the element names are the names of the columns and the values are the values in the fields):

```
<phone>
     <manufacturer>Ericsson</manufacturer>
<model>R320</model>
     <network>GSM 900</network>
</phone>
```

Now, we want to translate this information into an HTML table that looks like the following:

```
<table xmlns="http://www.w3.org/1999/xhtml">
<tr><th>Manufacturer</th><td>Ericsson</td></tr>
<tr><th>Model</th><td>R320</td></tr>
<tr><th>Network</th><td>GSM 900</td></tr>
</table>
```

Here is the transformation sheet that will perform this action:

```
<table xmlns="http://www.w3.org/1999/xhtml"
       xmlns:xsl="http://www.w3.org/1999/XSL/Transform">
     <tr>
          <th>Manufacturer</th>
          <td><xsl:value-of select="/phone/manufacturer" /></td>
     </tr>
     <tr>
          <th>Model</th>
          <td><xsl:value-of select="/phone/model" /></td>
     </tr>
     <tr>
          <th>Network</th>
          <td><xsl:value-of select="/phone/network" /></td>
     </tr>
</table>
```

When the XSLT processor processes the transformation sheet, the xsl:value-of element selects an element from the source XML document, takes the text from inside the element, and outputs the text as the result. The HTML elements are copied to the output stream as unchanged. The resulting document is, as expected, an XHTML table that has the same values as the XML document:

```
<table xmlns="http://www.w3.org/1999/xhtml">
<tr><th>Manufacturer</th><td>Ericsson</td></tr>
<tr><th>Model</th><td>R320</td></tr>
<tr><th>Network</th><td>GSM 900</td></tr>
</table>
```

The xmlns attributes and the xsl prefixes are part of XML namespaces and are essential for a transformation sheet to work. We will return to the topic of XML names later, but because they are such an essential part of XSLT, here is a short explanation.

A namespace is just a set of names that can be arbitrary. The set has a unique name, identified by the *Uniform Resource Indicator* (URI), as shown earlier. One way of thinking about this concept is that the URI anchors the namespace. Because all URIs are unique (they are unique because they are based on the Domain Name System, or DNS, a central registry that assures that Internet domains do not occur in different places), the names in the namespace will also be unique. In the transformation sheet that we showed earlier, the xmlns:xsl attribute declares that all names that are prefixed with xsl belong to the XSLT namespace. The xmlns attribute declares that all names that do not have prefixes belong to the HTML namespace. Because namespaces have unique names, it is possible for the XSLT processor to distinguish between the names that are part of the XSLT language and the names that are part of the XML documents that the transformation sheet is going to transform from and to.

Why XML and Not C?

We will look more closely at how a transformation takes place and will examine the XSLT language more in Chapter 3, "Simple Transformations." But as you might have noted, the XSLT language, which is used to transform XML documents, is itself expressed in XML. A transformation sheet is an XML document. In other words, if you use an XML editor to edit the documents that you need to transform, you can use the same editor to also edit the transformation sheet. Also, as we saw in the example, XSLT language constructs (for example, the xsl:value-of element) can be embedded into an XML document. In other words, you can transform transformation sheets. It is all XML.

It is not necessary to use XSLT to transform XML documents. It is possible to write a C or Java program or to use your favorite script language to perform all of the transformations described previously without using XSLT. Most programming languages today have standard libraries that you can use to change XML documents. So, why use XSLT? Why learn a new language?

As more and more information is stored as XML, the need for tools to create and change XML documents increases. As the need increases, it spreads from advanced developers that use C or Java every day to HTML authors and people who do not want to learn a complete programming language just to make a simple change in a few XML documents.

Not everyone is familiar with programming languages such as C or Java. And, using any of these languages—even for a very simple transformation—requires that the developer must pay attention to more concepts than the transformation itself: memory management, variables, compilation, and all of the concepts that come with it. Because you are reading this book, you are either not satisfied with using C or Java or script to change XML documents or you are not an expert in those fully fledged programming languages.

The XML transformation sheet, as we noted earlier, is also an XML document. In other words, it can be managed by using the same mechanisms and tools that you use to manage your other XML documents. If you just have a few files, you might not need anything except the file system and the Web server to handle your document management. But if you have many documents and use a content-management system, you will recognize the advantage of being able to handle all documents by using the same system.

When to Use XSLT

What XSLT provides is a simple tool for performing simple actions. Here is a summary of what a transformation sheet can do:

- **Change the structure of the XML document.** This function might mean changing the place of elements, inserting new elements, and removing elements. If in a new version of a document type a new element with more functionality has replaced an old one, it is easy to transform the old document to the new one.

- **Name elements and attributes**. This action might mean to map names from one namespace into another. Or, one company might call paragraphs "paragraphs" while another company calls them "p" and a third company calls them "para." A simple transformation sheet can change the vocabulary into the desired one. It is also possible to rename elements to attributes.

- Fragment one XML document into several smaller ones.

In practice, the transformations that can be done to an XML document depend on how much structure the document has. In a document that has a pronounced structure, where almost every character is inside its own element and attributes, a transformation sheet has many places to "hook into" and change. In a document that has a sparse structure, however (perhaps just one element with text inside), there is not much that a transformation sheet can do. As a rule, it is easy to transform "down" from much structure into less structure, but it is difficult to transform "up."

As we described previously, the formatting of the output does not have to be associated with the elements. There are other types of meanings, however, that can be associated with the element name. Some XML languages contain element types that are associated with semantic meaning. The WML language that is used for *Wireless Access Protocol* (WAP) phones has element types that represent complex logic that must be executed when the element is processed by the application (WAP browser). Element types that come with a heavy baggage of logic cannot, without losing functionality on the way, be transformed into another element from a different language unless that other element has equivalent or more functionality as the original. It is easy to transform "dumb" XML documents that have little semantics in them into documents that have many semantics. The opposite is, however, difficult.

XSLT is unidirectional. Transformations are not reversible. This concept is something that you need to consider—not when writing transformation sheets, but when writing the content and selecting the markup language that you will use for the original content.

Style Sheets and XSL

As we mentioned in the introduction, one of the advantages of XML is the separation of the markup and the formatting. For online formatting of documents, the advantage is the association of element names with formatting through a *Cascading Style Sheet* (CSS). CSS is the most popular style sheet language on the Web and is intended for lightweight formatting of documents, which means that the formatting can be adapted to different presentation devices.

CSS is much less capable than XSL, the other formatting language of the W3C, but is easier to learn. XSL consists of two pieces: XSLT and XSL-FO (formatting objects, which are used to format an XML document with XSL). A CSS style sheet cannot change the structure of the source document or rename any of the names; rather, it can only format the presentation. Actually, CSS can do very little of what XSLT can do but is implemented in several browsers (although the quality of the implementation varies), which means that it is more suited for on-screen display formatting than XSL. XSLT and CSS are often used together. The classic use case is to transform a data-centric XML document into an HTML document plus a CSS style sheet. You can change links to style sheets in a document by using XSLT.

One special scenario of styling use is to use XSLT to transform an XML document into formatting objects, as defined by the *XSL Formatting Objects* (XSL-FO) language. Originally, XSL Transformation and XSL Formatting Objects were one language called XSL. But as the work on XSL progressed, the transformation part was factored out and became XSLT. What was left of XSL was the definition of the formatting objects. This information explains the origin of the name, XSLT, or XSL Transformations.

CSS is not written in an XML-based language because it was defined before XML existed. In other words, CSS style sheets are not XML documents. They cannot be handled with the same tools as other XML documents—something that is a disadvantage if you are trying to create a consistent data environment.

If you want to do more advanced formatting of the document (for instance, format it as a book that will be printed), you will want to look at transformations into XML-based formatting. XSL demands more in terms of processing power and is more suited for use on large documents (for instance, manuals that are to be printed from an electronic storage format).

We will talk more about CSS and XSL Formatting Objects in Chapter 8, "XSLT and Style." But now, we will look more at the XML technologies behind XSLT.

XML Technologies: XML, XHTML, and WML

There are many other benefits of XML over HTML. Not only that you, as the author, can define your own markup, but XML has syntactical rules that makes it more robust and safer as a language. With XML it is easier to check whether the document is complete and syntactically correct—a sure benefit for many e-commerce applications. Because we can define any markup we want as XML, it is of course possible to define all the well-known HTML elements as XML. This is what the World Wide Web Consortium (W3C) has done, and called it XHTML. So HTML and XHTML is actually the same language, but XHTML, being an XML language, has a more strict syntax.

An XML document can be seen as a tree, where the root is the top element, and the branches are the other elements nested in it (we will cover this at some length in Chapter 4, "Xpath"). In an XML document, the information tree consists of a set of nodes of different types. The most common types of nodes are elements and attributes. Each element has a name and can contain a set of other element nodes or plain text. An element consists of two tags: a start tag and an end tag. The difference from HTML is that there are no end tags in many HTML elements (those that were introduced before HTML 4). <p> is perfectly valid HTML markup, but in an XML-based markup language, you have to use both the start and end tags to describe the element. A paragraph in

XHTML, the XML version of HTML, has to be written as <p></p>. Otherwise, the computer has no way of knowing where the paragraph ends.

An element can have attributes, which are written inside the start tag <p class="paragraph"></p>. Each attribute has a name and a value. Usually, the element name gives a hint about what type the element is and says something about what kind of data is inside the content of the element, and the attribute values say something about the element itself. Programs that will affect the document in some way (for instance, an XSLT transformation) can use this information.

With XML, companies and organizations on the Web have a common markup language that can be extended to support their own needs. A book publishing company may use XML to markup books. A mobile phone manufacturer may use XML to markup information about the phones. *Extensible Markup Language* (XML) is a universal data format. XML is a rule set for defining markup languages (called XML applications). In a markup language, you do not actually work with the data itself; rather, you create elements that have contents (which are the actual data) and work with them. The structures of the documents are expressed through the nesting of the elements. The content of the elements can be almost anything because this content does not affect the workings of the XML application itself. For instance, SMIL, the Synchronized Multimedia Integration Language, is an XML application that is used to handle multimedia data, that is, synchronize and integrate presentations of video, audio, text, and images.

XML can be used to mark up almost any information. Today, XML is used to describe the primitives of communication protocols, documents, multimedia presentations, images, and the state of a computer system, user interfaces, and much more. There is no central registry according to the principle of the Web and the Internet that there should not be a central point of control. So there is no one central place where information about XML applications can be found. Without a central authority that controls the birth of new XML applications, there is a risk that two or many applications use the same element name to mean different things. To avoid naming conflicts, XML supports a simple namespace mechanism. More about this in the section about namespaces later in this chapter.

Almost every data model that can be expressed in XML can be represented as a tree. An XML document contains a tree of elements. Each element has an element type name and zero or many attributes, and each attribute consists of a name and a value. Let's again look at the example with the phone description:

```
<phone>
    <manufacturer>Ericsson</manufacturer>
<model>R320</model>
    <network>GSM 900</network>
</phone>
```

Elements have relationships with each other that will be familiar to anyone who has worked with object-oriented programming. The manufacturer, model, and network elements are called children of the phone element, which then becomes the parent of these elements. In terms of the tree, as the tree branches out, the leaves and twigs become children of the branches. Elements that are on the same level in the documents are called siblings. In this example, the phone element is also the root of the XML document.

The start and end tags are together called an element, and elements can have attributes, as well, as in the following example:

```
<phone type="mobile">
    <manufacturer type="name"
identifier="brand">Ericsson</manufacturer>
<model type="name"
model_reference="manufacturer_reference">R320</model>
      <network type="string" network_type="ITU_definition">GSM
900</network>
</phone>
```

Attributes can be used to enhance the data, like in the previous example, where they declare what type the content of the different elements is. There can be multiple attributes of one element, and the content of the element and the values of the attributes are to a very large degree interchangeable. The name of the elements and the attributes, what data types they can contain, and the structure into which they can be combined (in other words, which elements can be parents and which can be children) are together called a document type and are defined in a *Document Type Definition* (DTD). The DTD is actually not an XML document, however, because the mechanism was inherited from SGML. This situation can cause problems if you are trying to find consistent ways of dealing with data sets, because you cannot use the same tools to work with DTDs as with the XML documents themselves. This situation is one reason why the W3C created XML schemas. Another reason was to create better descriptions of the data (because the DTD enables a very limited set of data types, for instance). The schema language of XML Schema can also be used to describe names and structures—in essence, declaring what element structures are allowed.

Elements can be nested in other elements, creating a structure within the document. This structure is mandatory for an XML document that has to have a root element in which the other elements are nested. A document cannot be in XML without having this structure.

When a program or a human being checks whether the names and the structure of a document matches that in the DTD, that process is called validation. An application that checks whether a particular document breaks any of the rules in the DTD and the XML specification is called a validating XML parser. An application that does not validate the document is, not surprisingly, called a non-validating XML parser. Both types of parsers check that the document follows the basic rules that make the XML document different from plain text and other data formats (the number of < must be equal to the number of > and so forth).

A well-formed document satisfies all of the requirements of the XML format (but does not have to be valid). A document that is not well formed is not an XML document. An XML document does not actually have to be valid to be used, but it must be well formed. Otherwise, the parser will stop and will throw an error.

There are two ways to declare the elements and attributes of an XML document. The first is the DTD, which is used to associate an XML document with a document type. This function is performed at the start of the document. A document is an instance of a document type, which is defined with a DTD. This relation is similar to the relation between an interface and an object:

```
<!DOCTYPE html PUBLIC "-//W3C//DTD XHTML Basic 1.0//EN"
"xhtml-basic10.dtd">
<html>
(É)
</html>
```

The string after the word PUBLIC is a global identifier that identifies the DTD. It can be used by an application that has the DTD built-in and that does not have to read the DTD from the specified file; in this example, xhtml-basic10.dtd.

When you create an XML application, you create an information model that accurately describes your information set instead of using an all-purpose model or one developed for some other purpose (the problem that has plagued the artificial intelligence, or AI industry). This model is expressed in the DTD or the XML schema—a document that describes the elements in an XML language. In the DTD or the XML schema, you specify a set of elements that will contain your information, declare which rules they have to follow, and give them names that are globally unique (which is possible because you are using the global URI naming system). XML makes sure that all new languages follow the same basic rules (if this process sounds confusing, you can play football, rugby, and soccer on the same field, but the rules for how and when you can use the field are the same, and you have teams that use a ball and score goals in all of the games). Belonging to a family of common rules enables you to transform one XML language into another (by using XSLT, which is another standard in the XML family), and it enables you to write software that can work with the markup without having to be rewritten for each new markup language with which you want to work. It is impossible to say how many different types of XML applications there are, because there is no central registry (indeed, one of the central ideas for XML is that there should not be a central registry, although several organizations have undertaken to register XML applications in their domains).

It is not necessary to have a DTD in order to write XML documents. And, whether it is necessary to validate the document, if you have a DTD, depends on the situation in which the document is used. The following example shows a DTD for the XML document in the phone example that we have been using:

```
<!ELEMENT phone (model, network)>
<!ELEMENT model (#PCDATA)>
<!ELEMENT network (#PCDATA)>
<!ELEMENT manufacturer (#PCDATA)>
```

How to create a good DTD deserves its own book. So we will not further go into any DTD adventures. That does not mean that we do not care about the DTD, only that the whole area of developing a good DTD is out of scope for a book on XSLT. Still, you need to know what DTD is and what it looks like. Ultimately, transformations of XML documents can be seen as transformations between DTDs (because you are replacing one markup structure with another). For practical purposes, however, we do not need to go that deep into the specifics of DTDs. It is enough that you know that it exists.

Because the DTD is an SGML document, it cannot be handled with XML tools. But the W3C has created another format, XML Schema, which can be used to describe the document format you are using. It fulfills the same functions as the DTD, but it is an XML format (and somewhat modernized). Since XML Schemas are XML documents, they can be transformed using XSLT–for instance, into DTDs. We will look a little more at how to transform an XML Schema into other formats in Chapter 7, "XSLT and Document Structure: Databases, DOM, and XML Schema."

The character set in the element names, attribute names, and attribute values of an XML document is always Unicode or a subset of Unicode, such as UTF-16 (the data itself can be binary). The first octets of the document always indicate the character encoding. An XML document does not rely on an external type system to indicate the character encoding.

Unicode is a character-encoding system that was originally developed in cooperation with a number of international standards organizations but is now developed and maintained by a consortium of organizations and companies (the Unicode consortium). It is a 16-bit format, which means that there is space for almost all characters that are used in writing systems today (almost, because Chinese actually has an enormous number of characters if you start looking at the unusual ones). The character encoding that was originally used on the Web, 7-bit ASCII, does not have space to encode more than the 26 letters of the Latin alphabet in lower and upper case, plus some special characters. This situation causes a problem for languages that use accented characters and umlauts (such as the ö, ä, and å, which are characters of the native Swedish of the writers), and it is an enormous headache for the Japanese, who have several mutually incompatible encodings in 7-bit ASCII of their rich character set. (Japanese actually uses three different sets of characters in writing, plus the letters of the Latin alphabet. But that definitely merits its own book, and we will not go into it now.)

As the Web (actually, the MIME types that are used to carry the information of the Web) has developed, character encodings in other formats have been brought in to enable non-English languages to use the system (first, Latin-1, which is an 8-bit encoding of the Latin alphabet; then UTF-8 and UTF-16, both of which have been defined as subsets of Unicode).

Because Unicode does actually contain most of the characters that are in use today, it is possible to have element names in XML that are not in English or that even use Latin letters. In other words, it is quite possible to have a Japanese document that has Japanese element names, for instance. If documents are to be used by an international audience, however, the fallback language is English, and that is also what (in reality) is used in most element names. If the document is not to be read by humans, however, any bit string will do. Computers cannot perceive meaning.

Different DTDs can be used to create different XML applications, such as XHTML, WML, and XSLT.

XML, HTML, and SGML

Like HTML, XML makes use of tags (words bracketed by < and >) and attributes (of the form *name="value"*), but while HTML specifies what each tag and attribute means (and often how the text between them will look in a browser), XML uses the tags only to delimit pieces of data and leaves the interpretation of the data completely to the application that reads it. The XML specification specifies neither semantics nor a tag set. In other words, if you see <p> in an XML file, do not assume that it is a paragraph. In fact, XML is really a meta-language for describing markup languages. In other words, XML provides a facility to define tags and the structural relationships between them. This information goes into the DTD or the XML schema. Because there is no predefined tag set, there cannot be any preconceived semantics. All of the semantics of an XML document will either be defined by the applications that process them or by style sheets. RDF, the Resource Description Framework, is an application that adds semantics to XML (actually, RDF Schema adds the semantics).

Development of XML started in 1996, and it has been a W3C recommendation since February 1998. SGML was developed in the early 1980s and has been an *International Standards Organization* (ISO) standard since 1986. XML is defined as an application profile of the *Standard*

Generalized Markup Language (SGML) defined by ISO 8879, but it is also defined as an application of itself. DTDs express the XML application as an application of SGML and XML schemas as an application of XML. XML is, roughly speaking, a restricted form of SGML. The designers of XML simply took the best parts of SGML, guided by the experience with HTML, and produced something that is no less powerful than SGML.

XML is different from HTML in many more ways than being an application profile of SGML. It uses Unicode, which is a 16-bit format for representing almost all characters that are being used all over the world (it was really intended to be used for all characters, but there are some that are not mapped into the character set, mostly in Japanese and traditional Chinese writing—although the most frequently used characters are covered). HTML up to version 4.0, on the other hand, used 7-bit ASCII as its least common denominator. The reason why HTML used 7-bit ASCII is the same as for mail systems, where some older mail servers are not equipped to handle modern character sets. 7-bit ASCII misses many characters that are important to people outside the United States, however, such as inflections, accents, and umlauts, and it is very complicated to represent Chinese and Japanese characters. This situation is one reason for using Unicode: it is possible to parse all XML content by using the same parsers, regardless of the language in which the content is written. URIs, however, which identify the resources, still have to be 7-bit ASCII on the insistence of the *Internet Engineering Task Force* (IETF). And the URI encoding excludes some characters, as well.

Writing XML is also different from HTML in that it requires that the elements—the combination of start and end markup tags—be closed. Open-ended tags such as <P> are not allowed; rather, they have to be closed, such as <p> . . . </p> (and element names must be in lower case, according to the XML convention——although technically, they could as well be upper case). Elements can either be structured with a start and end tag (<tag> content </tag>) or as an empty element with the end tag included in the start tag (<tag/>). The first type is elements with content, and the second is elements with no content (used for elements with attributes only). Figure 2.1 shows an XSLT document in an XML editor.

In XML, as in HTML 4.0, it is possible to have attributes on markup. Attributes are placed inside the start tag, so <start beginning="now"> means that the element start has an attribute name of *beginning* and an

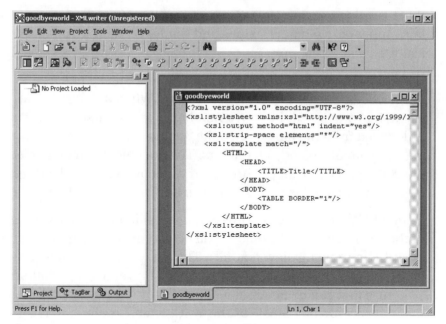

Figure 2.1 An XSLT document in an XML editor.

attribute value that is *now*. The attribute value must be in quotes. Attributes, though, have a much larger role to play in XML than in HTML. They also play a very large role in RDF.

Element names describe what the element is about while attributes provide further information (which can be used in the processing of the content or the application). Attribute values give you control over the element, but the element drives the application. You can, for instance, define an alternate representation, when it should be used, and in what ways (you recognize the alt element from HTML). This function can be used to facilitate transformations, to control how the content is applied, and to do many other things. Note, however, that in applications such as *Wireless Markup Language* (WML), the interpretation in the device is very restricted, and you cannot use attributes as you like.

XML is case-sensitive, so Creator, creator, CREATOR, and cREATOR are interpreted as four totally different elements. Putting element names in lower case is the existing best practice (so creator, not Creator), but the practice that has developed is also to use capitalization in elements where it increases readability (documentCreator, not documentcreator, for instance), something called the interCap convention. The important thing is to watch this capitalization very carefully, because you cannot take upper-case element names and render them in lower-case automatically.

HTML browsers normally render a document line by line as it is received at the client. The XML model is different. When a document arrives at a client, it is processed through a number of steps. First, the character data is decoded from the binary encoding that is used over the network, creating a stream of Unicode characters. The document is then parsed; that is, the XML processor steps through the document and identifies the elements that it contains and determines how they should be handled.

Unlike HTML documents, XML documents do not have to be structured in the order that they should be displayed or processed (you might not want them to be displayed at all). That they are ordered as they should be processed, instead of as they should be rendered, results in a tree structure that can be manipulated by programs and scripts via the *Document Object Model* (DOM) of the W3C, which essentially is an *Application Programming Interface* (API) to the data in the document. There have been discussions about APIs for RDF, but so far, there do not seem to be any winners.

To further confuse things, an XML document actually has two different object structures. Each XML document has both a logical and a physical structure. Physically, the document is composed of units called entities. An entity can refer to other entities in order to cause their inclusion in the document (an inline reference). A document begins in a root or document entity. Logically, the document is composed of declarations, elements, comments, character references, and processing instructions—all of which are indicated in the document by explicit markup. The logical and physical structures must nest properly within each other.

A document has to contain one or more elements. There must be one element, called the root or document element, that does not appear in the content of any other element. The document entity serves as the root of the entity tree and as a starting point for an XML processor. For all other elements, if the start tag is in the content of another element, the end tag is in the content of the same element. More simply stated, the elements, delimited by start and end tags, nest properly within each other. (Figure 2.2 illustrates the relationships between some of the many XML applications that exist.)

XHTML

Most of the documents on the Web today are HTML documents. HTML is not XML. Instead, the documents are SGML documents, which might look like XML from a distance but are more complicated (some would even say more powerful). In reality, very few people understand all of the ins and outs of SGML, and to become useful, it had to be simplified. When Tim Berners-Lee started creating the World Wide Web, he decided that HTML should be an application of SGML because he intended it to have the structured features of SGML.

Once XML had become a W3C recommendation, work began to create a new HTML based on XML instead of on SGML. HTML had developed quite extensively since the first version was presented in 1991, and HTML 4.0 represents a full-blown markup language with elements and attributes that enable content management through the markup.

The new version of HTML, a rendering of HTML 4.01 in XML, is called XHTML and is defined in the W3C Recommendation "XHTML 1.0." There are no new functions in XHTML compared to HTML 4.0, but all elements, attributes, and everything in XHTML 1.0 are defined in HTML 4.01 (which, in turn, merely contains corrections to HTML 4.0 and does not have any new functions). The expectation is that XML will be adopted as the universal data format on the Web, and because HTML is the most common type of data, XHTML fits better into this architecture than HTML. Languages that use XML as the data format are said to be applications of XML. So, XHTML is an application of XML. Figure 2.2 illustrates the relationships between the different modules of XHTML.

Many document editing programs still produce HTML, but if the HTML is correctly written, it is relatively easy to transform it into XHTML. You

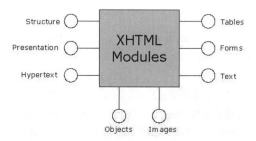

Figure 2.2   The relationship between different modules in XHTML.

cannot perform this action by using XSLT, however, because HTML is not an XML application. But if you write your documents in XHTML, you can transform them into different HTML variants (for instance, Compact HTML, which is used in the older Japanese iMode phones) by using XSLT.

Wireless Markup Language (WML)

One of the first XML applications was WML. So, WML and XHTML have XML in common. When WML was defined as an XML application back in early 1998, the XML recommendation had just been released and many of the related XML specifications that followed were naturally never adopted by WML.

Wireless Markup Language (WML) is defined by the WAP Forum, not by the W3C. WAP is an abbreviation of Wireless Application Protocol, and it was developed to be used with microbrowsers in mobile devices, which the forum standardizes. It has some special features, like the card and deck paradigm (where user interactions are marked up in individual cards and are grouped together in decks that can be transmitted over a slow wireless link).

WML contains many features that are similar to early versions of HTML but also has more advanced functions such as variables, which are used (among other things) for the history function, similar to the history function in Web browsers on PCs (but standardized). There are several good books about WML, among them Johan Hjelm's book *Designing Wireless Information Services* and Steve Mann's *Programming Applications with the Wireless Application Protocol*, both published by John Wiley & Sons (the same company that published this book).

Other XML Applications

Today, there are hundreds of XML applications used on the Web (refer to Figure 2.3). Some of the most important, apart from WML and XHTML, are WAP Push (the language that the WAP Forum has defined to create services that send information to the user without the user requesting it first); SMIL, the Synchronized Multimedia Integration Language (which is used to define how multimedia streams should interrelate), Xforms (the language that the W3C has defined as a replacement for the current forms mechanism on the Web); SVG (Scalable Vector Graphics, the for-

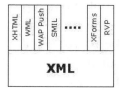

Figure 2.3 XML and XML applications.

mat defined by the W3C to represent images as vectors), RDF (the Resource Description Framework), SyncML (the Synchronization Markup Language), and many more.

As Figure 2.3 illustrates, XML is used for much more than XHTML and WML. It is also used for protocols (WAP Push, RSVP, and SOAP) to synchronize multimedia objects (SMIL) and the next generation of forms on the Web (Xform). Several markup languages can be mixed together in one document. This function is a feature of XML, but it is more or less useful depending on what the markup is intended to do. XHTML, for instance, is actually intended to function as a "host language" for other languages.

Namespaces

When you mix elements from several markup languages in a document, you need some way of keeping them apart. Otherwise, how would you know that the <a></a> element that you are using is a WML element and not an element from XHTML (because the same element name is used in both languages)? The way of separating them is to use XML namespaces.

A style sheet might contain elements and attributes from many different XML applications. A style sheet that transforms WML documents into XHTML documents will contain elements from three different XML applications: WML, XHTML, and XSLT. When elements and attributes from different XML applications are present in the same style sheet, there is a risk that an element or an attribute exists in more than one application but with a different meaning. If this situation happens, the XSLT processor cannot tell the difference between the names.

Applications use the element type name to determine how to process the element. In a distributed environment like the Web, names must be globally unique, or otherwise one name might accidentally be used for different purposes. For example, originally the element type VAR was used in WML to bind a value to a variable name, but in HTML an element type with the same name was used to describe that the following text was the name of a variable. Because the WML specification had not been published yet, it was possible to change the name to SETVAR. In practice, it is not always possible to check that a particular name is not used somewhere else for a different purpose. For this reason, namespaces are a part of most computer languages.

The W3C "XML Namespace Recommendation" specifies how names in an XML document can be associated with a URI that is globally unique. The name that is used inside the document is called a local name, and the name plus the associated URI is called a qualified name. That URIs are unique, by virtue of their association with the DNS, means that the qualified name will be globally unique and that the elements will also be globally unique. The URI is actually only used to identify the element names, however. There is no requirement that there should be a description, schema, DTD, or something else behind it.

XML namespaces are used to resolve naming conflicts between XML applications. In an XSLT style sheet, every element and attribute belongs to an XML namespace. A namespace is a set of names that has a unique identifier. The identifier can be a URL. All element and attribute names in XHTML belong to the namespace identified by the http://www.w3.org/1999/xhtml URL. All element and attribute names in XSLT belong to the http://www.w3.org/1999/XSL/Transform URL. By comparing both the names and the respective namespaces, the XSLT processor can distinguish between two elements that have the same name but that belong to two different namespaces. It is, however, up to the one that is responsible for the namespace to make sure that there are no names that conflict in the same namespace.

The standard for XML namespaces is published in a separate specification, not part of the core XML specification, at http://www.w3.org/TR/REC-xml-names/. Since its publication in January 1999, most new XML applications use XML namespaces.

Qualified Names

A qualified name is an element or attribute name that can be associated with an XML namespace. In an XSLT style sheet, all element and attribute names are qualified names.

A qualified name consists of two parts. The local part is the name used inside the document and distinguishes the element or attribute name inside its namespace. Names such as style sheet, template, value-of, and copy-of are all local names inside the XSLT namespace.

The namespace name is the second part of the qualified name. It distinguishes the name globally and is typically a URL because URLs are globally unique. The namespace name for XSLT is http://www.w3.org/1999/XSL/Transform. It is part of every element and attribute name in XSLT.

So, the fully qualified name of the <stylesheet> element in XSLT is "stylesheet" plus the http://www.w3.org/1999/XSL/Transform URL. The fully qualified name of the <template> element is "template" plus the http://www.w3.org/1999/XSL/Transform URL. The fully qualified name of the <a> element in XHTML is "a" plus the http://www.w3.org/1999/xhtml URL (and so on).

Qualified names are essential for interoperability on the Web. XML documents—and an XSLT style sheet is an XML document—are shared by many users who use different XML applications defined by different people, organizations, and companies. It is unavoidable that the same name will be used in different XML applications. By qualifying names with a unique URI, conflicts will be avoided.

Declaring and Using Namespaces

Every element and attribute name in an XSLT style sheet is a qualified name. Also, many other objects of an XSLT style sheet are identified by using qualified names (for example, variables, named templates, and attribute sets).

The xmlns and xmlns: Attributes

Before a qualified name can be used in an XML document, the namespace must be declared. To achieve this task, use a special attribute whose name starts with either xmlns: or xmlns.

The XML specification reserves names that start with the letters "xml" (both lower- and upper-case).

The xmlns: attribute declares a namespace prefix and a namespace name. Elements and attribute names that use the prefix in their name get associated with the namespace. In the following XSLT style sheet, all element names get associated with the XSLT namespace name:

```
<xsl:stylesheet
xmlns:xsl="http://www.w3.org/1999/XSL/Transform">
    <xsl:template match="/">
        <xsl:copy-of select="." />
    </xsl:template>
</xsl:stylesheet>
```

The xmlns attribute declares a default namespace. Every element that does not have a prefix is bound to the namespace. In the following example, all elements are bound to the XHTML namespace:

```
<html xmlns="http://www.w3.org/1999/xhtml">
    <head>
        <title>An XHTML document</title>
    </head>
    <body>
    ...
    </body>
</html>
```

The default namespace does not apply to attributes. It is a common mistake to think that it does. An attribute belongs to the element on which it is declared, and that element can be in any namespace declared in the document. An attribute that has a prefix, however, belongs to the namespace to which the prefix is bound.

Many XSLT attributes can contain references to element or attribute names. The references are qualified names. In the following example, the names in the match and select attributes refer to the elements in the XHTML namespace:

```
<xsl:stylesheet
    xmlns:xsl="http://www.w3.org/1999/XSL/Transform"
    xmlns:html="http://www.w3.org/1999/xhtml">
    <xsl:template match="html:ol">
        <xsl:value-of select="html:li" />
    </xsl:template>
</xsl:stylesheet>
```

The default namespace does not apply to names in attributes values. In the following modified example, the names in the match and select attributes refer to the <ol> and <li> elements in no particular namespace.

```
<xsl:stylesheet
    xmlns:xsl="http://www.w3.org/1999/XSL/Transform"
    xmlns="http://www.w3.org/1999/xhtml">
    <xsl:template match="ol">
        <xsl:value-of select="li" />
    </xsl:template>
</xsl:stylesheet>
```

The default namespace does not apply to names in attribute values.

The commonly used attributes xml:lang and xml:space are in the "XML namespace." It is an implied namespace that is never explicitly declared in the document. The namespace is controlled by the W3C, the organization that specifies XML. More names can be added to the namespace in the future.

The scope of a namespace declaration is the element on which it is declared and all descendant elements until it is overridden by another declaration that declares either the same namespace prefix (or, in the case of the default namespace, a new namespace) as the default.

In the following example, each template has a different default namespace:

```
<xsl:stylesheet
    xmlns:xsl="http://www.w3.org/1999/XSL/Transform">
    <xsl:template
        match="html-version"
        xmlns="http://www.w3.org/1999/xhtml">
        <body>
            <xsl:value-of select="." />
        </body>
    </xsl:template>
    <xsl:template
        match="wml-version"
        xmlns="http://www.wapforum.org/2001/wml">
        <card>
            <xsl:value-of select="." />
        </card>
    </xsl:template>
</xsl:stylesheet>
```

For readability, it is common to put all namespace declarations in the beginning of the document. Also, it is common practice to always use the same namespace prefix for a namespace name. For XSLT, we always use xsl as the namespace prefix. Sometimes XSLT elements are referred to with the xsl prefix, as in the <xsl:stylesheet> element and the

<xsl:value-of> element. The namespace prefix, however, does nothing more than associate the name with a namespace declaration. The prefix must be declared in each document where it is used.

Transformations across Namespaces

You will need to transform XML documents from one namespace into another (for example, a WML document into an XHTML document, or a document in your own private namespace into the XHTML or WML namespaces). All you need to do is to declare the namespaces you want to use in the beginning of the style sheet.

The following example transforms a WML <card> element into an XHTML <body> element:

```
<xsl:stylesheet
     xmlns:xsl="http://www.w3.org/1999/XSL/Transform"
     xmlns:wml="http://www.wapforum.org/2001/wml"
     xmlns="http://www.w3.org/1999/xhtml">
     <xsl:template match="wml:card" >
         <body>
             <xsl:apply-templates />
         </body>
     </xsl:template>
</xsl:stylesheet>
```

The following example illustrates how XML namespaces can be used to embed an XHTML anchor element inside of our now familiar phone description:

```
<?xml version="1.0" encoding="UTF-8"?>
<?xml-stylesheet type="text/css" href="phone.css" ?>
<phone xmlns ="http://www.ericsson.com/phones"
  xmlns:html="http://www.w3.org/1999/xhtml">
<manufacturer>
<html:a href="http://www.ericsson.com/">
Ericsson
</html:a>
</manufacturer>
<model>R320</model>
     <network>GSM 900</network>
</phone>
```

The prefix is used as the link between the local name and the name-space name. There is also a default namespace that does not use any prefixes. In this example, names in the XHTML namespace use html as the prefix while all of the names in our own invented "phone description language" are in the default namespace and do not use any prefix. Without the prefix, it would have been necessary to include the namespace name (the URI) in front of every local name, which would have been very inconvenient.

Hybrid Document Types

The Web browser Internet Explorer 5.5 presents documents that contain a mix of HTML and SMIL. Two different document types exist: HTML, which is familiar to everyone when describing documents, and another, SMIL, which is less familiar and describes how multimedia objects are synchronized. The document types are mixed in order to create new document types. This class of document types has been given a special name: hybrid document types. The motivation for creating new document types from existing ones is the classic argument of reuse.

The basis for all hybrid document types is a core set of document types that represent functions that a large number of content authors need. Here are some examples:

Create presentations with different kinds of multimedia objects (for example, images, video, and sound) that are synchronized with each other and with events from the user interface. This task can be done with the *Synchronized Multimedia Markup Language* (SMIL).

Create maps and simple logos with vector graphics that are defined directly in the markup. This task can be done with the *Scalable Vector Graphics* (SVG) image format.

In a structured way, include information about the document. For example, the name of the author, copyright information, and so on. This task can be done with the *Resource Definition Format* (RDF).

Control presentation and layout of the markup. This task can be done with style sheets; either with *Cascading Style Sheets* (CSS) or *Extensible Style Sheets* (XSL).

Present a document as a set of cards and maintain state between cards and documents. This task can be done with the *Wireless Markup Language* (WML).

> **Describe text structures such as paragraphs and headers and include links to other documents.** This task can be done with *Hypertext Markup Language* (HTML).

It is possible to mix and match markup in different XML formats by using namespaces in order to create truly multimedial or multimodal presentations.

One document instance can be presented in different ways (so-called presentation instances). The step from document to presentation is controlled with a style sheet. Presentation in different formats is not the entire solution, however. Often, the markup needs to be transformed into a different markup language. For instance, most WAP phones do not have the memory capacity to receive even a modestly long XHTML document. If it is transformed to WML instead, the card and deck mechanisms can be used to make sure that the document does not overflow the memory. The walk from one document type to another is where transformation sheets fit into the equation. It can also be used to do some primitive filtering.

Validity and Well-Formedness

If a document is not well formed, it is not XML, and the XML processor cannot handle it. This knowledge is very important when you write WML and XHTML: Documents that are not well formed will not be allowed. Well-formedness is, in turn, a subset of validity. A document can do without both the processing instruction at the start and the DTD, but it is then neither well formed nor valid. XML documents must be well formed, which is a minimum conformance level for the WML parser, for instance. They can also be valid. The validity check is basically a check of the document elements, their placement, and ordering against the DTD of the document. There is no automated way to check the content of a document (and indeed, it would be quite dangerous for our right to express ourselves if this situation were possible).

XML elements are defined in the DTD. Unlike SGML, an XML document is not required to have a DTD. Neither the XML declaration nor the DTD are required for an XML document to be well formed, which is all that is needed for a document to be read by the XML processor and rendered on the screen by the browser. An XML document always begins with a processing instruction, which is a way to define a document as an XML document and declare in which version of XML it is authored.

A well-formed XML document contains start tags, end tags, and content. A start tag contains a descriptive name (the "element name") surrounded by angle brackets: <french_army>. An end tag looks similar to a start tag except that it has a slash before the element name: </french_army>. Content is everything between the start tag and the end tag.

Another aspect of well formedness is that document elements must be properly nested. You cannot have one element inside another. The sequence <french_army><prussian_army> Battle of Waterloo </french_army></prussian_army> is incorrect because the <prussian_army> tag is not nested in the <french_army> element. If the processing is to work, you have to take great care to make sure that all of the tags you use in the document nest properly inside each other—including the root of the document, <html>.</html> in classic HTML.

A well-formed XML document must have a single "root" element that contains the rest of the document. This root element cannot exist anywhere else inside the document. If you are used to writing HTML, you will recognize that the HTML element is the root element because it surrounds the HEAD and BODY elements.

At the top of the document, you can place an "XML Declaration" to indicate the version of XML you are using and which character encoding the document has. XML documents start with the XML declaration <?xml ...?>. This declaration tells which version of XML is used and identifies that XML is being used. Apart from the xml version declaration, this declaration can also contain the character encoding, which is important if the document is to be rendered correctly. Here is an example:

```
<?xml version="1.0" encoding="UTF-8"?>
```

The XML declaration looks like a processing instruction, which is a way to provide information to an application. Processing instructions are not part of the document (in the same way as a comment), but the XML processor is required to pass them on to the application. Processing instructions contain the name of the instruction, which is how it is identified by the application. They also contain the data that are the parameters for the name. The application should process only the instructions that are directed at itself and leave all others aside. Any data after the name is optional, because what it is and how it is treated is up to the application. There are also processing instructions that have names that are prefaced with xml: and those are reserved for future XML standardization.

Therefore, you should also include any comments enclosed by <!-- and -->. Comments can contain any data except the two minus signs (the literal string --). Also, comments are not part of the textual content of the XML document, which means that an XML processor will not pass the content of a comment on to an application (unless there are other instructions saying so). In other words, you cannot include comments inside a document unless you are certain that the document will be used only in the current form or unless the comments do not matter. In that case, it might be a bit silly to include them anyway.

To be well formed, a document has to obey the syntax of XML. If the document cannot be parsed because it misuses markup characters, it cannot be well formed. That also applies if it does not follow the grammar for XML documents. Some types of markup, like parameter entity references, are allowed only in specific places and circumstances. If the document has them in other places, it is not well formed (even if it is well formed from all other points of view). In other words, you have to be careful about where you use parameter entity references, which are used for variable substitution in WML (among other things).

If the replacement text for parameter entities referenced inside a markup declaration is not correct, for instance, consisting only of a part of the markup declaration, the document cannot be well formed. All entities except &, <, >, ', and " must be declared (and remember, those were declared in the XML specification). The document is also not well formed if an attribute appears more than once on the same start tag. And, because string attribute values are restricted to internal elements, they cannot contain references to external entities. The content flow also cannot reference binary entities (which are allowed only in an attribute that is declared as ENTITY or ENTITIES). Although the binary entity might contain information that can be used by the application, it will not be possible for other applications to understand it. Finally, no parameters or text entities are allowed to be recursive (directly or indirectly).

Strange though it might sound, a document can be well formed and invalid. A document is valid only if it contains a proper document type declaration (either in the document or referenced) and if the document obeys the constraints of the declaration (for instance, that element sequences and nesting of elements are correct and that required attributes are provided and attribute values are of the correct type). If you want the XML parser to ensure that all of your XML documents adhere to the same structure, make sure that your XML documents are valid. Valid XML requires the *Document Type Definition* (DTD) or XML Schema that specifies the structure of the document in a very unambiguous, machine-readable way. You do not have to write this yourself; it can be referenced. When you are writing in a predefined format like WML or XHTML, you can just reference the DTD (or XML Schema).

To determine whether a document is valid, the XML processor has to read the entire DTD (both internal and external subsets). The big hurdle is whether a document is well formed. That it is valid does not become a requirement until it is transformed into something else, in which case the schema of the document has to be transformed (which puts very different requirements on what is needed in the document—in essence, all that is covered by the DTD).

Modular Recommendations

In the beginning of the Web, there was simplicity. One markup language, HTML, was used by all documents on the Web and was supported by all Web browsers. As the Web evolved, it became complex. The W3C standardized HTML through its recommendations (which do not have the official standing as standards but which, in theory, are recommendations to the members of the consortium——in practice, however, they have the force of standards). First, more and more functions were added to the HTML recommendation, then vendor-specific functions were added to some Web browsers but not to the official recommendation. It was getting harder to create Web documents that would run equally well in all Web browsers.

In 1997, the WAP Forum created a new markup language, WML, with many functions taken from the de-facto Web standard HTML. In 1999 and 2000, mobile phones with WML browsers began to appear. In Japan, a subset of HTML, Compact HTML, became successful as markup language for microbrowsers in mobile phones under the brand name iMode. In addition, new markup languages were being defined by the W3C and other organizations, and the company that was responsible for Web TV began to specify television-specific additions to HTML. Also, the level of implementation varies between browsers. Now, it is not only hard to create Web documents that will run equally well in all browsers, but it is also impossible.

One solution would have been to take it all in and to add everything to HTML. This action would have created a monstrously thick specification, which would most likely not have been implemented by any browser vendors (especially given that they often design browsers to handle errors in HTML, and the difficulty of this task increases exponentially with the complexity of the specification). Compounding this problem is that there was no mandatory validation of which functions from a W3C recommendation a browser implements or any control whatsoever).

The solution that the W3C decided to use was to create modularized recommendations. A module is a collection of semantically related element types. The HTML working group was the first group in the W3C to adopt this concept. From having been one very big specification, the functions of HTML are now broken down into smaller modules. There is one module for tables and another for fill-in forms and so on. This setup permits external organizations to customize XHTML in a controlled fashion.

Think of a module as an interface that has a certain number of related functions (elements) and their respective attributes. The entire specification consists of all of the modules, as shown in Figure 2.4. See the "Modularized XHTML" recommendation for a complete list and description of all modules.

It is possible to select which modules to implement. As in an object-oriented environment where it is not useful to just have a large number of objects, having a large number of independent modules is not very useful either. So, profiles are defined as a set of modules that make sense together and that serve the need from the industry. Here are some examples of profiles:

Figure 2.4   An XML source document.

"XHTML 1.1" Recommendation—the full set of XHTML elements

"XHTML Basic" Recommendation—a subset of all the XHTML 1.1
 elements

"XHTML+SMIL" Recommendation—adds timing to XHTML 1.1

Because these profiles are defined from modules in the XHTML specification, they are all parts of an XML application, and it is possible to
define transformation sheets that transform one set of modules into
another. And, because most content on the Web is in HTML (which can
be converted to XHTML with a few rather simple operations), this situation will most likely be one of the more popular transformations. We will
look more at transformations and demonstrate how a simple transformation works in Chapter 3, "Simple Transformations."

XSLT: Rules Declarations for Transformations

The biggest change to the computing industry that XML brings is that it
enables the programmer (or more properly, the system designer—who
can be a programmer, a Web site designer, or someone else) to declare
the rules for how information should be processed and handled. The
XML application itself describes the rules for how information should be
structured and how the markup should be constructed. The representation of the information is shaped by the use of a markup vocabulary

determined by the designer, which also declares the data type of the markup vocabulary (note that the markup is separated from the actual content of the document). This situation enables our tools to constrain the creation of an instance of our information and enables our users to validate a properly created instance of information against a set of constraints. The rule set for how to handle information is described in XSLT.

The generic XML processor has no idea what is "meant" by the XML, and the XML markup does not (usually) include formatting information. The information in an XML document might not be in the form in which it is desired to present it, but this information has to be described somewhere else.

An XML document is just an instance of well-formed XML. The two terms *document* and *instance* could be used interchangeably. A document is an object collection (of instances of the objects defined in the DTD or XML schema), where the content is held in elements (which are described in the schema or DTD).

The XML family of standards is starting to grow quite large, and in this book we will concentrate on four of them: Xpath, XSLT, and style sheets (XSL, which is an XML standard; and CSS, which is not an XML document type but still is used with XML documents). There are a few supporting standards that we also have mentioned already, such as XML namespaces and URIs. XSLT is (for purposes of transformation) the most important. The other two are Xpath, which is used to define patterns (or parts of an XML document), and XSL Formatting Objects, which define how XML documents should be displayed (to a viewer or to a listener). To confuse things, the W3C has another display language as well, called *Cascading Style Sheets* (CSS). It is not an XML-based language, but it can still interact with XML documents. We will talk more about this concept in Chapter 8, "XSLT and Style."

We declare our choice of an associated style sheet for an XML instance by embedding the construct described in the Stylesheet Association Recommendation. Recipients of the document and applications that process it can choose to respect or ignore this choice, but the declaration indicates that we have tied some process (typically, rendering) to our data, which specifies how to consume or work with our information. In the case of rendering, this process will normally be a CSS style sheet.

With XML, we can use any elements (combinations of starttags and endtags) we want. We can write documents by using our own element names—names that are meaningful where we intend to use them and that offer us greater control not only over presentation but also over the way in which the document will be processed. But this freedom comes at a price: XML tag names have no predefined semantics. An <h1> might just as legitimately identify a tall hedge as a first-level heading. Is <img> an image or an imaginary number? Who knows. You have to look in the DTD or XML schema to find out.

The characteristics of an XML element are declared in the XML schema (or DTD), but the presentation semantics are not part of the element's characteristics. If the content of the element <nuts> always had to be displayed as 10-point Times Roman, it would be impossible to import it into a database and process it automatically, to say nothing of importing it into a voice browser and rendering it as speech. Style sheets create a mechanism for how to present content, and different style sheets can be applied to the same content (depending on the circumstances).

In simplest terms, a style sheet contains instructions that tell a processor (such as a Web browser, print composition engine, or document reader) how to translate the logical structure of a source document into a presentational structure.

Style sheets typically contain instructions such as the following:

- Display hypertext links in blue.
- Start chapters on a new, left-hand page.
- Number figures sequentially throughout the document.
- Speak emphasized text in a slightly louder voice.

Many style-sheet languages augment the presentation of elements that have a built-in semantic meaning. For example, a Microsoft Word paragraph style can change the presentation of a paragraph, but even without the style, Word knows that the object in question is a paragraph.

The challenge for XSL, the XML Style Language which was the immediate origin of XSLT, is slightly greater. It is used for presentation of entire documents or document sets, transforming them to the relevant format in the process. Because there is no underlying semantic for an XML element, XSL must specify how each element should be presented and what the element is. For this reason, XSL defines not only a language for expressing style sheets but also a vocabulary of "formatting objects" that have the necessary base semantics.

The definition from the specification is actually as follows: "An XSL style sheet specifies the presentation of a class of XML documents by describing how an instance of the class is transformed into an XML document that uses the formatting vocabulary." In other words, a style sheet tells a processor how to convert logical structures (the source XML document represented as a tree) into a presentational structure (the result tree). An XSL style sheet is, in itself, an XML document, and during processing it is handled by the XML processor before it is handed to the XSL processor.

The key to understanding XSLT, as well as XSL and how it is different from CSS, is to understand XML documents in terms of tree structures. When you are creating a transformation sheet, you are creating an instruction for how a source tree should be transformed into a result tree. You are not manipulating the file itself, however. The original is still unchanged after the transformation.

In a WML document, for instance, the card element is nested in the deck element. It can be seen as a tree, where the deck is the root element and the card is a branch. Multiple cards will mean multiple branches. A branch is, in object-oriented terminology, a child of the root element. The root will then, of course, be the parent. As an aside, the tree can only branch further and branches cannot cross. An instance of an element in a tree cannot be the child of two parents (there can be other instances with the same element name, of course). If you have an element, which is the child of two (or more) parents, you no longer have a tree but a graph. And, to express graphs in XML, you need the *Resource Description Format* (RDF). But one of us has written another book about that.

Contrasted with a file format where information identification relies on some proprietary hidden format, predetermined ordering, or some kind of explicit labeling, the tree-like hierarchical storage structure infers relationships by the scope of values encompassing the scopes of other values. The addressing of elements is done by using the Xpath language, which we will describe in Chapter 4.

Although trees shape a number of areas of XML, both logically (markup) and physically (entities such as files or other resources), they are not the only means by which relationships are specified. For example, an information object (such as an element) can arbitrarily point to other information elsewhere by using *Universal Resource Identifiers* (URIs).

Because an XML application has to be well formed, applications also provide a language for specifying how a system can constrain the allowed logical hierarchy of information structures. Well-formed XML does not only dictate a certain syntax and use of characters in a certain way, but it also creates an implicit document model that is defined by the way elements are nested. There is no need to declare this model separately, because the syntax rules governing well-formedness guarantee the information to be seen as a hierarchy. The hierarchy also translates into a tree structure, which can be described in object-oriented terms. As with all hierarchies, there are family tree-like relationships of parent, child, and sibling constructs relative to each element.

Take, for instance, this simple XML example:

```
<?xml version="1.0"?>
 <purchase id="p001">
   <customer db="cust123"/>
   <product db="prod345">
        <amount>23.45</amount>
   </product>
 </purchase>
```

If you were to draw this code as a tree, it would look something like the following:

```
purchase -- customer
       |
product-amount
```

The hierarchy is implicit in the nesting of the elements. The customer element is a child of the document element, which is named purchase, and so is the product element. Amount, in turn, is the child of the product element. The elements nest in each other from the root out, and the element that does not nest in the others is the leaf node—the final tip of the tree.

The formal model does not affect the structural model of the document, and it does not really influence the interpretation of content. It is useful for an XML processor in handling the document or for other types of systems that work with the XML document. This statement is true regardless of whether the model is expressed as a DTD or as a schema. References to the DTD or schema can be used for validation, to check that the information content conforms not only to the lexical rules that apply to XML in general (well-formedness), but also that content follows the syntax rules that are dictated by the model described in the schema or DTD (validity).

There is also other information that can be derived from the document model (such as the data type of an element or that it is required).

XML semantics, while one of the foundations of XSLT, is actually a gray area. The document model is only one of many components that is used to describe the semantics of the information found in the document. Although well-formed documents do not have to have a formal document model (because there does not have to be a schema or a DTD), the names of the elements and attributes themselves will give hints to the associated semantics. There is currently no way of expressing these formally, however. You have to describe them in comments to the schema.

The XML 1.0 Recommendation only describes what an XML processor acting on an XML stream should do, including how it should identify the data and provide it to the application that is using the processor. Because there are no formalized semantic description facilities in XML, any XML that is used is not tied to any one particular concept or application. One way of looking at it is that the only purpose of XML is to unambiguously identify and deliver constituent components of data. Nothing is imposed by any process when creating a new XML vocabulary. Applications using XML processors to access XML information must be instructed how to interpret and implement the semantics because there is nothing to stop several applications from using the same names.

The first working draft of XSLT from the W3C was produced in August 1998, and in November it became a formal recommendation of that organization. Its companion recommendation Xpath is about the same age.

XML by itself does not actually do anything. XSLT makes it possible to match the output form of one process to the input form of another process or application.

Xpath was designed to be used together with XSLT. It is actually used with several other XML languages, as well. Xpath is a language to address parts of XML documents, and we will cover this topic in Chapter 4, "Xpath." Xpath is also used in the XPointer W3C recommendation and in the emerging XML Query Language.

There is no special description of XML Formatting Objects (at least, not yet) except inside the XSL specification. We will not cover the formatting part of XSL in this book (other than providing a cursory glance at the topic).

It is important when we think about styling information to remember that two distinct processes are involved, not just one. First, we must transform the information from the organization when it was created into the organization needed for consumption. Second, when rendering we must express, whatever the target medium, the aspects of the appearance of the reorganized information.

XSLT can be used to create output markup in any format that can be structured as characters. This format can, for instance, mean HTML but not binary formats. XML is based on Unicode, and that means it encompasses practically all character formats in existence. XSLT can also remove elements as well as add completely new elements. Elements can be rearranged and sorted, and elements can be tested against preconditions in order to make decisions about which elements to display.

The XSLT 1.0 Recommendation describes a transformation instruction vocabulary of constructs that can be expressed in an XML model of elements and attributes. One way of describing XSLT is "transformation by example," as opposed to other techniques such as "transformation by program logic." We tell an XSLT processor what we want as an end result, rather than describing how to do the changes, and it is the responsibility of the processor itself to do the actual work.

The XSLT Recommendation contains a vocabulary for specifying templates that function as "examples of the result." Based on how we instruct the XSLT processor to access the source of the data being transformed, the processor will incrementally build the result by adding the filled-in templates. It takes the source tree, applies the rules in the transformation sheet, and creates the result tree.

XSLT is similar to other forms of content transformation in that it deals with the documents as trees of abstract nodes. XSLT, or rather Xpath, enables you to identify structures and to make as many passes as required over them, modifying the structures in the source information (or rather, the markup of the information). The information being transformed can be traversed in any order needed and as many times as required to produce the desired result. The algorithms are declared in the XSLT code and are handled by the XSLT processor. It only works with the markup as abstract nodes, not with the source data or with the semantics of the markup.

The XSLT processor handles the mechanics of the operations. High-level functions such as sorting and counting are available when required as functions in the language. The XSLT processor handles low-level functions such as memory-management, node manipulation, how nodes are node traversed and created, and garbage collection. In other words, the XSLT programmer does not have to think about the mechanics of the operations. Nor do you have to consider the mechanics of the presentation, which can be left to the browser and the style sheet processor.

Writing a style sheet is actually a way of using markup to declare the behavior of the XSLT processor, much like HTML is used to declare the behavior of the Web browser to paint information on the screen. One effect is that XSLT might be more accessible to non-programmers (although doubtful, because programmers tend to underestimate the complexity of what they do).

While XSLT is declarative, there are procedural constructs as well. You can use it to write just about any program you can imagine. XSLT is (in theory) "Turing complete." It is possible to implement any algorithm, however complex it is. But this implementation will come at the price of considerable verbosity——the more complex the algorithm, the more verbose the XSLT code. Implementing business rules and semantic processing in XSLT is exactly what it is intended for (although it has its constraints).

XSLT does not actually transform the original document. It works with a copy of the source tree, which is transformed into the result tree. Or, if you will, the XSLT transformation sheet is an instruction for how to turn the source document into the result document (although it does not work with the actual source document, but only with the representation in memory). It only affects the parts that are to be transformed. The parts of the source document that are not addressed in the transformation sheet are unchanged and are passed on directly to the result tree. The fact that it works with a "virtual" document also means that it is possible for an XSLT transformation sheet to work with documents which are dynamically composed—for instance, created by another transformation sheet.

A transformation sheet consists of a set of templates (the instructions to the processor) that are matched to the source document (by addressing them by using Xpath). When a match is found, the matching part of the source document will be transformed to the result document.

One way of parameterizing an element is by its place in the tree structure. Another way is by giving it attributes. The attributes of an XML element are part of the element, not the content. Content in XML elements can be anything, and it can basically be binary—it does not concern the element structure. In other words, if a document has the same structure but the content is different, it can be processed as part of the presentation and the content will be the same as for the instance of the document. For instance, pages presenting flight information resulting from a request containing a flight number can be presented in WML on a WAP phone but in XHTML in a browser. The content will still be the same.

The most common usage of XSLT is probably producing human-readable forms of XML source documents. XSLT can be used to produce plain ASCII text through HTML, XML, and WML as well as formatted print documents in PDF and Postscript. XSLT is a general-purpose transformation language for XML-based content. It works fine for manipulating basic markup. It can be used to transform the content, but in XML, content can be binary, so if the content is not characters, it can be passed through untouched. What constitutes a character, however, is a different problem, which we will talk more about in Chapter 8, "XSLT and Style."

On the other hand, XSLT cannot be used to access system resources. There is no way to call subroutines that are written in other languages (although there is an extension mechanism that enables the processor to handle code from other declarative languages). It cannot deal with binary files (although the element content of the XML element can be binary). It is also an interpreted language, which is slower than compiled processing (although there are compilers available to speed up processing).

Because an XSLT style sheet is an XML document, it is no harder than creating any other XML document. Any text editor will suffice, although it is easier to use an XML editor (because it will give you a warning if you are trying to create a document that is not well-formed).

The following is a simple example that runs in most XSLT processors. There is no source document, or if you prefer, the source document is in the style sheet. It will generate a piece of content. It is embedded in HTML tags, but it is actually an XSL document that will generate the text "Welcome. This is an XSLT example" on the screen.

```
<HTML xsl:version="1.0"
xmlns:xsl="http://www.w3.org/1999/XSL/Transform">
  <HEAD>
    <TITLE>Welcome</TITLE>
  </HEAD>
  <BODY>
<P>This is an XSLT example</P>
  </BODY>
</HTML>
```

The namespace xsl:version="1.0" xmlns:xsl="http://www.w3.org/1999/XSL/Transform" tells the processor that this document is a style sheet document. The processor will then look for elements in that namespace (in other words, <xsl:....>) and do something with them. Because there are no such elements, nothing happens.

This rule is actually the first rule of XSLT processors: If there is no XSLT, do nothing. The second rule for processors is that anything that is not in the XSLT namespace is passed straight through to the output and is included in the result tree. We are actually cheating a bit in this case.

If we instead create a source file like the following (and call it example1.xml) and apply a style sheet to it, the result will be different. Here is example1.xml:

```
<?xml version="1.0" ?>
<example1>
<h1>The title goes here</h1>
<p>And this is the first paragraph</p>
</example1>
and the style sheet is:
<?xml version="1.0"?>
```

This style sheet will generate some content and put it together with the content from the source document into an HTML document:

```
<xsl:stylesheet version="1.0"

xmlns:xsl="http://www.w3.org/1999/XSL/Transform">
  <xsl:template match="/example1">
    <html>
      <head><title>Test Document</title></head>
      <body>
        <xsl:apply-templates/>
        <i>More content generated by the style sheet</i>
      </body>
    </html>
  </xsl:template>
```

```
<xsl:template match="head">
  <h1><xsl:apply-templates/></h1>
</xsl:template>
<xsl:template match="para">
  <p><xsl:apply-templates/></p>
</xsl:template>
</xsl:stylesheet>
```

Now, this coding is already a bit verbose, as you can see. Each iteration through the source document has to be described separately, which means that when you want to change <head> to <h1>, you have to write three lines of code and another three lines of code for changing <para> to <p>. This situation would be bad if it were not for the fact that the same template could be applied to every instance of <head> or <para>. The example will produce the following document:

```
<html>
<head><title>Test Document</title></head>
<body>
<h1>The title goes here</h1>
<p>And this is the first paragraph</p>
<i>More content generated by the style sheet</i>
</body>
    </html>
```

You can also embed the XSLT style sheet in the XML document. To perform this action, you have to use the xml-stylesheet processing instruction for that document. You also have to have a DTD that defines the xsl:stylesheet element as having an id attribute of type ID—otherwise, the href pseudo-attribute in the xml-stylesheet processing instruction won't be able to find the style sheet.

You also need a template matching xsl:stylesheet that does nothing so that the style sheet is ignored when it runs. Otherwise, it will try to run on itself.

Here is an example of an XML document with an embedded style sheet:

```
<?xml version="1.0"?>
<?xml-stylesheet type="text/xml" href="#stylesheet"?>
<!DOCTYPE doc [
<!ATTLIST xsl:stylesheet
  id ID   #REQUIRED>
]>
<doc>
<xsl:stylesheet id="stylesheet"
                version="1.0"
xmlns:xsl="http://www.w3.org/1999/XSL/Transform">
```

```
    <!-- xsl:import elements to include content -->
    <xsl:template match="xsl:stylesheet" />
    <!- the rest of the stylesheet -->
</xsl:stylesheet>
<!- the rest of the XML document -->
</doc>
```

Because there are no reserved element names in XSL or in any other XML document (except for those containing the letters X, M, and L and the prefix xmlns:), it is necessary to use some other mechanism to distinguish between elements that have XSL semantics and other elements. Namespaces were designed to solve this problem.

Namespaces are defined in the W3C recommendation, "Namespaces in XML" (www.w3.org/TR/WD-xml-names). In a document, they are given by using the colon-delimited prefixes. The prefix is significant when comparing element names within a document; therefore, xsl:template and template are different. The prefix can vary between documents, however. The important thing is the association of a prefix string with a URI. That is the function of the xmlns: attribute in the style sheets. For instance, the namespace declaration "xmlns:xsl="ttp://www.w3.org/TR/WD-xsl" " associates the namespace prefix xsl with the URI that follows it: "http://www.w3.org/TR/WD-xsl". Because the prefix is arbitrary, it could be xmlns:flasklock=http://www.w3.org/TR/WD-xsl instead. To follow convention, however, we will use xsl: as the namespace prefix for XSLT elements.

In this case, the XSLT style sheet is an XML fragment, not a document in itself. Fragments, however, preserve the context of the document, so the style sheet is still XSLT even while embedded in some other type of document. The style sheet is contained within a style sheet element, and its content is template elements. (Style sheets can contain elements in addition to the template, but most style sheets consist of mostly templates.)

Before discussing XSLT in more detail, we have to look at the XSL processing model. An XSLT processor takes over after the XML processor, or parser, which reads the byte sequences of the XML document from the input stream, resolves any entities or inline references (for example, fetches any included document fragments), and passes any well-formed XML structures that it finds to the application that called it. The XML processor is a program that is required to handle the processing, but it does not execute instructions in the same way as the XSLT processor (or a Java virtual machine) does. It only checks the well-formedness of the document and resolves the references and entities. The input to the XML processor can be either as static entities in the notation described in the XML recommendation (that is, files using tags following the XML definition of "well-formed"), or more generally, as "documents" constructed through some other method (for example, presented by some other application such as a pre-built DOM tree or fired as a series of SAX events). Popular XML processor implementations produce either a stream of SAX events such as "begin element foo, begin CDATA, CDATA bar, end element foo . . . " or a DOM object. In other words, the XSLT processor is dependent on the XML processor. It will take the stream (or DOM objects, but most XSLT processors use streams) and uses that information in a node tree (the style sheet tree) to create a new node tree (the result tree), possibly using several other node trees as input (the source tree or trees).

Most XSLT processors accept SAX events generated by some XML processors as input, and some accept DOM objects that might be generated by other XML parsers or created from scratch. The SAX events or DOM objects are used as the basis for the node trees that follow the Xpath/XSLT data model.

Some XSLT processors are bundled with XML processors and are provided as standalone applications. Others are toolkits that application developers can integrate into their own software. In this book, we will assume that you are using one of the standalone XSLT processors, and we will not separate the XML and XSLT processing. XSLT processors are sometimes built so they can accept input in different forms. Because the XML notation is normative but an XML data model or "Infoset" is not, however, the usual case is for an XSLT processor to be combined with an XML processor to accept XML files by using the XML notation as input.

The XSLT processing can be done in the browser but also in the server. It has turned out to be done more economically in the server, especially for formats that are to be displayed in devices that are less capable in terms of display and processor (such as a mobile phone).

Conceptually, the XSL processor begins at the root node in the source tree and processes it by finding the template in the style sheet that describes how that element should be displayed. Each node is then processed in turn until there are no more nodes left to be processed. (In fact, it is a little more complicated than this situation, because each template can specify which nodes to process—so some nodes might be processed more than once and some might not be processed at all. We will examine this topic later.)

MSXML, for instance, provides both an XML parser and an XSL processor in one Windows DLL. IE 5.0 is an application that utilizes MSXML to handle the processing of XML documents that have been associated with a style sheet by means of a processing instruction in the XML. The version of MSXML that ships with IE 5.0 does not fully implement XSLT but is instead based on an older working draft of the XSL specification, before XSL was split into XSLT, XSLFO, and Xpath. This version is the source of much confusion among people who are new to XSLT. We will try to avoid using this version in this book, other than for examples.

Contrary to the case of browsers, where designers often feel that it is necessary to create a specific version of the document for each browser, the programmer can create an XSLT transformation sheet that will work on all processors by avoiding the differences.

The XML processor reads the XML input. The XSLT processor performs the actual XSL transformations. It will have to use an XML processor to read the source XML and the XSLT. An XML processor (often called a parser, but called a processor in the XML recommendation) reads a source XML file and identifies the syntactic units (such as elements, attributes, and text content).

An XSLT processor takes a style sheet and applies it to the tree representation of a source XML document (produced by an XML parser) and generates a tree representation of an output XML document.

Because XSLT transformations operate on the tree-like document data model described in the Xpath specification, inputs and outputs to the XSLT processor will be a representation of a tree. These trees often start and end life as documents in an XML notation. In other words, it might look like we are taking the document and changing the tags, but that is not how it works. XML tags (elements, actually) are only a way of representing underlying data structures. So, XSLT actually works with the underlying tree structure through the XML elements. You must realize this fact, because many misconceptions about how XSLT style sheets are best written come from looking at them as a way of switching around tags.

The product of the XSLT processing is a "result tree." If the result tree is composed of XSL formatting objects, then it describes how to present the source document. There is nothing, however, that says that the result tree has to be composed of XSL formatting objects. It can be composed of any elements, and it does not have to be XML, either. When HTML is used in the result tree, XSL will transform an XML source document into an HTML document. There are some restrictions, however: empty elements, for instance, will use the XML syntax for empty elements.

While checking source documents for validity can be very useful for diagnostic purposes, all of the hierarchical relationships of content are based on what is found inside the specific document that is being input into the processing (the instance), not on the document data model. An XSLT style sheet is independent of any DTD or other explicit schema that defines the abstract model of the instance. In other words, XSLT can process well-formed XML that does not have an explicit data model (for example, a DTD or schema).

If there is a DTD or an XML Schema describing the document, however, certain information such as attribute types and defaulted values can be used to improve the processing. Without this information, the processor can still perform style sheet processing as long as the absence of the information does not influence the desired results.

Because we do not depend on a specific DTD for the current document, we can design a single style sheet that can process different (but similar) documents. For instance, if you have a damage report for cars, which will include certain elements when the car has a diesel engine and others when it has a gasoline engine, the same style sheet can be used to process them. When the models are very similar, much of the style sheet operates the same way each time and the rest of the style sheet only processes that which it finds in the sources.

The corollary is that one single source file can be processed with multiple style sheets for different purposes. In other words, it is possible to process a source file with a style sheet designed for an entirely different vocabulary. The results will probably be very inappropriate, but there is nothing inherent to an instance that ties it to a single style sheet or a set of style sheets. Style sheets can actually be used to validate input as well as present output, but this topic is beyond the scope of this book.

A style sheet can be the synthesis of the starting style sheet and a number of supplemental files that are included or imported by the main file. There are restrictions, however. It is not possible to build style sheets that are dynamically composed, for instance.

All of the inputs to an XSLT transformation process must be well-formed (but not necessarily valid) XML documents. In other words, HTML, text, and other formats that are not XML cannot be used. If you want to use an existing HTML file as input to the process, you have to transform it to XHTML.

The input to the transformation can be one or more style sheet files and one or more source files, but the processing always starts with one single style sheet file and a single source file. Other style sheet files are included in the first one before the first source file is processed. The XML processor will then access other source files according to the XML content of the first file (including the style sheet, if that is being used as source code). The names of these supplementary resources can be hard-wired into the style sheet and passed to the style sheet as a parameter, or the style sheet can find them in the source files (by using Xpath addressing). Next, the XSLT processor will access other source files under the control of the style sheet. The first source file that is fed to the XSLT processor defines the first abstract tree of nodes that the style sheet uses (in other words, the current context, although there are functions that can change these nodes, as we will see in Chapters 5, "Programming Basics in XSLT," and 6, "More XSLT Programming: Import, Include, and Extensions to XSLT").

For each source file, there will be a separate node tree that will have its own set of unique node identifiers and global values. When a given resource is identified more than once as a source file, the XSLT processor uses only a single representation for that resource. In this way, a style sheet is guaranteed to work unambiguously with source information (because all of the source documents and style sheets are copied into the processor's memory area before processing begins——although this action is not stated in the specification).

A single source file does not have to contain all of the necessary information. It is often (actually, almost always) necessary to supplement the source with boilerplate or other hard-wired information in the style sheet. In other words, it is very rare for a style sheet to be applicable across different services. You normally have to modify it for each site, even if the processing is largely the same.

XSLT is defined in the XSLT specification, but the specification includes functions for extending it by using different languages. We will look more at how that happens in Chapter 8, "XSLT and Style." A conforming processor might or might not support such extensions and is only obliged to accommodate error and fallback processing in such a way that a style sheet writer can reconcile the behavior if needed.

The XSLT specification provides a set of built-in templates to take care of cases where extensions are not supported or when the style sheet author has made an error. The XSLT processor has to contain these situations, but there are also ways for the style sheet designer to override them.

For instance, the recursive processing of a document can continue although a processor does not find a match for a previous pattern (element, attribute, or value) that has been explicitly stated in the style sheet. This template rule applies to both element nodes and to the root node. The following shows the equivalent of the built-in template rule (using the Xpath notation):

```
<xsl:template match="*|/">
  <xsl:apply-templates/>
</xsl:template>
```

There is also a built-in template rule for each mode (a way of creating conditional recursive processing, which we will look at in Chapter 6). This template rule applies to both element nodes and to the root node. The following code shows the equivalent of the built-in template rule for mode m.

```
<xsl:template match="*|/" mode="m">
  <xsl:apply-templates mode="m"/>
</xsl:template>
```

There is also a built-in template rule for text and attribute nodes that copies text through the following:

```
<xsl:template match="text()|@*">
  <xsl:value-of select="."/>
</xsl:template>
```

The built-in template rule for processing instructions and comments is to do nothing.

```
<xsl:template match="processing-instruction()|comment()"/>
```

The built-in template rule for namespace nodes is also to do nothing. There is no pattern that can match a namespace node. The built-in template rule is the only template rule that is applied to namespace nodes.

The built-in template rules are treated as if they were imported implicitly before the style sheet and therefore have a lower import precedence than all other template rules. In other words, you can override a built-in template rule by including an explicit template rule.

If you only want text in particular elements to be outputted, you will have to override the built-in template.

To summarize, the built-in template rules for each of the seven Xpath node types are listed in Table 2.1.

Unless you do selective processing of the nodes by using the "select" attribute of <xsl:apply-templates/>, the only nodes you have to worry about are those that qualify as children (the first four in this list). Because the built-in rules for comments and processing instructions are to do nothing, all you really have to worry about is being aware of how built-in rules will be applied to elements and text.

To avoid processing white space nodes in the source tree, you can use <xsl:strip-space/> in your stylesheet—the details of which we will come back to in Chapter 5, "Programming Basics in XSLT."

Table 2.1 Actions of Default Rules

NODE TYPE	RULE
Elements	Apply templates to children
Text	Copy text to the result tree
Comments	Do nothing
Processing instructions	Do nothing
Attributes	Copy the value of the attribute to the result tree
Namespace	Do nothing
Root	Apply templates to children

Before we continue, let's look a little at the Internet Explorer XML parser (MSXML 2.0). But first, be warned that the following examples are not standard XSLT, and we will go back to it after this description.

An XML document begins with the namespace declaration, which tells where the elements come from (and where to find the XML Schema or DTD that declares their meaning). The namespace declaration in documents, which will work in regular XSLT processors, is as follows:

```
<xsl:stylesheet
xmlns:xsl="http://www.w3.org/1999/XSL/Transform">
```

But for Internet Explorer, it is as follows:

```
<xsl:stylesheet
xmlns:xsl="http://www.w3.org/TR/WD-xsl">
```

MSXML uses the *Simple API for XML* (SAX), which is used in most XML implementations. First, you start with the XML document that you want to transform into HTML:

```
<?xml version="1.0"?>
<directory>
  <employee>
    <department>Internal Sanitation</department>
    <name>Bob Dylan</name>
    <country>USA</country>
    <position>Director</position>
    <phone>451-2571090</phone>
    <room_number>985</room_number>
  </employee>
</directory>
```

If you use Internet Explorer 5.0 or later (or an XML editor), you can view the XML file (Figure 2.4).

Then, you create an XSL style sheet with a transformation template:

```
<?xml version='1.0'?>
<xsl:stylesheet xmlns:xsl="http://www.w3.org/TR/WD-xsl">
<xsl:template match="/">
  <html>
  <body>
    <table border="2" bgcolor="yellow">
      <tr>
        <th>Department</th>
        <th>Name</th>
      </tr>
```

```
      <xsl:for-each select="department/employee">
      <tr>
        <td><xsl:value-of select="department"/></td>
        <td><xsl:value-of select="name"/></td>
      </tr>
      </xsl:for-each>
    </table>
  </body>
  </html>
</xsl:template>
</xsl:stylesheet>
```

If you use Internet Explorer 5.0 or later, you can view the XSL file (Figure 2.5).

An XML document has no internal presentation semantics (they are added by the style sheet, either by applying XSL Formatting Objects or by applying CSS). The reference to the style sheet has to be added to the XML document. This link is done in the same way as the namespace dec-

Figure 2.5 The XSLT transformation sheet.

Figure 2.6   The HTML document.

laration, and the style sheet will be looked up when the document is to be presented to the user. If the document is to be processed by another computer, it is different, of course—then, no presentation semantics are needed. The HTML has no inherent presentation semantics either (other than those that you have programmed into your browser as part of its settings). But it is clearer how the content of <H1> should be presented in relation to the rest of the document <phone>.

```
<?xml version="1.0"?>
<?xml-stylesheet type="text/xsl" href="employee_directory.xsl"?>
<directory>
  <employee>
    <department>Internal Sanitation</department>
    <name>Bob Dylan</name>
    <country>USA</country>
    <position>Director</position>
    <phone>451-2571090</phone>
    <room_number>985</room_number>
  </employee>
</directory>
```

If you have an XSL-compliant browser, such as Internet Explorer 5.0 or later, your browser will nicely transform your XML into HTML when it is loaded by using the style sheet we just saw and will display the result in Figure 2.6.

This function solves the problem of adding presentation to documents (and can be done selectively, for instance, by enclosing a number of style sheets with one document and applying the one that is adapted to the browser at hand). But in the process, the document is changed from one structure to another. This document can be used for much more than only adding a presentation format, as we will see in Chapter 3, "Simple Transformations."

Simple Transformations

This chapter presents a quick introduction to XSLT. This chapter is not complete, however. The purpose is to demonstrate the most rudimentary features of XSLT. For the sake of simplicity, we have left out many important features of XSLT for later chapters.

After having read this chapter, if you are new to XML and XSLT, you should be able to write a simple XSLT transformation sheet. Experienced XML developers should understand how to use XSLT to solve their needs. More detailed descriptions begin in Chapter 5, "Programming Basics in XSLT."

Applying Templates

Because you have to know the structure of the input to create the output, XSLT works best when it can be applied to documents that are made up of content that is well structured, such as tables, forms, or other standardized objects. To transform them into another format, you create a template that contains instructions for how the source nodes should be processed. Then, the template is processed until no new source nodes remain to be selected for processing.

The way the template rules identify the nodes to which they apply is by using a pattern. Patterns are created with the match attribute. Patterns are defined in the Xpath language, which we will talk more about in Chapter 4, "Xpath."

A transformation sheet is a set of rules expressed in the XSLT language for how an XML document should be transformed or renamed. Each rule identifies a set of nodes from the source XML document and then the rules that should be applied; for example, move this element here, change the name of that element, and so on. According to the XSLT specification, the correct term is style sheet, but because style sheets traditionally are used to declare the formatting of a document and XSLT can be used for so much more, we will use it interchangeably with the term transformation sheet throughout this book.

A set of transformation rules is called a template. Each template defines for itself a set of nodes that it matches by using the Xpath language (more about that in Chapter 4); for example, elements of a given element type, or elements with a given name. When a matching element shows up in the source XML document, the XSLT processor applies the rules to the element. Every element in the template is either an XSLT processing instruction or is copied literally into the result tree. For each node that has an element name, it finds the matching template and instantiates it. The sequence of instantiated templates is placed in the result tree at the location of the node with the element name in the template.

A template is similar to a method in an object-oriented programming language. It enables a single XSLT style sheet to be broken down in logical units, each of which performs a specific transformation. The xsl:apply-templates element (which contains all of the template rules) then recursively processes the children of the source element in order to generate the result tree fragment that is created by the template rule (and finally, the result tree itself).

Templates can have either a match attribute or a name attribute. If a template has a match attribute, it will be invoked when the pattern specified as the value of the attribute matches one or more nodes in the source tree. If a template has a name attribute, it can be invoked by calling the template explicitly by name. By using a sequence of xsl:call-template instructions (which calls named templates) to perform the transformations, you can push all of the complexity out of the first template (or style sheet) and into the named templates. When there is no select attribute, the xsl:apply-templates instruction processes all of the children of the current node, including text nodes.

Text nodes that have been stripped as specified by using white space stripping will not be processed, however. If stripping of white space nodes has not been enabled for an element, then all white space in the content of the element will be processed as text, and the white space between child elements will count in determining the position of a child element as returned by the Xpath position function.

xsl:apply-templates can have a select attribute that can be used to process nodes selected by an expression instead of processing all children. The value of the select attribute is an Xpath expression. The expression must evaluate to an Xpath node set. The selected set of nodes is processed in document order unless a sorting specification is present. The following example processes all of the author children of the author-group:

```
<xsl:template match="author-group">
    <xsl:apply-templates select="author"/>
</xsl:template>
```

The following example processes all of the given names of the authors that are children of the author-group:

```
<xsl:template match="author-group">
    <xsl:apply-templates select="author/given-name"/>
</xsl:template>
```

This example processes all of the heading descendent elements of the book element:

```
<xsl:template match="book">
    <xsl:apply-templates select=".//heading"/>
</xsl:template>
```

It is also possible to process elements that are not descendents of the current node (in other words, elements that do not branch out from it in the XML tree). This example assumes that a department element has group children and employee descendents. It finds an employee's department and then processes the group children of the department:

```
<xsl:template match="employee">
  <fo:block>
    Employee <xsl:apply-templates select="name"/> belongs to group
    <xsl:apply-templates select="ancestor::department/group"/>
  </fo:block>
</xsl:template>
```

XSLT is not really a programming language, but that is increasingly how it is used. It is declarative, whereas traditional programming languages are procedural. It is interpreted (like Basic) but not compiled (like C), which means that performance will suffer if there is a high number of transformations that are to take place simultaneously (although this situation depends on the processor). There are XSLT compilers that speed up the processing but only work with one processor.

The following transformation sheet is simple; it is just one big template:

```
<table xmlns="http://www.w3.org/1999/xhtml"
    xmlns:xsl="http://www.w3.org/1999/XSL/Transform">
    <tr>
        <th>Manufacturer</th>
        <td><xsl:value-of select="/phone/manufacturer" /></td>
    </tr>
    <tr>
        <th>Model</th>
        <td><xsl:value-of select="/phone/model" /></td>
    </tr>
    <tr>
        <th>Network</th>
        <td><xsl:value-of select="/phone/network" /></td>
    </tr>
</table>
```

This transformation sheet contains only one element type from the XSLT language, and most of the elements are just copied right through the XSLT processor. Each template in our style sheet "instantiates" a small part of the result tree. XSLT knits all of these fragments together to form the complete result tree.

It is perfectly legitimate for a template to contain more than one occurrence of an element. There are also ways for the processor to apply the template conditionally, as we will see in Chapter 6, "More XSLT Programming: Import, Include, and Extensions to XSLT." The same processing is performed each time, however.

Here is a more complex transformation sheet:

```
<xsl:transform
      version="1.0"
      xmlns:xsl="http://www.w3.org/1999/XSL/Transform"
      xmlns="http://www.w3.org/1999/xhtml">
      <xsl:template match="/phone">
      <table><tr>
            <xsl:apply-templates />
      </tr></table>
      </xsl:template>

      <xsl:template match="manufacturer">
              <th>Manufacturer</th>
              <td><xsl:value-of select="." /></td>
      </xsl:template>

      <xsl:template match="model">
              <th>Model</th>
              <td><xsl:value-of select="/phone/model" /></td>
      </xsl:template>
      <xsl:template match="model">
              <th>Network</th>
              <td><xsl:value-of select="/phone/network" /></td>
      </xsl:template>
  </xsl:transform>
```

This transformation sheet contains four templates, each matching an element type from the source XML document and containing rules for how to transform the elements that match. Also, the transformation sheet is contained inside the xsl:transform element, which acts as a container for the templates. Templates are defined inside the xsl:template element.

The first template in the example matches the root phone element (using the value-of element with the select attribute). It goes off and creates the first part of the table by adding the <th> and <td> around the selected values and then applies the other templates. When they all have been checked, it creates the last part of the table. The result is the same as for the previous transformation sheet.

This process looks more complicated than the first one, but in reality, this method is how most transformation sheets are built: as a set of templates that get invoked one after another over the source document. Note that you do not have to know anything about the contents of the source document, only its structure.

A template rule is specified with the xsl:template element. It has a match attribute, which identifies the source node or nodes to which the rule applies. The match attribute is required unless the xsl:template element has a name attribute, and it can not contain a variable reference. The xsl:template element contains the template that is applied when the template rule is applied. For example, an XML document might contain the following:

```
This is an <emph>important</emph> point.
```

The following template rule matches emph elements and produces a fo:inline-sequence formatting object with a font-weight property of bold in the source tree, essentially replacing the <emph> with bold text:

```
<xsl:template match="emph">
  <fo:inline-sequence font-weight="bold">
    <xsl:apply-templates/>
  </fo:inline-sequence>
</xsl:template>
```

The `fo:` prefix is the namespace for formatting objects—a way of creating format elements in a document by using style sheets. The namespace for formatting objects is http://www.w3.org/1999/XSL/Format (which has to be declared in the namespace declaration in the beginning of the style sheet, as well as in the resulting XML document). More information about formatting objects, which do not have anything to do with transformations and which have everything to do with formatting, appears in Chapter 8, "XSLT and Style."

Multiple xsl:apply-templates elements can be used within a single template to perform simple reordering. The following example creates two HTML tables. The first table is filled with domestic sales while the second table is filled with foreign sales:

```
<xsl:template match="product">
  <table>
    <xsl:apply-templates select="sales/domestic"/>
  </table>
  <table>
    <xsl:apply-templates select="sales/foreign"/>
  </table>
</xsl:template>
```

Depending on the addressing of the element, there can be two matching descendents where one is a descendent of the other (they are on the same branch of the tree). Both descendents will be processed as usual and will not be processed differently in any way. For example, given a source document as follows,

```
<doc><div><div></div></div></doc>
```

the following rule

```
<xsl:template match="doc">
  <xsl:apply-templates select=".//div"/>
</xsl:template>
```

will process both the outer div and inner div elements.

It is possible to create loops in XSLT, which might become a problem. While xsl:apply-templates normally is used to process nodes that are descendents of the current node (further down in the tree on the same branch), any loops cannot be dangerous. When xsl:apply-templates is used to process elements that are not descendents of the current node, however, it is possible to create nonterminating loops. For example:

```
<xsl:template match="foo">
  <xsl:apply-templates select="."/>
</xsl:template>
```

This code will be nonterminating. Some processors might be capable of discovering such loops, but it is possible to create a nonterminating loop that might be a security risk (to speak nothing of being annoying).

Copying

The xsl:copy element provides an easy way of copying the current node. You do not have to know anything about it—the <xsl:copy> element copies it through to the result tree. According to the value of the match attribute, it can be applied to any kind of node. If the current node is an element, <xsl:copy> will construct an element in the result tree. If it is an attribute, <xsl:copy> will construct an attribute and put it inside the containing element. The <xsl:copy> element handles the other types of nodes, as well.

The namespace nodes of the current node are automatically copied as well, but the attributes and children of the node are not automatically copied (in other words, only the branch in the tree where you currently are will get copied). xsl:copy will create a template that applies to the attributes and children of the created node. It can only be applied to nodes of types that can have attributes or children (in other words, root nodes and element nodes).

The xsl:copy element might have a use-attribute-sets attribute. This attribute is used only when copying element nodes.

Because you do not need to define the root node of the result tree (but the node is created automatically), that node is treated differently. When the current node is the root node, xsl:copy will not create a root node but just apply the content template.

For example, the identity transformation can be written by using xsl:copy as follows:

```
<xsl:template match="@*|node()">
  <xsl:copy>
    <xsl:apply-templates select="@*|node()"/>
  </xsl:copy>
</xsl:template>
```

If you apply xsl:attribute to create an attribute that has the same name as the current node, it might cause an error. Applying xsl:copy in the same situation will also cause an error. It is very useful to copy an attribute from the source tree to the result tree, however—for instance, in the case of XML attributes that do not change. xml:lang is a good example. It gives the language of the element, and if you are not changing the language of the content in the result tree, it can be copied through from the source to the result. The following template is named "apply-templates-copy-lang," and it will be applied by calling it when you want to copy the language attribute.

```
<xsl:template name="apply-templates-copy-lang">
 <xsl:for-each select="@xml:lang">
   <xsl:copy/>
 </xsl:for-each>
 <xsl:apply-templates/>
</xsl:template>
```

When you want to apply it in the result tree, simply write the following:

```
<xsl:call-template name="apply-templates-copy-lang"/>
```

This code calls a named template. This action is simpler than creating a separate template to copy the attribute.

Suppose that you have an XML document with an element and its descendents that you want to remove. Suppose the name of the element is called "remove." You want to keep the rest of the XML tree in the result tree. Essentially, you want to copy the rest of the tree and just remove the remove element.

Here is a template that will perform that task:

```
<xsl:template match='/'>
  <xsl:apply-templates/>
</xsl:template>
<xsl:template match='remove'/>
<xsl:template match='@* | node()'>
  <xsl:copy>
    <xsl:apply-templates select='@* | node()'/>
  </xsl:copy>
</xsl:template>
```

An Example: Hello, World

Starting an XSLT tutorial with a classic "Hello, world" program is awkward. Programming with XSLT is not like computer programming with compilers and programs. It is more similar to scripting languages like PERL, but there is no concept of a "program" in XSLT. Let's see how XSLT writes "Hello, world" on the screen.

In XSLT, you author *transformation sheets*, which are fed into a *transformation processor* together with a *source document*, which is always an XML document. The transformation sheet contains rules for how the source document will be transformed. The transformation processor applies the rules in the transformation sheet to the source document and generates the result. The process can be described as a function of the XSLT transformation processor, which takes two arguments (the source document and the transformation sheet) and returns a result (the result document):

XSLT processor (*source document, transformation sheet*) → *result document*

The transformation sheet is the "program" in XSLT. If the source document contains the text "Hello, world," we can write a transformation sheet that selects the classic sentence and returns the words in the form of a plain-text string, rather than as an XML document. Here is the source document (not complete, as you will note, since it is missing the XML declaration—but XSLT can be used to transform fragments from documents, as well):

```
<message>Hello, world</message>
```

To transform this XML document into the "Hello, world" text, we need to instruct the transformation processor to select the value of the *text* element, to ignore everything else in the source document, and to insert the value of that element (the "Hello, world" text) as plain text into the result document.

In XSLT, a transformation sheet that performs this action looks like the following:

```
<xsl:transform version="1.0"
xmlns:xsl="http://www.w3.org/1999/XSL/Transform">
    <xsl:output method="text" />
    <xsl:template match="message">
        <xsl:value-of select="."/>
    </xsl:template>
</xsl:transform>
```

Now, we need to input the source document and the transformation sheet into a transformation processor. The ways by which the transformation sheet can be associated with the source document are many. If you have an *Integrated Development Environment* (IDE) that supports XSLT, all you might have to do is select the source document and press a button or select "Transform" in a menu (for example, XML Spy is available from www.xmlspy.com). Alternatively, you can download XT for free from http://www.jclark.com and transform the XML document with the following command:

```
xt  hello.xml  hello-to-text.xslt  hello.txt
```

The `hello.xml` is the source XML document. The `hello-to-text.xslt` is the transformation sheet. Also, the `hello.txt` is the result document that XT generates. If the transformation went through without any errors, the `hello.txt` file will contain the following line:

```
Hello, World
```

If you are using a different transformation processor, you must consult its documentation to see how transformation sheets and source documents are made available to the processor, since this is not standardized.

How the Transformation Sheet Works

How do transformation sheets work? The transformation sheet consists of a set of rules. As you probably have noticed, the syntax of the rules is XML: the transformation sheet that specifies how the source XML document will be transformed is also an XML document; everything that goes into the transformation processor is XML. The result could have been an XML document as well, but in this case we choose to generate a plain-text file. At first, this situation sounds confusing because typically one thinks of XML as a language to mark up data, in order to provide data about the data; as in the source document, the message element indicated that the following text was some sort of message. In XSLT, however, XML is used as the syntax of the transformation language.

In order to understand how the transformation processor transforms the source document, we must not think of the XML document as a text file (as a sequence of characters). Instead, we must look at the XML from the perspective of a computer program that has read the XML document into its memory. Here is the source document again:

```
<message>Hello, world</message>
```

The transformation processor, once it has read the document, will see the XML as a hierarchical tree structure. The message element is located immediately under the root, and one more step down in the hierarchy the processor will find the "Hello, world" text string. The element and the text are called *nodes* and represent XML information items. Other information items, in addition to text and elements, include attributes, processing instructions, and comments. Here is an illustration of what the transformation processor sees once it has read the source document:

```
----- message
    |
    ----- 'Hello, world'-----
```

Here is an XML document that has more structure and thus has a more complex hierarchy:

```
<program>
        <message xml:lang="en">Hello, world</message>
        <message xml:lang="se">Hej, v_rlden</message>
</program>
```

If this code had been the source document, the transformation processor would have seen the following hierarchy of nodes:

```
----- program
    |
    ----- message
          |
          ----- xml:lang="en"
         |
          ----- 'Hello, world'
    ----- message
          |
          ----- xml:lang="se"
         |
          ----- 'Hej, v_rlden'-----
```

So, now we know that the transformation processor views the XML source document not as sequential text, but rather as a hierarchy of different types of nodes (elements, attributes, text, and so on) and that this structure of nodes is being transformed. The XSLT processor does not work directly on the source document, but on the representation in memory, which is key to some of the operations we will look at in Chapters 5 and 6, as well as the addressing mechanisms of Xpath, which we will look at more in Chapter 4. The rules in the transformation sheet will be applied to the structure of nodes. When you, the author, are in the transformation sheet, and you want to select specific nodes in the source document for transformation, you can do so based on their type and their location in the hierarchy.

Now, let's take a closer look at the actual transformation sheet:

```
<!--
| State that we use XSLT version 1.0 and
| that the prefix "xsl" shall be bound to the unique
| XSLT namespace name,http://www.w3.org/1999/XSL/Transform.
| In this XML document, element names starting with "xsl"
| will be interpreted as XSLT operations.
+-->
<xsl:transform version="1.0"
```

```
xmlns:xsl="http://www.w3.org/1999/XSL/Transform">

<!--
| State that output shall be formatted as plain text
+-->
<xsl:output method="text" />

<!--
| Select the message element for transformation
+-->
<xsl:template match="message">
<!--
| Take the value of the selected element (".") and insert it
|   into the result document
+-->
     <xsl:value-of select="." />

</xsl:template>
</xsl:transform>
```

The text between `<!--` and `-->`__is *comments* and is ignored by the transformation processor.

The first element, the `xsl:transform`, is a container and specifies that the transformation processor must support XSLT version 1.0 (the version used in this book). All XSLT transformation processors support version 1.0 because it is the first version of the language. The `xmlns:xsl` attribute indicates that all element names with the xsl prefix will be associated with the unique http://www.w3.org/1999/XSL/ Transform URL and treated as XSLT operations. Another prefix than xsl could have been used, but using xsl is common practice for XSLT transformation sheets. If you include non-XSLT elements in the transformation sheet, they must use another prefix bound to a different URL. Otherwise, the transformation processor cannot distinguish XSLT operations from elements with the same name but different meanings that accidentally might exist in other XML languages. The `xsl:transform` element and its attributes are used by the processor to recognize the document as a transformation sheet, and thus must always be present.

The `xsl:output` element specifies that the result will be formatted as plain text. In order to generate the result as XML, we can change the output method to xml:

```
<xsl:transform version="1.0"
xmlns:xsl="http://www.w3.org/1999/XSL/Transform">
```

```
<xsl:output method="xml" />

<xsl:template match="message">
    <xsl:value-of select="."/>
</xsl:template>

</xsl:transform>
```

Instead of only the "Hello, world" text string, the result will now become the following:

```
<?xml version="1.0" encoding="UTF-8" ?>
Hello, World
```

The transformation processor added the XML declaration before the actual result of the transformation. If you know XML, you will notice that the result is not a correct, well-formed, XML document; it does not contain any elements, only the XML declaration and some text. So, if the processor did not produce correct XML, then what was the point of using the xsl:output element? As we will see later, the xsl:output element is a convenient way of letting the transformation processor take care of some of the low-level syntactical details (for example, adding the XML declaration) for known output formats (in other words, text and XML). It does not, however, guarantee that the result always is correct. That is still determined by the transformation rules in the transformation sheet.

The xsl:template element is perhaps the most important one (and one that we will return to often). Templates are at the core of XSLT programming (sometimes called template-based programming). The template matches a set of nodes in the source document and holds the transformation rules that will be applied to the matching nodes. During the transformation, the processor walks through the templates in the transformation sheet and applies the rules on the source document as it finds matching elements. Typically, a transformation sheet contains many templates.

The value of the match attribute on the xsl:template element is a pattern. A pattern has a special syntax that we will return to shortly. Patterns are used to associate nodes of the source document with templates in the transformation sheet. The message pattern matches the element node with the same name. The selected node is called the current node. Patterns inside the template are evaluated relative to the current node. The pattern syntax is a language of its own. We will discuss this topic in Chapter 5, "Programming Basics in XSLT."

The actual transformation rules are located inside the template. One transformation rule is the `xsl:value-of` operation. It selects a node as specified with the pattern in the `select` attribute, takes its value, and inserts it as text into the result document. The pattern in the `select` attribute selects the current node. In this case, it is the `message` element. The value of the `message` element is the "Hello, world" text.

After the processor has found all message nodes in the source document, there is only one, and the transformation is done.

Loops and Conditional Processing

The next transformation sheet will select text nodes in the source document based on the language, as indicated in the `xml:lang` attribute, and will insert a language-specific text before each message. Also, the result will be XHTML, not plain text:

```
<?xml version="1.0" encoding="utf-8" ?>
<html>
<head>
  <title>Hello, World</title>
</head>
<body>
  <h1>English:</h1>
  <p>Hello, world</p>
  <h1>Svenska:</h1>
  <p>Hej, v_rlden</p>
</body>
</html>
```

This concept makes the transformation sheet more complicated, but not by much.

```
<xsl:transform version="1.0"
xmlns:xsl="http://www.w3.org/1999/XSL/Transform">

    <xsl:output method="xml" encoding="ISO-8859-1"/>

    <xsl:template match="program" >
```

```
<html>
    <head>
    <title>Hello, World</title>
    </head>
    <body>

    <xsl:for-each select="message">
        <h1>
        <xsl:choose>
            <xsl:when test="lang('se')">
                <xsl:text>Svenska: </xsl:text>
            </xsl:when>
            <xsl:when test="lang('en')">
                <xsl:text>English: </xsl:text>
            </xsl:when>                     <xsl:otherwise>
                <xsl:text>Unknown: </xsl:text>
            </xsl:otherwise>               </xsl:choose>
        </h1>
        <p>
            <xsl:copy-of select="text()" />
        </p>
    </xsl:for-each>

    </body>
    </html>
```

This transformation sheet introduces a couple of new concepts. It inserts literal XHTML elements, uses a loop, uses conditional processing, creates text and inserts it into the result, and uses patterns (not only on the template).

Because they are not prefixed with xsl, the XHTML elements in the template—html, head, title, h1, p, and body—are inserted as they are into the result document. Using literal elements this way is the easiest way of creating and inserting elements into the result document. As we will see later, XSLT offers other mechanisms for creating elements and also other types of XML information items that are more appropriate in some situations. But in most cases, literal elements are sufficient. As in this case, literal XHTML elements are used as a template for the result document.

The xsl:for-each element is a loop and works in the following way. First, the pattern in the select attribute is evaluated. The operations inside the xsl:for-each element are then applied on each node that matches the pattern. In the program element, there are two nodes that will match the message elements. Thus, the operations inside the `xsl:for-each` element will be executed for each `message` element. The For-each loop is available in other languages as well (for example, PERL and C#).

The `xsl:choose` element, together with the `xsl:when` and `xsl:otherwise` elements, is used for conditional processing. The test attribute contains an expression that is evaluated to a boolean value (*true* or *false*). If *true*, then the operations inside the `xsl:when` element are executed. The operations inside the `xsl:otherwise` element are evaluated only when none of the `xsl:when` elements were executed. If you are familiar with other programming languages, you have already recognized this statement as a classic Switch statement.

The `xsl:text` element is easy to understand. It generates a text node and inserts it into the result document. This method is an easy way of getting plain text into the result document. In this case, we use it to insert the language-specific text and to write "unknown" when we do not know what the language is.

Patterns have been used at various places in the transformation sheets:

- The *lang('en')* pattern was used to match elements for which the `xml:space` attribute had the value of 'en'.
- The *message* and *program* patterns were used to match elements with the same name.
- The . pattern was used to match the current node.

The XSLT patterns are based on the XML path expression (XPath) language—a separate language that spun off from the work on XSLT and that can be used on its own to address nodes in an XML document.

Things That XSLT Cannot Do

Despite its power, XSLT is not a general programming language (although it is Turing-complete). It cannot do some things (and other things less well). For instance, you can not construct Xpath expressions in run time, which means that you can not refer to the style sheet you are using (for instance, to obtain a variable value). Variables get their value at run time, when the template is applied to the source tree. This value also applies to style sheets and templates, which cannot be called dynamically (although they can be called at run time).

When XSL was being designed, it was decided that the advantages of having a side effects-free language (in other words, without the ability to change the value of variables once the style sheet has gone through the parser) outweighed the annoyance of old school programmers (who are used to changing the value of variables). The idea is that if you parse your document once and only once and ban any changes to the style sheet, you will get (in theory) much faster processing. This question is also a philosophical one, of course. Do you regard the result tree as a fixed entity or not? Another thing is that it is possible to chain several source trees, result trees, and style sheets in order to create the same result.

XSLT also does not know anything about the source tree and style sheets before they were parsed. In other words, it will not know anything about entity definitions or entity references used in XML.

Another restriction is that XSLT sources can be XML and XML only. The content of an XML element can be binary, text, or whatever is required. But the element itself has to be Unicode. This condition excludes all characters in the C0 group except TAB, CR, and LF. &#27; should be rejected by the XML parser before XSL gets a chance to do anything with it. In other words, you cannot use XSLT to perform transformations on an HTML document. HTML is not XML, so it cannot be used as input to a transformation. It has to be transformed to XML (for instance, to XHTML by using HTML Tidy) first.

It is also not possible to have any variable reference in the match attribute of a template. In general, in XSLT you cannot use variables to contain expressions, patterns, or parts thereof—you can only use them to hold strings, numbers, node-sets, and Booleans. <xsl:number> is the one place in XSLT where variables can be used within a predicate that forms part of a pattern. There is no way in standard XSLT of saying "sort by the value of the XPath expression represented by the string value of $param."

The XPath data types are as follows: string, number, node-set, and boolean. XSLT adds an additional data type called the result tree fragment (whose days are numbered, because the next version of XSLT will likely do away with it). There is no XPath data type that corresponds to an Xpath expression. Likewise, there is no eval() function that will enable you to evaluate a string as an Xpath expression. The first thing to remember is that XSLT variables do not store Xpath expressions; instead, they always store one of the five data types. How Xpath works, and how it interacts with these data types, will be the subject of the next chapter.

Xpath

I n this chapter, we will examine the *XML Path Language* (Xpath), which XSLT uses to select the nodes in the source document that are going to be used in the transformation process.

In the previous chapter, you saw that we frequently had to use Xpath addresses to get to the elements and attributes in the source document. This situation is actually unavoidable in XSLT. The language is actually not about transformation; rather, it is about creating a node tree and transforming it into another. This process involves accessing one or more node trees that are derived from input XML documents. Think of it as the XSLT processor creating the tree in memory when it reads the source document and applying the transformation sheet to it in order to create the result tree. The result tree does not have to have any relationship with the source tree(s) at all. At the end of the process, a serialized output is derived from your result tree automatically, creating the result document.

In other words, locating information in an XML document is critical to both transforming it and to associating or relating it to other information (for instance, to parameterize the transformation by attributes or content of the elements). Because an XML document is a tree and the tree structure is known, it is possible to address parts of the tree. More properly, you are addressing the data model of interlinked nodes that are arranged hierarchically, echoing the tree-shape of the nested elements in an instance (a mouthful, but true), creating a subtree. We will continue to talk about the XML document as a tree in itself.

The XML document tree is made up of nodes of different types. Actually, it is addressing the parsed result of the bit stream that the processor has received, but there is no need to look at it at that level. To be able to address the components of the document—the nodes in the tree—you have to know how the components are arranged. Viewing the document as a tree makes the actual syntax of the markup irrelevant.

Apart from addressing parts of documents, Xpath also provides some facilities to handle the manipulation of strings, numbers, and Boolean attributes (true and false). The presence of datatypes and expressions makes XSLT and Xpath look like a proper programming language. The W3C XML Stylesheet and the W3C XML Linking work groups created this language jointly. Both groups extend the core Xpath facilities to meet the needs they had in each of their domains: The style sheet group uses Xpath as the core of expressions in XSLT, and the linking group uses Xpath as the core of expressions in the XPointer recommendation. Xpath gets its name from its use of a path notation (the same as in Uniform Resource Indicators, or URIs) for navigating through the hierarchical structure of an XML document.

If the nodes of the tree have unique identifiers (for instance, XML fragment IDs), those can be used for the addressing (by using URIs). Some types of nodes also have names that can be XML identifiers. Xpath also supports XML namespaces, which means that the name of a component of the tree—a node—consists of a local part and a namespace part, which can be a null namespace URI (in case it is not used outside the current document). The combination of the local part of the name and the namespace part is called an expanded name. Addressing is most often done by using the abstract location path syntax, however.

The key to Xpath is that the order of components in the tree (the hierarchical position in the tree) can be used to address the components. In other words, the tree is organized in the order the elements nest in each other. This ordering is referred to as document order in Xpath (in other cases, it is called parse order or depth-first order). It is the order in which the first character of the XML representation of each node occurs in the XML representation of the document after the expansion of general entities. The root node will be the first node followed by the element nodes. Element nodes will occur before their children. Attribute nodes and namespace nodes of an element occur before the children of the element. Namespace nodes occur before attribute nodes, but the relative order of namespace nodes and attribute nodes is implementation dependent. The document order can also be reversed.

If that sounds difficult to understand, look at the following example:

```
<first_element>
  <second_element>
    <third_element first_attribute="thirtyone">
      <fourth_element second_attribute="fortytwo">
        <fifth_element third_attribute="fiftythree">
        </fifth_element>
      </fourth_element>
    </third_element>
    <sixth_element>
      <seventh_element>
        <eighth_element>
          <ninth_element>
          </ninth_element>
        </eighth_element>
      </seventh_element>
    </sixth_element>
  </second_element>
</first_element>
```

The order of this document is as follows:

```
1: first_element
2: second_element
3: third_element
4: thirtyone
5: sixth_element
6: fourth_element
7: fortytwo
8: seventh_element
9: fifth_element
10: fiftythree
11: eighth_element
12: ninth_element
```

The tree consists of the root node and its child nodes. The children can be elements which, in turn, can have children. The nodes never share children, because the fact that they have different parents will make the child nodes unique. All nodes except the root have one and only one parent, which is either an element node or the root node. The descendants of a node are the children of the node and the descendants of the children of the node.

In this example, the root is <first_element>. It has one child, <second_element>, which has two children: <third_element> and <sixth_element>. <third_element> has one child: <fourth_element> (and so on).

If you bring it up in an editor that enables you to visualize the tree structure, it will look like Figure 4.1.

For clarity, I have added the tree structure on top of the document in Figure 4.2.

An Xpath address (an expression) starts in the context node (the node that is the root of the address). It tells you where to find the members of a node set by identifying the locations of those nodes relative to an initial set of nodes (which you have specified). It is a "path" because it says, essentially, that to find all of the nodes in the set that you want, "start at the nodes that match this pattern, then go in this direction (along an axis) to all nodes that match this other pattern, then go in this other direction (along another axis) to the nodes that match this other pattern." Beyond the internal addresses in the document, Xpath uses XML namespaces.

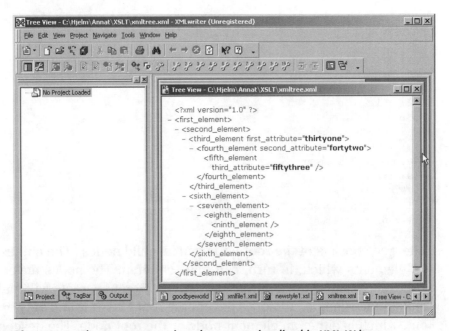

Figure 4.1 The tree structure in a document visualized in XML Writer.

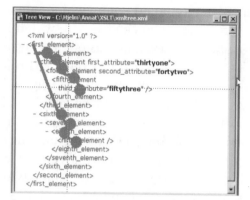

Figure 4.2 The tree structure overlaid on the text.

In other words, you have to construct one style sheet per source document, because the addressing can vary between documents (unless, as we noted in the previous chapter, they are very similar).

Xpath Nodes in the Document Tree

There are seven types of nodes in Xpath:

- Root nodes
- Element nodes
- Text nodes
- Attribute nodes
- Namespace nodes
- Processing instruction nodes
- Comment nodes

For every type of node, there is a way of determining a string value for a node of that type. For some types of nodes, the string value is part of the node; for other types of nodes, the string value is computed from the string value of descendant nodes (the children and their children). For element nodes and root nodes, the string value of a node is not the same as the string returned by the DOM nodeValue method. String values are used in some XSLT operations, as you will see in Chapters 5 and 6.

Some types of nodes also have an expanded name, which consists of a local part (a string of characters) and a namespace URI, which is either null (in other words, does not show) or a string (although strictly speaking, URIs are not strings). The namespace URI can be a URI reference, which can have a fragment identifier (which has the hash sign # in front of it) and can be relative. A relative URI should be resolved into an absolute URI during namespace processing (preferably by the XSLT processor). Relative URIs can cause problems if you are moving components between style sheets (unless you do not have a very strict document system). If you are going to use components to build style sheets (a very good and simple method of accomplishing a lot of things quickly), it is better to use absolute URIs to address your documents.

Element nodes can have a *unique identifier* (ID) if there is an ID attribute declared in the DTD or XML Schema for the document. If there are two IDs that are the same (not unique), the document is not valid. The namespace URIs of expanded names of nodes in the data model should be absolute. Note that even if you are using expanded names, you can have conflicting IDs. If the values are the same but the only thing differentiating them is the namespace, because two expanded names are equal if they have the same local part, they can be the same if either both have a null namespace URI or if both have non-null namespace URIs that are equal. If a document does not have a DTD, then no element in the document will have a unique ID.

Root Node

The root node is the root of the tree. There can only be a root node at the top of the tree and not anywhere else (confusingly enough, trees are upside down). In this example, <first_element> is the root node. If there had been other elements at the same level as <first_element>, XSLT would construct a root node to be the parent. Think of the root node as the (nonexistent) element that is marked up with the xml declaration. The element nodes for the elements in the document are children of the root node. Processing instruction and comment nodes that occur in, before, and after the end of the document element are also children to the root node. Because the root node occurs before the namespace declaration, it does not have an expanded-name.

Element Nodes

There is an element node for every element in the document. Each element node has a number of children, which are the element nodes, comment nodes, processing instruction nodes, and text nodes that it contains.

The element node has an expanded name that is created by taking the QName of each element as specified in the tag and expanding it. It will have a null namespace if there is no prefix on the QName, and there is no default namespace of the document (otherwise, the prefix will be the default namespace of the document).

Attribute Nodes

Each element node has an associated set of attribute nodes. The element is the parent of each of these attribute nodes, but the attribute node is not a child of its parent element (which means that it does not inherit properties from it). This situation is different from the DOM, where the element is not the parent of the attribute. If an attribute is declared in the DTD (in other words, there is a default attribute declared for the element), it is treated in the same way as an attribute for which the value is specified if the attribute is declared for the element type in the DTD. Elements cannot share attribute nodes.

Because elements cannot share attribute nodes, the = operator in Xpath does not determine whether two nodes are the same (only if they have the same value).

The attributes xml:lang and xml:space are defined in the XML specification. They can be used in any XML document type, if they are declared in the DTD. Their semantic is such that once defined on an element, the value is inherited by all descendant children. An element can have attribute nodes only for attributes that were explicitly specified in the start tag or empty element tag of the element, however, or that were explicitly declared in the DTD with a default value. In other words, if xml:lang and xml:space apply to the element, this tag might not show, and you have to look back into the tree to see it. The expanded name of an attribute is computed in the same way as for the element.

It is possible for default attributes to be declared in an external DTD or in an external parameter entity. The XML recommendation does not require an XML processor to read an external DTD or an external parameter unless it is validating the document. In other words, if your processor is assuming that the Xpath tree contains default attribute values that are declared in an external DTD or parameter entity, those values might not work with some nonvalidating XML processors.

Namespace Nodes

Namespaces are used to separate elements so that they do not have the same value although their tags stay the same. For each element, there is an associated set of namespace nodes—one for each namespace prefix that is used in the element (including the XML prefix, which is implicitly declared by the XML Namespaces Recommendation for all XML documents) and one for the default namespace (if the element does not have a namespace prefix of its own). There can be more than one, because the element can have children that can be in a different namespace than itself. The `xmlns=""` attribute "undeclares" the default namespace and sets the namespace to the one declared in the xmlns attribute instead.

The element is the parent of each of these namespace nodes, but a namespace node is not a child of its parent element (because it does not inherit its properties even if it follows it in the document order). Elements never share namespace nodes, so there will be one namespace node for an element for the following:

- Every attribute on the element whose name starts with xmlns:
- Every attribute on an ancestor element whose name starts with xmlns: (unless the element itself or a nearer ancestor redeclares the prefix)
- If the element or some ancestor has an xmlns attribute and the value of the xmlns attribute for the nearest such element is not empty

A namespace node has an expanded name. The local part is the namespace prefix (empty if the namespace node is for the default namespace), and the namespace URI is always null.

Processing Instruction Nodes

There is a processing instruction node for every processing instruction except those that occur within the document type declaration. The XML declaration, which starts the document, is not a processing instruction, so there is no processing instruction node corresponding to the XML declaration.

The local part of the expanded name of the processing instruction is the processing instructions target; the namespace URI is null. The local part of the expanded name of the node comes from the target property. (The namespace URI part of the expanded name of the node is null.)

Comment Nodes

Every comment has a comment node, except for any comment that occurs within the DTD. A comment node does not have an expanded name. The comment nodes are children of the elements where they occur.

Text Nodes

Character data in the CDATA section of the XML document is grouped into text nodes. As much character data as possible is grouped into each text node. A text node never has an immediately following or preceding sibling that is a text node.

Characters inside comments, processing instructions, and attribute values do not produce text nodes. Line endings in external entities are normalized to #xA as specified in the XML recommendation.

Text nodes do not have expanded names.

Xpath Data Types: Boolean, Numerical Expressions, Node Sets, and Strings

Xpath has four data types: number, string, Boolean, and node set. XSLT 1.0 adds a fifth: result tree fragment (it is a node set in a different context, which will most likely disappear in version 1.1).

The number can be an IEEE 754 number but not null. A number in Xpath represents a floating-point number and can have any double-precision 64-bit format IEEE 754 value. These include a special *Not-a-Number* (NaN) value, positive and negative infinity, and positive and negative zero.

The string can be any string, including an empty string, but not null. The Boolean can only have two values, true or false. The node set can have a node set as a value, and it can be empty (no nodes in the set) but not null. The result tree fragment can contain a result tree and can be empty (no nodes in the set) but not null.

In Xpath, there is no concept of "null" per se. You either have an object of one of those types or you do not. It is an error if you reference an object that is not defined. A Boolean object (of type Boolean) can have one of two values, true or false. An "or" expression is evaluated by evaluating each operand and converting its value to a Boolean as if by a call to the Boolean function. The result is true if either value is true and false otherwise. The right operand is not evaluated if the left operand evaluates to true.

Strings consist of a sequence of zero or more characters, where a character is defined as in the XML recommendation. A single character in Xpath corresponds to a single Unicode abstract character with a single corresponding Unicode scalar value. This situation is not the same as a 16-bit Unicode code value, however. The Unicode-coded character representation for an abstract character with a Unicode scalar value greater than U+FFFF is a pair of 16-bit Unicode code values (a surrogate pair). In many programming languages, a string is represented by a sequence of 16-bit Unicode code values; implementations of Xpath in such languages must take care to ensure that a surrogate pair is correctly treated as a single Xpath character. In Unicode, two strings should be treated as identical although they consist of the distinct sequences of Unicode abstract characters. For example, some accented characters can be represented in either a precomposed or decomposed form. If both of the characters in the Xpath expression and in the XML document have been normalized into a canonical form, it will be correct—but otherwise, you might get unexpected results.

String Values

Xpath defines a way to compute a string value for each type of node. In many cases, the string value of a node is used in Xpath. It is computed differently for the different types of nodes.

The string value of the root node is the concatenation of the string values of all text node descendants of the root node in document order.

The string value of an element node is the concatenation of the string values of all text node descendants of the element node in document order. Entity references to both internal and external entities have to be expanded before the expanded name or the string value are computed. Character references have to be resolved.

The string value of an attribute node is the normalized value as specified by the XML recommendation. Attributes whose normalized value is a zero-length string are not treated specially; rather, they result in an attribute node whose string value is a zero-length string.

The string value of a namespace node is the namespace URI that is being bound to the namespace prefix. If it is a relative URI, it must be resolved just like a namespace URI in an expanded name.

The string value of a processing instruction node is the part of the processing instruction following the target and any white space. It does not include the terminating ?>.

The string value of comment is the content of the comment not including the opening <!-- and the closing -->.

The string value of a text node is the character data. A text node always has at least one character of data. Each character within a CDATA section is treated as character data. <![CDATA[<]]> in the source document will be treated in the same way as <. Both will result in a single < character in a text node in the tree. When a text node that contains a < character is written as XML, the < character must be escaped by, for example, using < or including it in a CDATA section.

Context Nodes

Xpath defines addresses of nodes relative to the current context node. Context in Xpath is specified by the application (XSLT in our case). xsl:apply-templates selects a set of nodes that become the "current node list." The XSLT processor looks at each node in the list one by one in document order, finds the template that best matches that node, and instantiates the instructions found in that template—using the node as the "current node."

xsl:for-each does the same thing, but the XSLT processor uses the contents of the for-each element as the best matching template.

For xsl:apply-templates, you can have many templates that match a given node, but there are rules that the XSLT processor follows to determine which of the matching templates is the "best" match. This conflict resolution is described in section 5.5 of the XSLT 1.0 Recommendation. xsl:call-template keeps the current node the same and goes to the named template, honoring similar conflict resolution rules.

In XSLT, an outermost expression (in other words, an expression that is not part of another expression) gets its context from the current node. When a template is instantiated, it is always instantiated with respect to a current node and a current node list. The current node is always a member of the current node list. Many operations in XSLT are relative to the current node. Only a few instructions change the current node list or the current node; during the instantiation of one of these instructions, the current node list changes to a new list of nodes, and each member of this new list becomes the current node in turn. After the instantiation of the instruction is complete, the current node and current node list revert to what they were before the instruction was instantiated.

Templates are not instantiated in a predictable order. Processing always begins with the current node list being just the root node of the main source tree. The best matching template for that one node is found, and its instructions are instantiated with that node as the current node. The best matching template is usually going to be the one that has match="/", and there is a built-in one (assuming that you are not using IE 5.0) for this purpose.

"Navigating" from template to template, if you want to call it that, is a matter of encountering an apply-templates element in the instructions within a template, selecting new nodes, finding a matching template for each node, and executing the instructions therein.

The context position comes from the position of the current node in the current node list. The first position is 1. The context size comes from the size of the current node list. The variable bindings are the bindings in scope on the element, which has the attribute in which the expression occurs.

The set of namespace declarations are those in scope on the element that has the attribute in which the expression occurs; this set includes the implicit declaration of the prefix XML required by the XML Namespaces Recommendation; the default namespace (as declared by xmlns) is not part of this set.

The function library consists of the core function library together with the additional functions and extension functions. It is an error for an expression to include a call to any other function.

Patterns and Location Paths

Patterns in XSLT are used to address and describe nodes. You can understand the patterns without knowing Xpath, however. In a pattern, | indicates alternatives; a pattern that has one or more | symbols separates alternatives that match if any of the alternatives match. A pattern that consists of a sequence of StepPatterns, paths to locations that are separated by / or //, is matched from right to left. StepPatterns only match if the pattern farthest to the right matches, and there are matches for the rest of the pattern. If the separator is /, then only the parent element can be a match. If the separator is //, then any ancestor element can be a match.

A StepPattern matches along the child axis if the Xpath NodeTest returns a true value for the node and the node is not an attribute node (a node test checks that the type and name of the node are the same as those given in the address, which is a predicate in this case). A StepPattern that uses the attribute axis matches if the NodeTest is true for the node and if the node is an attribute node. When the expression is enclosed in square brackets [], then the context node is evaluated against the first predicate expression in a StepPattern, and the siblings of the context node that match the NodeTest are used as the context node list. This situation is true unless the node being matched is an attribute node, in which case the context node list is all of the attributes that have the same parent as the attribute being matched and that match the NameTest.

There are two kinds of location paths: relative location paths and absolute location paths:

A relative location path consists of a sequence of one or more location steps separated by /. The steps in a relative location path are composed from left to right. Each step selects a set of nodes that are relative to a context node in turn, and then an initial sequence of steps is composed together with the following step. The initial sequence of steps selects a set of nodes relative to a context node. Each node in that set is used as a context node for the following step. The sets of nodes identified by that step are merged (by forming a union). This union is the set of nodes identified by the composition of the steps. For example, `child::div/child::para` selects the `para` element children of the `div` element children of the context node (or, in other words, the `para` element grandchildren that have `div` parents).

An absolute location path consists of /, which can be followed by a relative location path. A / by itself selects the root node of the document that contains the context node (in other words, the root node of the current document). If a relative location path follows it, then the nodes selected are the same as what would be selected if the location path were relative to the root node of the current document.

Location Steps

A location step has three parts:

- An axis, which specifies the tree relationship between the nodes selected by the location step and the context node
- A node test, which specifies the node type and expanded name of the nodes selected by the location step
- Zero or more predicates, which use arbitrary expressions to further refine the set of nodes selected by the location step

The syntax for a location step is the axis name and node test separated by a double colon, followed by zero or more expressions each in square brackets. For example, in `child::para[position()=1]`, `child` is the name of the axis, `para` is the node test, and `[position()=1]` is a predicate.

The node set selected by the location step is the node set that results from generating an initial node set from the axis and node test and then filtering that node set by each of the predicates in turn.

The initial node set consists of the nodes having the relationship to the context node specified by the axis and having the node type and expanded name specified by the node test. For example, a location step `descendant::para` selects the `para` element descendants of the context node. `descendant` specifies that each node in the initial node set must be a descendant of the context, and `para` specifies that each node in the initial node set must be an element named `para`. The meaning of some node tests is dependent on the axis.

The initial node set is filtered by the first predicate in order to generate a new node set; this new node set is then filtered by using the second predicate and so on. The final node set is the node set selected by the location step. The axis affects how the expression in each predicate is evaluated, and therefore the semantics of a predicate are defined with respect to an axis. Alternatively, we can access an arbitrary location in the tree based on points in the tree that have unique identifiers.

For example,

```
appendix//ulist/item[position()=1]
```

matches a node if and only if all of the following statements are true:

- The NodeTest item evaluates as "true" for the node, and the node is not an attribute.

- You get a "true" result when evaluating the PredicateExpr `position()=1` with the node as context node, as well as the siblings of the node.

- The node has a parent that matches `appendix//ulist`; this statement will be true if the parent is a ulist element that has an appendix ancestor element.

A pattern is a set of location path patterns separated by |. A location path pattern is a location path whose steps use only the child or attribute axes. Although patterns must not use the `descendant-or-self` axis, patterns can use the // operator as well as the / operator (we will learn more about *axis* later). Location path patterns can also start with an id or key function call with a literal argument. Predicates in a pattern can use arbitrary expressions just like predicates in a location path. You cannot end an Xpath with / (or //); instead, you have to have the final step specified. The grammar says what expressions are allowed, and by implication, that anything that is not in the list is not allowed.

A pattern is defined to match a node if there is a context that the node can be in, and it becomes a member of the node set that is a result of the evaluation if there is a pattern that can be evaluated as an expression with that context. There will be a context node for the possible contexts that consist of the node that is being matched (or an ancestor of that node and a list of context nodes that contains just that node).

For example, p matches any p element. In other words, if you evaluate p with the parent of that element as the context node, then the resulting set of nodes will contain p as one of its members. This resulting set matches even a p element that is the document element, because the document root is the parent of the document element. The syntax for Xpath is, confusingly enough, not XML. The basic Xpath syntax is similar to file system addressing and is the same as is used in URIs (which is based on the ISO9660 file system). If the path starts with a slash /, then it represents an absolute path to the required element. If the path starts with //, then all elements in the document that fulfill the following criteria are selected. The star * (or asterisk) selects all elements located by the preceding path. Several paths can be combined with a | separator. Attributes are specified by the @ (at sign) prefix.

Values of attributes can be used as selection criteria. The function "normalize-space" removes leading and trailing spaces and replaces sequences of white space characters with a single space.

Expressions in square brackets can further specify an element. A number in the brackets gives the position of the element in the selected set. The function last() selects the last element in the selection. Never use curly braces inside an Xpath expression, and never use anything inside an <xsl:value-of> instruction (it must be empty).

Here are some examples of patterns. There is also an abbreviated syntax, which we will talk about later. But to understand how Xpath works, it is easier to look at these examples:

`para` matches any para element.

`*` matches any element (and is an Xpath operand)

`chapter|appendix` matches any chapter element and any appendix element (the | is an Xpath operand).

`olist/item` matches any item element that has an olist parent (again, / is an Xpath operand).

`appendix//para` matches any para element that has an appendix ancestor element (`//` is an Xpath operand).

`/` matches the root node.

`text()` matches any text node.

`processing-instruction()` matches any processing instruction.

`node()` matches any node other than an attribute node and the root node.

`id("W11")` matches the element that has a unique ID W11.

`para[1]` matches any para element that is the first para child element of its parent.

`*[position()=1 and self::para]` matches any para element that is the first child element of its parent.

`para[last()=1]` matches any para element that is the only para child element of its parent.

`items/item[position()>1]` matches any item element that has an items parent and that is not the first item child of its parent.

`item[position() mod 2 = 1]` would be true for any item element that is an odd-numbered item child of its parent.

`div[@class="appendix"]//p` matches any p element that has a div ancestor element that has a class attribute with value `appendix`.

`@class` matches any class attribute (not any element that has a class attribute).

`@*` matches any attribute.

The following list describes some examples of location paths. The location path is used to express how the node you want to find relates to the current node (the context node).

`child::para` selects the para element children of the context node.

`child::*` selects all element children of the context node.

`child::text()` selects all text node children of the context node.

`child::node()` selects all of the children of the context node, whatever their node types.

`attribute::name` selects the name attribute of the context node.

`attribute::*` selects all of the attributes of the context node.

`descendant::para` selects the para element descendants of the context node.

`ancestor::div` selects all div ancestors of the context node.

`ancestor-or-self::div` selects the div ancestors of the context node, and if the context node is a div element, the context node as well.

`descendant-or-self::para` selects the para element descendants of the context node, and if the context node is a para element, the context node as well.

`self::para` selects the context node if it is a para element or otherwise selects nothing.

`child::chapter/descendant::para` selects the para element descendants of the chapter element children of the context node.

`child::*/child::para` selects all para grandchildren of the context node.

`/` selects the document root (which is always the parent of the document element).

`/descendant::para` selects all of the para elements in the same document as the context node.

`/descendant::olist/child::item` selects all of the item elements that have an olist parent and that are in the same document as the context node.

`child::para[position()=1]` selects the first para child of the context node.

`child::para[position()=last()]` selects the last para child of the context node.

`child::para[position()=last()-1]` selects the last but one para child of the context node.

`child::para[position()>1]` selects all of the para children of the context node other than the first para child of the context node.

`following-sibling::chapter[position()=1]` selects the next chapter sibling of the context node.

`preceding-sibling::chapter[position()=1]` selects the previous chapter sibling of the context node.

`/descendant::figure[position()=42]` selects the forty-second figure element in the document.

`/child::doc/child::chapter[position()=5]/child::section[position()=2]` selects the second section of the fifth chapter of the doc document element.

`child::para[attribute::type="warning"]` selects all para children of the context node that have a type attribute with the value warning.

`child::para[attribute::type='warning'][position()=5]` selects the fifth para child of the context node that has a type attribute with a value of warning.

`child::para[position()=5][attribute::type="warning"]` selects the fifth para child of the context node if that child has a type attribute with a value of warning (the result here is the same as the previous example, but note that the selection here is the fifth para child, and it gets selected only if the attribute is of the type warning, whereas in the previous example, the selection would be done only among the para children which had an attribute of the type warning, and then the fifth would be selected).

`child::chapter[child::title='Introduction']` selects the chapter children of the context node that have one or more title children with a string value equal to Introduction.

`child::chapter[child::title]` selects the chapter children of the context node that have one or more title children.

`child::*[self::chapter or self::appendix]` selects the chapter and appendix children of the context node.

`child::*[self::chapter or self::appendix][position()=last()]` selects the last chapter or appendix child of the context node.

The URI (Universal Resource Identifier)

The ideas of Tim Berners-Lee that are at the basis of the World Wide Web hinge on the use of *Universal Resource Identifiers* (URIs) to address objects. What is more, his idea is that in principle, not only is a URI a unique address, but the resource it points to is also unique and is referenced, rather than copied, whenever needed. He has borrowed this particular thought from Ted Nelson, the visionary who invented hypertext. In essence, what it means is that there will be no degradation through copying and that the resource will always be under the control of the originator. It is not how the Web is used in practice. But the theory is reflected both in the XML Namespaces specification and in Xpath, which is why you must have some knowledge about it.

URIs are not restricted to referencing information objects, but they can also be proxies for a physical entity that in itself does not have a URI. This method is how a physical device description can be created in the *Composite Capability/Preferences Profile* (CC/PP) format, just to give an example. In CC/PP, the statements relate to the URI where the device description is found, and by splitting it up into components (which are fragments of the RDF description), CC/PP can handle the different aspects of the device's capabilities. If the URI in the resource identifier contains a fragment identifier (the hash mark, #), it is only a subcomponent (a fragment) that is identified by the anchor id for the fragment of the resource to which the URI refers.

The URI itself is a string of characters that identifies an abstract or physical resource according to the specification that describes URIs, RFC 2396. This situation is not strictly true anymore, however, because RFC 2396 was based on the versions of the *Domain Name System* (DNS) that handled characters only (and only 7-bit ASCII at that). A URI today is really a bit string, but because the standards are not quite set yet, I will assume that the old standard still applies and will refer to URIs as if they were composed of characters. By the time that you read this text, however, it is very likely that there will be a new version of the DNS that handles Chinese characters (which, strictly speaking, are not characters but ideograms) as well as other alphabets and writing systems. This situation would mean that you could have a proper Chinese or Thai name for your site, for instance. That, in turn, would imply that they are Unicode characters, and are probably handled as strings of bits by the DNS server. However, the technology is not there at this moment.

The three parts of the URI name represent the three important parts of the concept: URIs are uniform, they identify resources, and the resources are resources. Okay, that sounds like a tautology if there ever was one. But here is how it works.

A resource can be anything that has an identity. And, because any object can have an identity, any object can be a resource. This reasoning is circular, and there have so far not been any real attempts to resolve it. Nor are they needed, because in practice the identity is being regulated by the scheme describing the resource.

Because the URI is an identifier, it should not be used for parameterization unless the parameters are part of the unique identity of the object. If you create a URI for each step you take, the coordinates are part of the identity of the footsteps. But when you request an object, you should not put your position in the URI. It has nothing to do with the object because it comes from you. This request is often misused (you have probably seen URIs that are 254 characters long, generated by lazy database programmers). But while it might look like a quick fix that takes care of an immediate problem, it creates more problems in the end.

Because a URI can address anything, you could create resource descriptions for anything—such as the direction of your steps (or, more practically, perhaps, and a real-use case) the books in a library. What most often happens is that the identifier points to an information object that, in turn, describes the object about which you are actually making statements. When you talk about a library book, you most often point to the card catalog in the library (actually, the computerized version of it), not the library book itself (which will cause a problem if the location of the book is a part of the URI—what if it has been checked out? Will its URI change second by second as you carry it home? As you can see, parameterizations do not belong in the URI).

Another aspect of the URI is its recognizability. In theory, a URI can be 255 characters (256 minus one, the root dot) long, but in practice, nobody could remember a URI like that. This feature matters, although Tim Berners-Lee intended that URIs should not be visible to humans (in particular, the protocol part should be something you should never have to care about); but as it happens, URIs have become as well-known as ZIP codes. Now, those of us who are old enough to remember when we started using ZIP codes will recognize how complicated it seemed to add a string of numbers to the address. Today, nobody even thinks about it. In the seven or so years since the Web was released upon humanity, URIs have become a fact of life—very much like ZIP codes. First, being a fashion item (this author had a laughing attack the first time he heard an announcer on the radio try to read a URI in 1995), they have become an indispensable part of an organization's address. Like brochures, business cards, and the sign on the door, it is an indispensable part of a company's identity. And indeed, it is not just an identifier, but it is also a part of both the identity and identification of the object.

A URI consists of a scheme and a scheme-specific part (the scheme depends on the protocol being used to access the object. There is one scheme for HTTP, one for *File Transfer Protocol* (FTP), one for the file system in Windows, and so on. "Scheme" is not the same as a "schema." A scheme is a way of writing things, whereas a schema is a way of describing things—for instance, an RDF schema). The URI scheme defines the name space of the URI. In the URI `http://www.history-buff.org/Napoleon`, the scheme part is `http`, the `://` differentiates the scheme from the scheme-specific part, and `www.historybuff.org/Napoleon` is scheme-specific. Actually, it is a path, as you recognize by now.

If you have been using the Web for a while, you probably wonder what happened to the *Uniform Resource Locator* (URL). The answer is that a URI can be a URL, but it does not have to be. In the URI `file://my_documents/RDF_book/ch03.doc`, the location of the file `ch03` of the type `doc` is in the subdirectory `RDF_book` of the directory `my_documents`. The operating system maps the filename to a location on the hard disk of the computer.

In the file scheme, the identification of an object is synonymous with its location. The URI is a URL. If you use a Web server to access the same file, however, the scheme for it could be `http://www.historybuff.org` because there will be a mapping between the file system and the Web server in your computer (actually, between the http scheme and the file scheme). Because an object can be anything (for instance, a library book, which is in the wrong format for the hard disk of your computer), the identifier does not have to be related to the location (what if somebody checked the book out? Is its location in the home of the borrower or in his bag as he takes the bus from the library, or forgotten at a café?). The scheme determines whether the location is a part of the identity of the object or not. In the file scheme, it is. In the http scheme, it is not.

The uniformity implies that the same type of identifier can be used for many different types of objects, regardless of the access method and how they are handled. Both `ftp://www.historybuff.org/Napoleon` and `http://www.historybuff.org/Napoleon` are valid resource identifiers although the access protocols are different (whether they refer to the same resource is a different question). Of course, the way this setup is structured is also dependent on the Internet way of doing things. Conceivably, you could have had different systems depending on whether you dialed in or had a fixed connection. But now, the separation of transport and application means that because the physical access method is translated into the *Internet Protocol* (IP) and the application protocol only works with the IP layer, the method you use to access the Internet is transparent to the system. It really is a question about which application protocol you use. Each application protocol contains systems to translate addresses to IP addresses (using the DNS).

You might have noted that the URI is the same for both FTP and HTTP. This situation is no coincidence, but the uniformity exists from the first part of the URI abbreviation. It might look like it refers to a file system, but there is nothing that says that it must. Indeed, there can be local mappings to whatever underlying identifier is used internally in the system. When you access a database-driven site such as CNN's Web site (http://www.cnn.com), for instance, the file does not exist previous to your requesting it. It is generated from a database by using a set of rules that are tied to the URI.

URIs are not tied to a specific protocol, which means that they can be used in different access protocols. In other words, when a new protocol is invented, it can use the same URI (except for the scheme, the protocol part) to address the resource(s) that can be handled by using that protocol.

Not all resources are network retrievable, however, because the access method might not be network connected (for instance, you or I can be considered resources—my employer does, as I hope yours does—but we are not downloadable). This situation has meant that there has been some contention about what you address when you dial a phone number (Is it the call or the terminal at the other end of the line that is being addressed?), and conceivably, you could have a URI for each memory you have or for each step you take (just three-dimensional coordinates plus time and your personal identity should do it). These are marginal aspects, and while the mechanism (strictly speaking) works for these edge cases as well, it is not really something you want to use for this purpose. It works best when referring to a network-accessible resource, and that is plenty enough.

The third part of the URI is the identifier part. An identifier is "an object that can act as a reference to something which has an identity," and because that can be anything, anything can be identified (at least, anything in a space of possible addresses that is as large as the number of the characters allowed with 256 as the exponent). In the URI, however, the identifying object is a sequence of characters with a restricted syntax (given that DNS only handles 7-bit ASCII and only in a certain way—at least, currently).

How XML Namespaces Work

XML namespaces identify a set of element names by using prefixes in the XML markup and declaring the namespace in the head of the document. Now, it is time to explain how XML namespaces work and why they are important. For instance, how do you create your own namespace?

If you are a programmer, you are probably familiar with the use of namespaces in programming languages. Namespaces in XML, however, are not quite the same thing as namespaces in programming languages. They are not sets of names but rather a mechanism to identify names and to make them unique. This uniqueness avoids collisions due to markup that is intended for some other software package by using the same element type or attribute name.

XML namespaces depend on URIs. The identification of the namespace is a URI, but that is the only function of the URI in this context. Namespaces are usually declared in the beginning of a document in the namespace declaration. It is quite possible to have a namespace declaration anywhere in the document, however. In that case, the namespace declaration is considered to apply to the element where it is specified and to all elements within the content of that element (that are nested within it), unless overridden by another namespace declaration with the same identifier part. Note that default namespaces do not apply directly to attributes.

A namespace is declared by using a family of reserved attributes. Such an attribute's name must either be xmlns or have xmlns: as a prefix (these two are reserved, but you can use any other prefix for your namespaces—however, the namespace declaration must be prefixed with xmlns). These attributes, like any other XML attributes, can be provided directly or by default. The attribute's value, a URI reference, is the namespace name identifying the namespace. There can actually be several names that have the same functionality but are identified by different URIs.

Because URI references can contain characters that are not allowed in names, they cannot be used directly as namespace prefixes. The namespace prefix serves as a proxy for a URI reference. It is the prefix, mapped to a URI reference, that selects a namespace. The combination of the universally managed URI namespace and the document's own namespace produces identifiers that are universally unique.

There can be several different namespaces in the same XML document. Namespace names are arbitrary and depend on the URI used, not on the prefix. Prefixes for the same namespace can vary between documents, because the scope of the declaration is only the current document. The default namespace can be set to the empty string. This function has the same effect, within the scope of the declaration, of there being no default namespace.

Here is a simple example (from the namespace specification) of two namespaces used in a document: bk and isbn. Both are declared by using the xmlns prefix and are then available throughout the document:

```
<?xml version="1.0"?>
  <!-- both namespace prefixes are available throughout -->
  <bk:book xmlns:bk='urn:loc.gov:books'
          xmlns:isbn='urn:ISBN:0-395-36341-6'>
     <bk:title>Cheaper by the Dozen</bk:title>
     <isbn:number>1568491379</isbn:number>
  </bk:book>
```

Using this mechanism, you can essentially expand any XML document with the elements and attributes from any other XML document. Because the XML processor has to resolve them, this situation might mean a delay in processing—but it does not mean that the processing slows down.

Xpath Axis

An axis is a set of nodes along which Xpath goes from the context node. It identifies a set of nodes relative to a context node. The self axis is the context node itself; the child axis is all of the child nodes of the context node; the parent axis is the node that is one level "above" the context node; and so on. Axes are followed based on predicates, which are filters for patterns, reducing the set of nodes matching the pattern to only those for which the expression in the predicate is true. Each combination of axis::pattern[predicate] is a location step, and location steps are separated by /. The predicates determine whether the axis is forward or reverse.

The proximity position of a member of a node set with respect to an axis is defined to be the position of the node in the node set ordered in document order if the axis is a forward axis and is ordered in reverse document order if the axis is a reverse axis. The first position is 1.

A predicate filters a node set with respect to an axis in order to produce a new node set. For each node in the node set to be filtered, the predicate is evaluated with that node as the context node, with the number of nodes in the node set as the context size, and with the proximity position of the node in the node set with respect to the axis as the context position. If the predicate evaluates to true for that node, the node is included in the new node set; otherwise, it is not included.

A predicate is evaluated by evaluating the predicate expression and converting the result to a Boolean. If the result is a number, the result will be converted to true if the number is equal to the context position and will be converted to false otherwise; if the result is not a number, then the result will be converted as if by a call to the Boolean function. Thus, a location path para[3] is equivalent to para[position()=3].

The following axes are defined in the specification:

ancestor: Ancestors of the current node (the context node); the ancestors of the context node consist of the parent of context node and the parent's parent and so on; thus, the ancestor axis will always include the root node unless the context node is the root node.

ancestor-or-self: Ancestors, including the current node (the context node) and the ancestors of the context node; thus, the ancestor axis will always include the root node.

attribute: Attributes of the current node (abbreviated "@") (the context node); the axis will be empty unless the context node is an element.

child: Children of the current, or context node (the default axis)

descendant: Descendants of the current node (the context node); a descendant is a child or a child of a child and so on; thus the descendant axis never contains attribute or namespace nodes.

descendant-or-self: Descendants, including the current node (abbreviated "//"), in other words, the context node and the descendants of the context node.

following-sibling: Elements that occur after the current node, in document order (all of the following siblings of the context node); if the context node is an attribute node or namespace node, the following-sibling axis is empty.

following: The following axis contains all nodes in the same document as the context node that are after the context node in document order, excluding any descendants and excluding attribute nodes and namespace nodes.

namespace: The namespace nodes of the current node (the context node); the axis will be empty unless the context node is an element.

parent: The parent axis contains the parent of the context node if there is one (abbreviated "..").

preceding: Elements that occur before the current node in document order (returned in reverse-document order), excluding any ancestors and excluding attribute nodes and namespace nodes.

self: The self axis contains just the context node itself (abbreviated as ".").

preceding-sibling: The preceding-sibling axis contains all of the preceding siblings of the context node; if the context node is an attribute node or namespace node, the preceding-sibling axis is empty.

Axes are used with node tests and determine what general category of nodes can be considered for the following node test. The document is partitioned by the ancestor, descendant, following, preceding, and self axes. They do not overlap, and together they contain all of the nodes in the document. The child axis is the default axis, and it can be omitted.

An axis that only contains the context node, or nodes that follow the context node, in document order is a forward axis. An axis that contains the context node, or nodes that are before the context node, in document order is a reverse axis. For example, when you are following the path along the attribute axis from one node (which is probably an element, because other types of nodes will not have attributes) to some other nodes matching the pattern you have stated (in other words, an element that has attributes that conform to the pattern), you can use a predicate to say that of those nodes, you really only want the ones for which the string value is something else. If the attribute value is foo and the string value is bar, then the expression will be attribute::foo[. = 'bar']. The predicate does not filter anything that is dependent on the axis, however.

The ancestor, ancestor-or-self, preceding, and preceding-sibling axes are reverse axes; all other axes are forward axes. Because the self axis always contains one node at most, it makes no difference whether it is a forward or reverse axis (in essence, its direction is null). position() returns the proximity of the node in the node set with respect to the context node. Applied to the preceding-sibling axis, this situation would mean that preceding-sibling::*[1] would return the immediately preceding sibling.

Node Tests Using Xpath

In addition to its use for addressing, Xpath can be used for matching (testing whether or not a node matches a pattern). This method is precisely the way Xpath is used in XSLT. Every axis has a principal node type. If an axis can contain elements, then the principal node type is element; otherwise, it is the type of the nodes that the axis can contain.

- For the attribute axis, the principal node type is attribute.
- For the namespace axis, the principal node type is namespace.
- For other axes, the principal node type is element.

For example, child::para selects the para element children of the context node. If the context node has no para children, it will select an empty set of nodes. attribute::href selects the href attribute of the context node. If the context node has no href attribute, it will select an empty set of nodes.

Going from an attribute to its element involves using the parent:: axis. So, if the context node is an attribute (as it is in a template that matches attribute nodes), then you can identify the element that attribute is on with the following expression:

```
parent::*
```

(the element that is the parent of this node), or:

```
parent::node()
```

(the *node* that is the parent of this node and that must be an element) or the abbreviation of the above:

```
..
```

To get the name of the parent, you can use the name() function, taking one of these expressions as an argument:

```
name(..)
```

So, to test whether the name of the parent element is FOO, you could use the following:

```
name(..) = 'FOO'
```

There is a corollary, however. You have tested whether the name of the parent element is FOO, but can you find out whether there is a parent of this attribute that is a FOO element? The expression to get to such a parent is:

```
parent::FOO
```

(the FOO element that is the parent of this node). If the parent element is a FOO element, then that node will be returned. If the parent element is not a FOO element, then no node will be returned because there is no parent FOO element. Within a test expression, if a node is returned, the test returns true; if no node is returned, the test returns false. In most situations, the following is equivalent:

`parent::FOO` **is equivalent to** `name(..) = 'FOO'`

The situation where they are not equivalent is where namespaces are involved. The name() of a node gives the exact name for the node within the XML source. Look at the following XML:

```
<foo:FOO xmlns:foo="http://www.foo.com/" />
```

In this coding, the `FOO` element is in the `http://www.foo.com/` namespace.

The `name()` of that element is as follows:

```
foo:FOO
```

So, if you are using `name()` to test the identity of the element, then you need to use the following coding:

```
name(..) = 'foo:FOO'
```

It might be, however, that in another document (or even in the same document), you have an element such as the following:

```
<bar:FOO xmlns:bar="http://www.foo.com/" />
```

The FOO element here is in the same namespace (`http://www.foo.com/`) but has a different prefix. Its name is:

```
bar:FOO
```

and it would have to be tested with the following:

```
name(..) = 'bar:FOO'
```

because the elements are not the same (if they are in different namespaces). When you use parent::FOO instead, it takes into account the fact that the prefix of a namespace is not important——it is the URI at which you have to look. If within your XSLT you have declared the foo prefix to be associated with the `http://www.foo.com/URI` by using the following:

```
xmlns:baz="http://www.foo.com/"
```

then the Xpath:

```
parent::baz:FOO
```

will match both the foo:FOO and the bar:FOO elements. It looks for the equivalence in the namespace URI rather than in the namespace prefix. For this reason, it is worth getting into the habit of testing for nodes that are called by a particular name by testing for whether the node exists, rather than testing whether the node is called that name.

A QName in the node test is expanded into an expanded name by using the namespace declarations from the expression context. This method is the same way that expansion is done for element type names in start tags and end tags, except that the default namespace declared with xmlns is not used. If the QName does not have a prefix, then the namespace URI is null. (This method is the same way that attribute names are expanded.) It is an error if the QName has a prefix for which there is no namespace declaration in the expression context.

A node test `*` is true for any node of the principal node type. For example, `child::*` will select all element children of the context node, and `attribute::*` will select all attributes of the context node.

A node test can have the form `NCName:*`. In this case, the prefix is expanded in the same way as with a QName by using the context namespace declarations. It is an error if there is no namespace declaration for the prefix in the expression context. The node test will be true for any node of the principal type whose expanded name has the namespace URI to which the prefix expands, regardless of the local part of the name.

The node test `text()` is true for any text node. For example, `child::text()` will select the text node children of the context node. Similarly, the node test `comment()` is true for any comment node, and the node test `processing-instruction()` is true for any processing instruction. The `processing-instruction()` test might have an argument that is literal; in this case, it is true for any processing instruction that has a name equal to the value of the literal.

A node test `node()` is true for any node of any type whatsoever.

If you have a template for an attribute and you want to specify a choice based on the name of the element in which the attribute occurs (for example, test="IF THE NAME OF YOUR ASSOCIATED_ELEMENT IS 'FOO'"), use `parent::FOO`.

Xpath Expressions

Xpath expressions can be used in attributes. In XSLT, expressions are used in the "select" attribute to select nodes from the source tree. To use Xpath, you first have to set the current context. Then, after you have identified that element, you can start walking along the axis to pick out other nodes that you want to use and create the current node set.

You perform this action by creating an expression, which is a pattern that will yield an object. Expressions can be constructed by using operators, which are or, and, = (equal to), != , (not equal to), <= (smaller or equal than), < (smaller than), >= (greater or equal than), and > (greater than). In addition, there are numerical operators, which are +, -, mod, and div.

The = comparison will be true if and only if the objects are equal; the != comparison will be true if and only if the objects are not equal. The operators all associate to the left. 3 > 2 > 1 is equivalent to (3 > 2) > 1, which evaluates to false. The expression is evaluated to yield an object, which can be one of the four XSLT basic data types: node-set (an unordered collection of nodes without duplicates), Boolean (true or false), number (a floating-point number), or string (a sequence of UCS characters).

The different types of operators are evaluated slightly differently. The and expression is evaluated by taking each operand and converting its value to a Boolean as if by a call to the Boolean function. The result is true if both values are true and false otherwise. The right operand is not evaluated if the left operand evaluates to false.

The numeric operators convert their operands to numbers as if by calling the number function. The + (plus sign) operator performs addition, and the − (minus sign) operator performs subtraction. Because XML allows in names, the operator typically needs to be preceded by white space. The div operator performs floating-point division according to IEEE 754. The mod operator returns the remainder from a truncating division, the same as the % operator in Java and ECMAScript. In other words, 5 mod 2 returns 1, and 5 mod −2 returns 1 and so on.

If both objects to be compared are node sets, then the comparison will be true if there is a node in the first node set and a node in the second node set that has the same string values (in other words, the comparison of the two string values evaluates to true).

If you are comparing a node set and a number, then the comparison will be true if the number and the node set are equal after you have converted the string value of the node set to a number (by using the number function). If you are comparing a node set and a string value, you must compare the string values of the node set and the string value. Comparing a Boolean value to a node set means that you first have to convert the string value to a Boolean value by using the Boolean function.

If neither object is a node set, then both must be converted to a common type. If one is Boolean, then that will be the common value. If one is a number, then that will be the common value. Otherwise, both are converted to strings (by using the string function).

When neither object to be compared is a node set nor the operator is <=, <, >= or >, then the objects are compared by converting both objects to numbers and comparing the numbers.

The effect of the above is that the order of precedence is (lowest precedence first):

- or
- and
- =, !=
- <=, <, >=, >

Note that when an Xpath expression occurs in an XML document, any < and <= operators must be quoted according to XML 1.0 rules by using, for example, < and <=.

In the following example, the value of the test attribute is an Xpath expression:

```
<xsl:if test="@value &lt; 10">...</xsl:if>
```

When you have found the element you are looking for with an Xpath expression, you get its value by using an xsl:value-of instruction. The following code is used to format the name given to a model into an XHTML <title> for the resulting page:

```
<!-- Title -->
<xsl:template match="model" mode="head">
    <title>
    <!-- Name of the model -->
        <xsl:value-of select="title_model"/>
    </title>
</xsl:template>
```

When this template is invoked, the current context is the model element. The name of the model is a child node of this element. We extract the name by using the `xsl:value-of` instruction and enclose it inside its new XHTML `<title>` tag. The Xpath expression to extract the name is '   ' and appears as the value of the `'select'` attribute in the `xsl:value-of` instruction.

You can also create an expression that enables you to find elements wherever they appear in a document. If we want to find the Class elements wherever they are in the document, we can use the following Xpath expression in an `xsl:apply-templates` instruction:

```
<!-- Classes -->
<xsl:apply-templates select="//Foundation.Core.Class[@xmi.id]">
```

The Xpath notation // instructs the processor to search for Class elements beginning from the root of the document and then continuing through each level of the node tree. This notation is actually an abbreviation for a longer axis specifier defined by the Xpath standard; however, because this notation is so convenient, it is usually used in place of the longer notation.

If you only want to find elements that contain a specific attribute, you use a predicate. Predicates are qualifying expressions that serve to constrain the result set returned.

If the Class element can have both definitions and references attributes, you select it by using the Xpath predicate notation, [ ]:

```
<!-- Classes -->
<xsl:apply-templates select="//Foundation.Core.Class[@definitions]">
```

The @ symbol identifies an attribute. Actually, it is an abbreviation for an axis specifier. In this case, the abbreviation is for the attribute axis. So, the way we read this full expression is as follows: Beginning from the root, find all Class elements in the document that contain the definitions attribute.

Having identified the attribute, we want to access it. To extract the value of the definitions attribute and assign the value to a variable, we use the following code:

```
<xsl:variable name="xmi_id" select="@xmi.id" />
```

Expression evaluation is done with respect to a context. XSLT and Xpointer specify how the context is determined for Xpath expressions used in XSLT and Xpointer, respectively. The context is more than just the current node. It consists of a node (the context node); a pair of non-zero positive integers (the context position and the context size); a set of variable bindings; a function library; and the set of namespace declarations in scope for the expression.

The context position is always less than or equal to the context size.

The variable bindings consist of a mapping from variable names to variable values. The value of a variable is an object, which can be of any of the types that are possible for the value of an expression and can also be of additional types not specified here (we will look more at variables in Chapter 6, "More XSLT Programming: Import, Include, and Extensions to XSLT").

The function library consists of a mapping from function names to functions. Each function takes zero or more arguments and returns a single result. The Xpath specification defines a core function library that all Xpath implementations must support. For a function in the core function library, arguments and results are of the four basic types. Both XSLT and XPointer extend Xpath by defining additional functions; some of these functions operate on the four basic types while others operate on additional data types defined by XSLT and XPointer.

Several kinds of expressions change the context node. Only predicates change the context position and context size.

When the evaluation of a kind of expression is described, it will always be explicitly stated if the context node, context position, and context size should change for the evaluation of subexpressions. If nothing is said about the context node, context position, and context size, they remain unchanged for the evaluation of subexpressions of that kind of expression.

Xpath expressions often occur in XML attributes. The Xpath specification specifies a grammar that applies to the attribute value after XML 1.0 normalization. So, for example, if the grammar uses the character <, this character must not appear in the XML source as < but must be quoted according to XML 1.0 rules by, for example, entering it as <. Within expressions, literal strings are delimited by single or double quotation marks, which are also used to delimit XML attributes. To avoid a quotation mark in an expression being interpreted by the XML processor as terminating the attribute value, the quotation mark can be entered as a character reference (" or '). Alternatively, the expression can use single quotation marks if the XML attribute is delimited with double quotation marks or vice-versa. You do not actually have to worry about this situation in practice, though, because the XML normalization takes place before the XSLT processing.

First, dividing the character string to be parsed into tokens and then parsing the resulting sequence of tokens parses expressions. White space can be freely used between tokens. One important kind of expression is a location path. The result of evaluating a location path is the node set containing the nodes selected by the location path. Location paths can recursively contain expressions that are used to filter sets of nodes. The | operator computes the union of its operands, which must be node sets.

In Xpath, the namespace definitions that are in scope for a particular element can be accessed with the function

```
namespace::*
```

The element a namespace is defined on is the top-most ancestor element that has a namespace:: with the same name() and string value, for example:

```
ancestor-or-self::*[namespace::*[name() = $namespace-prefix and
                            . = $namespace-uri]][last()]
```

So, for example, you can print what namespaces an element defines with the template:

```
<xsl:template match="*" mode="namespace">
   <xsl:for-each select="namespace::*">
      <xsl:if test="not(../ancestor::*[namespace::*[name() =
name(current()) and
                                    . = current()]][last()])">
         <xsl:value-of select="name(..)" /> defines <xsl:text />
         <xsl:choose>
            <xsl:when test="name()">xmlns:<xsl:value-of select="name()"
/></xsl:when>
            <xsl:otherwise>xmlns</xsl:otherwise>
         </xsl:choose>
         <xsl:text />="<xsl:value-of select="." />"&#xA;<xsl:text />
      </xsl:if>
   </xsl:for-each>
</xsl:template>
```

The 'XML' namespace is always declared on the top element (by default, because the source has to be an XML document) and needs to be filtered out if you want only those namespaces that are declared explicitly in the document.

A variable reference evaluates to the value to which the variable name is bound in the set of variable bindings in the context. It is an error if the variable name is not bound to any value in the set of variable bindings in the expression context. Parentheses can be used for grouping.

A FunctionCall expression is evaluated by using the FunctionName to identify a function in the expression evaluation context function library, evaluating each of the arguments, converting each argument to the type required by the function, and finally calling the function—passing it the converted arguments. It is an error if the number of arguments is wrong or if an argument cannot be converted to the required type. The result of the FunctionCall expression is the result returned by the function.

An argument is converted to type string as if by calling the string function. An argument is converted to type number as if by calling the number function. An argument is converted to type Boolean as if by calling the Boolean function. An argument that is not of type node set cannot be converted to a node set.

Predicates are used to filter expressions in the same way that they are used in location paths. It is an error if the expression to be filtered does not evaluate to a node set. The Predicate filters the node set with respect to the child axis. The meaning of a Predicate depends on which axis applies. For example, `preceding::foo[1]` returns the first foo element in reverse document order, because the axis that applies to the [1] predicate is the preceding axis; by contrast, `(preceding::foo)[1]` returns the first foo element in document order, because the axis that applies to the [1] predicate is the child axis.

The / and // operators compose an expression and a relative location path. It is an error if the expression does not evaluate to a node set. The / operator does composition in the same way as when / is used in a location path. As in location paths, // is short for `/descendant-or-self::node()/`.

There are no types of objects that can be converted to node sets.

Core Xpath Function Library

Apart from being an addressing mechanism, Xpath also contains mechanisms to compute an address. You write them with an argument and the function (for instance, name( ) or string translate(string, string, string)). The Xpath functions are as follows:

- Boolean, which converts its argument to a Boolean as follows: a number is true if and only if it is neither positive nor negative zero nor NaN; a node set is true if and only if it is non-empty; a string is true if and only if its length is non-zero; an object of a type other than the four basic types is converted to a Boolean in a way that is dependent on that type.

- ceiling, which returns the smallest (closest to negative infinity) number that is not less than the argument and that is an integer.

- concat, which returns the concatenation of its arguments (the strings to be concatenated).

- contains, which returns true if the first argument string contains the second argument string (otherwise, it returns false)

- count, which counts the number of selected elements. Its argument is a node-set.

- false, which returns false.

- floor, which returns the largest (closest to positive infinity) number that is not greater than the argument and that is an integer.

- lang, which returns true or false depending on whether the language of the context node as specified by xml:lang attributes is the same or a sublanguage of the language specified by the argument string (sublanguages are for instance American English, which is a sublanguage of English). The language of the context node is determined by the value of the xml:lang attribute on the context node, or if the context node has no xml:lang attribute by the value of the xml:lang attribute on the nearest ancestor of the context node. If there is no such attribute, then lang returns false.

- last() returns a number equal to the context size.

- local-name returns the local part of the expanded name of the node in the argument node set that is first in document order. If the argument node set is empty or the first node has no expanded name, an empty string is returned. If the argument is omitted, it defaults to a node set with the context node as its only member.

- `name` returns a string containing a QName representing the expanded name of the node in the argument node set that is first in document order. The QName must represent the expanded name with respect to the namespace declarations that are in effect on the node whose expanded name is being represented. Typically, this node will be the QName that occurred in the XML source. This situation need not be the case if there are namespace declarations in effect on the node that associate multiple prefixes with the same namespace. An implementation might include information about the original prefix in its representation of nodes, however; in this case, an implementation can ensure that the returned string is always the same as the QName used in the XML source. If the argument node set is empty or the first node has no expanded name, an empty string is returned. If the argument is omitted, it defaults to a node set with the context node as its only member. The string returned by the name function will be the same as the string returned by the local name function except for element nodes and attribute nodes.

- `name()`, which returns the name of the element

- `namespace-uri` returns the namespace URI of the expanded name of the node in the argument node set that is first in document order. If the argument node set is empty, the first node has no expanded name, or the namespace URI of the expanded name is null, an empty string is returned. If the argument is omitted, it defaults to a node set with the context node as its only member. The string returned by the namespace uri function will be empty except for element nodes and attribute nodes.

- `node-set id(object)` selects elements by their unique ID (the ID is the value of the attribute that is declared in the DTD or XML Schema as type ID. The ID has to be unique within the document). When the argument to ID is a node set, then the result is the union of the result of applying ID to the string value of each of the nodes in the argument node set. When the argument to ID is of any other type, the argument is converted to a string as if by a call to the string function; the string is split into a whitespace-separated list of tokens (whitespace is any sequence of characters matching the production

S); the result is a node set containing the elements in the same document as the context node that have a unique ID equal to any of the tokens in the list. id("foo") selects the element that has a unique ID foo, and `id("foo")/child::para[position()=5]` selects the fifth para child of the element with unique ID foo.

- `normalize-space`, which removes leading and trailing whitespaces and replaces sequences of whitespaces with one single space

- `not`, which returns true if its argument is false and false otherwise

- `number` converts its argument to a number as follows: a string that consists of optional white space followed by an optional minus sign followed by a number followed by white space is converted to the IEEE 754 number that is nearest (according to the IEEE 754 round-to-nearest rule) to the mathematical value represented by the string; any other string is converted to NaN. Boolean true is converted to 1; Boolean false is converted to 0. A node set is first converted to a string as if by a call to the string function and then converted in the same way as a string argument. An object of a type other than the four basic types is converted to a number in a way that is dependent on that type. If the argument is omitted, it defaults to a node set with the context node as its only member. The number function should not be used for conversion of numeric data occurring in an element in an XML document unless the element is of a type that represents numeric data in a language-neutral format (which would typically be transformed into a language-specific format for presentation to a user). In addition, the number function cannot be used unless the language-neutral format used by the element is consistent with the Xpath syntax for a number.

- `position()` returns a number equal to the context position.

- `round` returns the number that is closest to the argument and that is an integer. If there are two such numbers, then the one that is closest to positive infinity is returned. If the argument is NaN, then NaN is returned. If the argument is positive infinity, then positive infinity is returned. If the argument is negative infinity, then negative infinity is returned. If the argument is positive zero, then positive zero is returned. If the argument is negative zero, then negative zero is returned. If the argument is less than zero, but greater than or equal to -0.5, then negative zero is returned. For these last two cases, the result of calling the round function is not the same as the result of adding 0.5 and then calling the floor function.

- `starts-with`, which returns true if the first argument string starts with the second argument string.

- `string` converts an object to a string as follows: A node set is converted to a string by returning the string value of the node in the node set that is first in document order. If the node set is empty, an empty string is returned. A number is converted to a string as follows: NaN is converted to the string NaN. Positive zero is converted to the string 0. Negative zero is converted to the string 0. Positive infinity is converted to the string Infinity. Negative infinity is converted to the string -Infinity. If the number is an integer, the number is represented in decimal form as a Number with no decimal point and no leading zeros, preceded by a minus sign ( ) if the number is negative otherwise, the number is represented in decimal form as a Number including a decimal point with at least one digit before the decimal point and at least one digit after the decimal point, preceded by a minus sign ( ) if the number is negative; there must be no leading zeros before the decimal point apart possibly from the one required digit immediately before the decimal point; beyond the one required digit after the decimal point there must be as many, but only as many, more digits as are needed to uniquely distinguish the number from all other IEEE 754 numeric values. The Boolean false value is converted to the string false. The Boolean true value is converted to the string true. An object of a type other than the four basic types is converted to a string in a way that is dependent on that type. If the argument is omitted, it defaults to a node-set with the context node as its only member. The string function is not intended for converting numbers into strings for presentation to users. The format-number function and xsl:number element provide this functionality.

- `string-length` returns the number of characters in the string. Note that you must use < as a substitute for < and > as a substitute for >.

- `substring` returns the substring of the first argument starting at the position specified in the second argument with length specified in the third argument. For example, substring("12345",2,3) returns 234. If the third argument is not specified, it returns the substring starting at the position specified in the second argument and continuing to the end of the string. For example, substring("12345",2) returns 2345. More precisely, each character in the string is considered to have a numeric position: the position of the first character is 1, the position of the second character is 2, and so on. This situation differs from Java and ECMAScript, in which the String.substring method treats the position of the first character as 0. The returned substring contains those characters for which the position of the character is greater than or equal to the rounded value of the second argument, and if the third argument is specified, less than the sum of the rounded value of the second argument and the rounded value of the third argument; the comparisons and addition used for the above follow the standard IEEE 754 rules. Rounding is done as if by a call to the round function. The following examples illustrate various unusual cases: `substring("12345", 1.5, 2.6)` returns 234, `substring("12345", 0, 3)` returns 12, `substring("12345", 0 div 0, 3)` returns "", `substring("12345", 1, 0 div 0)` returns "", `substring("12345", -42, 1 div 0)` returns 12345, and `substring("12345", -1 div 0, 1 div 0)` returns "".

- `substring-after` returns the substring of the first argument string that follows the first occurrence of the second argument string in the first argument string, or the empty string if the first argument string does not contain the second argument string. For example, `substring-after("1999/04/01","/")` returns 04/01, and `substring-after("1999/04/01","19")` returns 99/04/01.

- `substring-before` returns the substring of the first argument string that precedes the first occurrence of the second argument string in the first argument string or the empty string if the first argument string does not contain the second argument string. For example, `substring-before("1999/04/01","/")` returns 1999.

- `sum` returns the sum for each node in the argument node set of the result of converting the string values of the node to a number.

- `translate` returns the first argument string with occurrences of characters in the second argument string replaced by the character at the corresponding position in the third argument string. For example, `translate("bar","abc","ABC")` returns the string BAr. If there is a character in the second argument string with no character at a corresponding position in the third argument string (because the second argument string is longer than the third argument string), then occurrences of that character in the first argument string are removed. For example, translate("--aaa--","abc-", "ABC") returns AAA. If a character occurs more than once in the second argument string, then the first occurrence determines the replacement character. If the third argument string is longer than the second argument string, then excess characters are ignored. The translate function is not a sufficient solution for case conversion in all languages. A future version of Xpath might provide additional functions for case conversion. See Table 4.1 where the functions and their arguments are listed in more detail.

In addition, there are a number of XSLT-specific functions that are not defined in the Xpath specification but rather in the XSLT specification (Table 4.2).

Note that it is an error to use `current()`, which returns the current node, in a pattern.

An example is to use `count(ancestor::*)` to give all of the ancestor elements, `count(ancestor::branch)` to give all the ancestor branch elements, and `count(ancestor::node())` to give all the ancestor nodes (including the root). Remember that when you use the `position()` function, it should look at the position of the current node in the current node list, not in the source file. Within the template, the current node is the node that is being matched. The current node list is set by the xsl:apply-templates that was used to apply the template.

Abbreviated Syntax

The Xpath syntax looks a lot like addressing subdirectories in a file system or as part of a URI. Multiple steps in a location path are separated by either one or two oblique "/" characters. Filters can be specified to further refine the nature of the components of our information being addressed.

Table 4.1 Functions in Xpath

FUNCTION	RETURN TYPE	ARGUMENT TYPE	ARGUMENT OPTIONAL
Boolean	Boolean	(object)	
ceiling	number	(number)	
concat	string	(string, string, string*)	
contains	Boolean	(string, string)	
count	number	(node-set)	
false	Boolean	()	
floor	number	(number)	
id	node-set	(object)	
lang	Boolean	(string)	
last	number	()	
local-name	string	(node-set)	yes
name	string	(node-set)	yes
namespace-uri	string	(node-set)	yes
normalize-space	string	(string)	yes
not	Boolean	(Boolean)	
number	number	(object)	yes
position	number	()	
round	number	(number)	
starts-with	Boolean	(string, string)	
string	string	(object)	yes
string-length	number	(string)	yes
substring	string	(string, number, number?)	
substring-after	string	(string, string)	
substring-before	string	(string, string)	
sum	number	(node-set)	
translate	string	(string, string, string)	
true	Boolean	()	

For instance, `select="question[3]/answer[1]"` selects only the first "answer" child of the third "question" child of the focus element. `match="question|answer"` expresses a test of an element being in the union of the element types named "question" and "answer." `select="id('start')//question[@answer='y']"` uses an Xpath address

Table 4.2 XSLT-Specific Xpath Functions

FUNCTION	RETURN TYPE	ARGUMENT TYPE	ARGUMENT OPTIONAL
current	node-set	()	
document	node-set	(object, node-set)	Yes
element-available	Boolean(string)		
format-number	string	(number, string, string)	Yes
function-available	Boolean	(string)	
generate-id	string	(node-set)	Yes
key	node-set	(string, object)	
system-property	object	(string)	
unparsed-entity-uri	string	(string)	

identifying some descendants of the element in the instance that has the unique identifier with the value "start." Those identified are the question elements whose answer attribute is equal to the string that is equal to the lower-case letter y. The value returned is the set of nodes representing the elements meeting the conditions expressed by the address. The address is used in a select attribute, which means that the XSLT processor will select all of the addressed elements for some kind of processing.

Within an Xpath expression you can use predicates; `/path/to/some-nodes[ foo ]` will evaluate to only those somenodes for which 'foo' is true.

```
document('otherdoc.xml')/otherdoc/stuff[ . = 'hello' ]
```
will be 'stuff' elements that have a string value of 'hello' and that are children of 'otherdoc' elements which, in turn, are children of the root node in the tree derived from otherdoc.xml.

The most important abbreviation in the abbreviated syntax is that `child::` can be omitted from a location step. In effect, child is the default axis. For example, a location path `div/para` is short for `child::div/child::para`.

There is also an abbreviation for attributes. attribute:: can be abbreviated to @. For example, a location path `para[@type="warning"]` is short for `child::para[attribute::type="warning"]` and so selects para children with a type attribute with value equal to warning.

`//` is short for `/descendant-or-self::node()/`. For example, `//para` is short for `/descendant-or-self::node()/child::para` and will select any para element in the document (even a para element that is a document element will be selected by `//para` because the document element node is a child of the root node); `div//para` is short for `div/descendant-or-self::node()/child::para` and will select all para descendants of div children.

The location path `//para[1]` does not mean the same as the location path `/descendant::para[1]`. The latter selects the first descendant para element; the former selects all descendant para elements that are the first para children of their parents.

A location step of `.` is short for `self::node()`. This abbreviation is particularly useful in conjunction with `//`. For example, the location path `.//para` is short for `self::node()/descendant-or-self::node()/child::para`. and so will select all para descendant elements of the context node.

Similarly, a location step of `..` is short for `parent::node()`. For example, `../title` is short for `parent::node()/child::title` and will select the title children of the parent of the context node.

When you use an axis that works backward (a 'reverse axis'), such as preceding, preceding-sibling, ancestor, or ancestor-or-self, then the node list is given in reverse document order until you take the next step in the Xpath. So, `preceding::row[1]` (which is exactly the same as `preceding::row[position()=1]`) gets the row immediately before the current node.

Here are some more examples of location paths using abbreviated syntaxes:

- `para` selects the para element children of the context node.
- `*` selects all element children of the context node.
- `text()` selects all text node children of the context node.
- `@name` selects the name attribute of the context node.
- `@*` selects all the attributes of the context node.
- `para[1]` selects the first para child of the context node.
- `para[last()]` selects the last para child of the context node.
- `*/para` selects all para grandchildren of the context node.

- `/doc/chapter[5]/section[2]` selects the second section of the fifth chapter of the doc.

- `chapter//para` selects the para element descendants of the chapter element children of the context node.

- `//para` selects all of the para descendants of the document root and thus selects all para elements in the same document as the context node.

- `//olist/item` selects all the item elements in the same document as the context node that have an olist parent.

- `.` selects the context node.

- `.//para` selects the para element descendants of the context node.

- `..` selects the parent of the context node.

- `../@lang` selects the lang attribute of the parent of the context node.

- `para[@type="warning"]` selects all para children of the context node that have a type attribute with value warning.

- `para[@type="warning"][5]` selects the fifth para child of the context node that has a type attribute with value warning.

- `para[5][@type="warning"]` selects the fifth para child of the context node if that child has a type attribute with value warning.

- `chapter[title="Introduction"]` selects the chapter children of the context node that have one or more title children with a string value equal to Introduction.

- `chapter[title]` selects the chapter children of the context node that have one or more title children.

- `employee[@secretary and @assistant]` selects all of the employee children of the context node that have both a secretary attribute and an assistant attribute.

Now that you know Xpath, we can start using it together with the functions of XSLT to create transformation sheets.

CHAPTER 5

Programming Basics in XSLT

X SLT is a programming language, albeit one that is designed for a specific purpose: to turn source trees derived from XML documents into result trees. In other words, it can be used in the same way as other programming languages to perform conditional processing of data. It also means that XSLT style sheets can be managed in the same way as program code. For instance, an organization can build libraries of components of style sheets for different processing examples, especially because style sheets (as a rule) have to be tied to the site. Style sheet writers can tweak the results of a transformation by writing shell specifications that include or import other style sheets known to solve the problems that they are addressing.

The library approach also means that style sheet fragments can be written for particular CC/PP vocabulary fragments. These fragments can subsequently be used to enable device independence and to create specific versions of the site for different browsers and other user agents (as we will see in Chapter 8, "XSLT and Style").

It is not necessary to embed everything in the style sheet. The source document can contain a lot of useful data. To restrict the source documents to house-only "content" is to forego many of the possibilities that you get by using XSL with XML documents. XSL can use data in the source documents as cues as to how to build the result tree.

For instance, you can use xsl:apply-templates to process a source document containing only a structural description of the site and a secondary source document (which can be retrieved via the Xpath expression document()) that contains presentational variables (style sheet parameters such as colors, text styles, image names, and attributes) that are referenced by the structural tree. You essentially quantify and act on presentational data alongside, but separate from, the content data. Good XSLT can transform XML in order to achieve greater degrees of specificity in the markup or can use XML marked up with an adequate degree of specificity in order to extract information. Good XML markup uses both elements and attributes to create as much specificity in the nodes as possible.

Of course, it is possible to create a spaghetti bowl of subroutines that cross and tangle. But that is a danger with any programming language, and there are well-established ways of managing the problem. You can also use a generator, such as XSL Invoker, illustrated in Figure 5.1.

Now is a good time to recapitulate the elements of XSLT and to see which ones we have not been using so far. We will go through the most frequently used ones and give examples of how you can apply them. See Table 5.1.

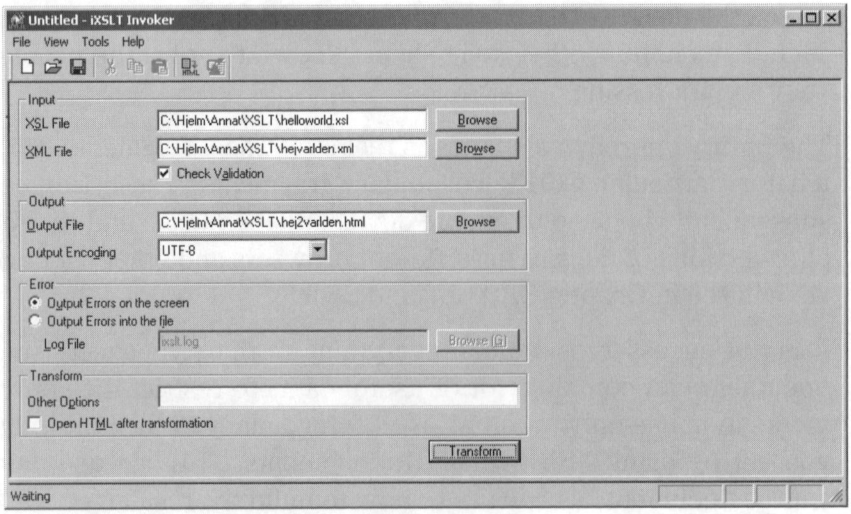

Figure 5.1 An example of an XSLT generator.

Table 5.1 Elements of XSLT

ELEMENT	ATTRIBUTES AND VALUES	REQUIRED ATTRIBUTES	CONTENT	TOP-LEVEL ELEMENT	FUNCTION
xsl:apply-imports	None		Empty element	No	Processes the current node using template rules which were imported using xsl:import
xsl:apply-templates	select = node-set-expression; mode = qname		xsl:sort | xsl:with-param	Yes	Declares that the template will be applied
xsl:attribute	name = { qname }; namespace = { uri-reference }	name	Template	No	Adds attributes to elements in the result tree; content is the template for the attribute
xsl:attribute-set	name = qname; use-attribute-sets = qnames	name	xsl:attribute*	Yes	Defines an attribute set (which is used by xsl: element, xsl:copy, and xsl:attribute-set by adding the attribute use-attribute-sets and a list of names)
xsl:call-template	name = qname	name	xsl:with-param*	No	Invokes a named template
xsl:choose	None		xsl:when+, xsl:otherwise?	No	Selects from among a set of xsl:when and xsl:otherwise elements, which are in its content
xsl:comment	None		Template	No	Creates a comment in the result tree. The content of the comment is the content of the template which is the content of the element.
xsl:copy	use-attribute-sets = qnames		Template	No	Copies the current node (including namespaces but not including attributes and child elements)

Table 5.1 Continued

ELEMENT	ATTRIBUTES AND VALUES	REQUIRED ATTRIBUTES	CONTENT	TOP-LEVEL ELEMENT	FUNCTION
xsl:copy-of	select = expression	select	None (empty element)	No	Inserts a copy of the value of the expression (a node set or result tree fragment) into the result tree, without converting it to a string.
xsl:decimal-format	name = qname; decimal-separator = char; grouping-separator = _char; infinity = string; minus-sign = char; NaN = string; percent = char; per-mille = char; zero-digit = _char; digit = char; pattern-separator = char		None (empty element)	No	Declares a decimal format, which controls the interpretation of a format pattern used by the format-number function
xsl:element	name = { qname }; namespace = { uri-reference };use-attribute-sets = qnames	name	Template	No	Allows an element to be created with a computed name
xsl:fallback	None		Template	No	Can be specified on an instruction element to declare in which order fallback should be instantiated (the children are instantiated in order)
xsl:for-each	select = node-set-expression	select template	xsl:sort*,	No	Contains a template that is instantiated for each node selected in the expression in the attribute

ELEMENT	ATTRIBUTES AND VALUES	REQUIRED ATTRIBUTES	CONTENT	TOP-LEVEL ELEMENT	FUNCTION
xsl:if	test = boolean-expression	test	Template	No	If the expression in the attribute template is true, then the template in the content is instantiated.
xsl:import	href = uri-reference	href	None (empty element)	Yes	Imports a style sheet (same as including, except that definitions and template rules in the importing style sheet take precedence over template rules and definitions in the imported style sheet).
xsl:include	href = uri-reference	href	None (empty element)	Yes	References an XSLT transformation sheet to be included.
xsl:key	name = qname; match = pattern; use = expression	name, match, use	None (empty element)	Yes	Declares keys for use when cross-references are not explicitly declared using ID and IDREFs. Keys are triples (but not RDF).
xsl:message	terminate = "yes" | "no"		Template	No	Passes a message that is specified in the template. The presentation is implementation dependent.
xsl:namespace-alias	stylesheet-prefix = prefix | "#default"; result-prefix = prefix | "#default"	stylesheet-prefix; result-prefix	Empty element	Yes	Declares that one namespace URI is the alias for another.
xsl:number	level = "single" | "multiple" | "any"; count = pattern; from = pattern;		None (empty element)	No	Inserts a formatted number into the result tree (can be done as a result of an expression).

Table 5.1 Continued

ELEMENT	ATTRIBUTES AND VALUES	REQUIRED ATTRIBUTES	CONTENT	TOP-LEVEL ELEMENT	FUNCTION
	value = number-expression format = { string }; lang = { nmtoken }; letter-value = { "alphabetic" | "traditional" }; grouping-separator = { char }; grouping-size = { number }				
xsl:otherwise	None		Template	No	If none of the xsl:when test attributes is true, then it is instantiated.
xsl:output	method = "xml" | "html" | "text" | qname-but-not-ncname; version = nmtoken; encoding = string; omit-xml-declaration = "yes" | "no"; standalone = "yes" | "no"; doctype-public = string; doctype-system = string; cdata-section-elements = qnames; indent = "yes" | "no"; media-type = string		None (empty element)	Yes	If the processor is capable of outputting the result tree as a byte sequence, the author of the style sheet can select the format here.
xsl:param	name = qname; select = expression	name	Template	Yes	Creates a variable that has the value of the expression. The variable value is a default value and can be overridden by expressions later on in the style sheet.

ELEMENT	ATTRIBUTES AND VALUES	REQUIRED ATTRIBUTES	CONTENT	TOP-LEVEL ELEMENT	FUNCTION
xsl:preserve-space	elements = tokens	elements	None (empty element)	Yes	Preserves whitespace.
xsl:processing-instruction	name = { ncname }	name	Template	No	Creates a processing instruction in the result tree. The name specifies the name of the processing instruction; the content is a template for the string value of the processing instruction node.
xsl:sort	select = string-expression; lang = { nmtoken }; data-type = { "text" | "number" |_qname-but-not-ncname }; order = { "ascending" | "descending" }; case-order = { "upper-first" | "lower-first" }		None (empty element)	No	Can be added to an xsl:apply-templates or xsl:for-each element in order to sort the content before processing (the content will be processed in the order it is sorted, not in the document order). The first child of the parent is the primary key; the second child is the secondary key.
xsl:strip-space	elements = tokens	elements	None (empty element)	Yes	Strips out white space
xsl:stylesheet	id = id; extension-element-prefixes = tokens; exclude-result-prefixes = tokens; version = number	version	xsl:import, other top-level-elements	No	Encapsulates the transformation sheet (root element).
xsl:template	match = pattern; name = qname; priority = number; mode = qname	xsl:param; template		Yes	Root element for the template.

Table 5.1 Continued

ELEMENT	ATTRIBUTES AND VALUES	REQUIRED ATTRIBUTES	CONTENT	TOP-LEVEL ELEMENT	FUNCTION
xsl:text	disable-output-escaping = "yes" | "no"		#PCDATA	No	Creates a text node in the result tree.
xsl:transform	id = id; extension-element-prefixes = tokens; exclude-result-prefixes = tokens; version_ = number	version	xsl:import; top-level-elements	No	Synonymous with xsl:stylesheet.
xsl:value-of	select = string-expression; disable-output-escaping = "yes" | "no"	select	None (empty element)	No	Creates a text node in the result tree. The select attribute contains an expression which will be converted to a string as if the string function was used.
xsl:variable	name = qname; select = expression	name	Template	Yes	Creates a variable that has the value of the expression.
xsl:when	test = boolean-expression	test	Template	No	The expression in the test is evaluated when an xsl:choose is instantiated, and if it is true, the template in the content is instantiated. Only the first of the xsl:when set that is true is instantiated.
xsl:with-param	name = qname; select = expression	name	Template	No	Passes a variable to a template; allowed within both xsl:call-template and xsl:apply-templates; if the parameter is to be used, the receiving template must have it specified by using xsl:param.

XSLT If and Choose

To be able to select an action based on a condition, you need to describe the condition (which is what Xpath is for), describe the action (which is what `xsl:apply-templates` is for), and describe that this action is predicated on the condition. You perform these actions by using `xsl:if` and `xsl:choose`.

xsl:if

The `xsl:if` element enables you to declare that an action should take place if an Xpath expression evaluates to true. If you are not sure whether an input XML document will contain certain elements or not, you can perform an XSLT transformation conditionally. If the element exists, then an output will be produced in the result tree. If it does not exist, however, either another output will be produced or no output will be produced at all.

The `xsl:if` element has a test attribute that specifies an expression (in Xpath). The expression is evaluated, and the resulting object is converted to a Boolean value as if by a call to the Boolean function. If the result is true, then the template is instantiated; otherwise, nothing is created. The content of the element is a template. In the following example, the names in a group of names are formatted as a comma-separated list:

```
<xsl:template match="namelist/name">
  <xsl:apply-templates/>
  <xsl:if test="not(position()=last())">, </xsl:if>
</xsl:template>
```

The following example colors every other table row yellow:

```
<xsl:template match="item">
  <tr>
    <xsl:if test="position() mod 2 = 0">
      <xsl:attribute name="bgcolor">yellow</xsl:attribute>
    </xsl:if>
    <xsl:apply-templates/>
  </tr>
</xsl:template>
```

For instance, if you want something to happen when a certain attribute is set to "true" (because the value of an attribute is a string, not a Boolean) and you want something else to happen when it is set to false, then simply write the following line: `<xsl:if test="@att='true'">`. If you instead want something to happen when a condition is true, you have to use `xsl:choose`.

If you want to create a list of elements that fulfill a condition (separated by a comma) and that exclude the comma after the last element, you can combine xsl:if with xsl:for-each in order to produce the following:

```
<xsl:for-each select=" item[@available='true']">
  <xsl:value-of select="@name" />
  <xsl:if test="position() != last()">, </xsl:if>
</xsl:for-each>
```

The usual way of omitting the trailing comma, however, is to use the position of the current node to determine whether to add the comma or not. This would look like the following:

```
<xsl:for-each select=" item ">
  <xsl:if test="@available='true'">
    <xsl:value-of select="@name" />
    <xsl:if test="position() != last()">, </xsl:if>
  </xsl:if>
</xsl:for-each>
```

Note that you are not allowed to use the Xpath abbreviated syntax inside the test attribute. Whenever an `xsl:if` tests true, then the contents of that `xsl:if` are processed.

Take, for instance, the following document:

```
<?xml version="1.0"?>
<catalog>
<cd>
<title>Exile On Main Street</title>
<artist>Rolling Stones</artist>
<country>USA</country>
<year>1972</year>
</cd>
</catalog>
```

To put a conditional "if" test against the content of the file, simply add an `xsl:if` element to your XSL document as follows:

```
<xsl:if match="artist='Rolling Stones'">
... some output ...
</xsl:if>
```

Now, look at your slightly adjusted XSL style sheet:

```
<?xml version='1.0'?>
<xsl:stylesheet
xmlns:xsl="http://www.w3.org/1999/XSL/Transformhttp://www.w3.org/1999/
XSL/Transform">
<xsl:template match="/">
  <html>
  <body>
    <table border="2" bgcolor="yellow">
      <tr>
        <th>Title</th>
        <th>Artist</th>
      </tr>
      <xsl:for-each select="catalog/cd">
          <xsl:if match="artist='Rolling Stones'">
            <tr>
          <td><xsl:value-of select="title"/></td>
          <td><xsl:value-of select="artist"/></td>
        </tr>
          </xsl:if>
        </xsl:for-each>
    </table>
  </body>
  </html>
</xsl:template>
</xsl:stylesheet>
```

You can use `xsl:if` to create a checkbox in the output document, which can be selected or not dependent on the content of the source document. The following style sheet will do just that:

```
<?xml version="1.0" standalone="yes"?>
<DemoMenu>
    <option strValue="A Check Box" textValue="N"/>
</DemoMenu>
<?xml version="1.0"?>
<xsl:stylesheet version="1.0"
xmlns:xsl='http://www.w3.org/1999/XSL/Transform'>
<xsl:template match="/"><html><head></head><body>
<xsl:apply-templates/></body></html>
</xsl:template>
<xsl:template match="DemoMenu">
<xsl:apply-templates/>
</xsl:template>
```

```
<xsl:template match="option">
<p align="center">
   <xsl:value-of select="@strValue"/>
   <xsl:if test="@textValue='Y'">  <!-- checked -->
         <input name="box1" type="checkbox" align="center" checked="Y"
value="Y"/>
   </xsl:if>
   <xsl:if test="not(@textValue='Y')">  <!-- not checked -->
         <input name="box1" type="checkbox" align="center" value="Y"/>
   </xsl:if>
</p>
</xsl:template>
<xsl:template match="*"/>
</xsl:stylesheet>
```

Note that XSLT does not have an `xsl:else` instruction. If you need multiple conditional branches, you will need to use `xsl:choose` with `xsl:when`.

xsl:choose

Another way of creating conditional processes in XSLT is using `xsl:choose`. The `xsl:choose` element selects one among a number of possible alternatives. It consists of a sequence of `xsl:when` elements followed by an optional `xsl:otherwise` element. Each `xsl:when` element has a single attribute, test, which specifies an Xpath expression. The content of each of the `xsl:when` and `xsl:otherwise` elements is a template.

When an `xsl:choose` element is processed, each of the `xsl:when` elements is tested in turn by evaluating the expression and converting the resulting object to a Boolean as if by a call to the Boolean function. The content of the first, and only the first, `xsl:when` element whose test is true is instantiated. If no `xsl:when` is true, the content of the `xsl:otherwise` element is instantiated. If no `xsl:when` element is true and no `xsl:otherwise` element is present, nothing is created.

Here is an example that selects among a set of alternatives based on the `$count` variable:

```
<xsl:choose>
  <xsl:when test="$count > 2"><xsl:text>, and
</xsl:text></xsl:when>
  <xsl:when test="$count > 1"><xsl:text> and
</xsl:text></xsl:when>
  <xsl:otherwise><xsl:text> </xsl:text></xsl:otherwise>
</xsl:choose>
```

The following example enumerates items in an ordered list by using Arabic numerals, letters, or Roman numerals (depending on the depth to which the ordered lists are nested):

```
<xsl:template match="orderedlist/listitem">
  <fo:list-item indent-start='2pi'>
    <fo:list-item-label>
      <xsl:variable name="level"
                   select="count(ancestor::orderedlist) mod 3"/>
      <xsl:choose>
        <xsl:when test='$level=1'>
          <xsl:number format="i"/>
        </xsl:when>
        <xsl:when test='$level=2'>
          <xsl:number format="a"/>
        </xsl:when>
        <xsl:otherwise>
          <xsl:number format="1"/>
        </xsl:otherwise>
      </xsl:choose>
      <xsl:text>. </xsl:text>
    </fo:list-item-label>
    <fo:list-item-body>
      <xsl:apply-templates/>
    </fo:list-item-body>
  </fo:list-item>
</xsl:template>
```

To insert a conditional choose test against the content of the file, simply add the `xsl:choose`, `xsl:when`, and `xsl:otherwise` elements to your XSL document. If you have a source document that looks like the following,

```
<?xml version="1.0"?>
<catalog>
<cd>
<title>Exile On Main Street</title>
<artist>Rolling Stones</artist>
<country>USA</country>
<year>1972</year>
</cd>
</catalog>
```

now look at your slightly adjusted XSL style sheet:

```
<?xml version='1.0'?>
<xsl:stylesheet
xmlns:xsl="http://www.w3.org/1999/XSL/Transform">
<xsl:template match="/">
```

```
<html>
<body>
  <table border="2" bgcolor="yellow">
    <tr>
      <th>Title</th>
      <th>Artist</th>
    </tr>
    <xsl:for-each select="catalog/cd">
        <tr>
      <td><xsl:value-of select="title"/></td>
        <xsl:choose>
        <xsl:when test="artist='Rolling Stones'">
          <td bgcolor="#ff0000">
           <xsl:value-of select="artist"/>
          </td>
        </xsl:when>
        <xsl:otherwise>
          <td><xsl:value-of select="artist"/></td>
        </xsl:otherwise>
        </xsl:choose>
    </tr>
      </xsl:for-each>
    </table>
  </body>
  </html>
</xsl:template>
</xsl:stylesheet>
```

If you want an action to be taken when some condition is not satisfied, you can do the following:

```
<xsl:choose>
  <xsl:when test="$someelement='true' and
                  otherelement='FALSE'"></xsl:when>
  <xsl:otherwise>
    <tr>...</tr>
  </xsl:otherwise>
</xsl:choose>
```

This will output a `<tr>...</tr>` if the variable `$someelement` is not true and if `otherelement` is false. The same effect can be accomplished with an `xsl:if`, however (and it is often the case that `xsl:if` and `xsl:choose` overlap):

```
<xsl:if test="not($someelement = 'true' and
                  otherelement = 'FALSE')">
  <tr>...</tr>
</xsl:if>
```

You can also use xsl:choose to enable a style sheet only to work with a certain version (for instance, XSLT 1.1). The following style sheet will output a message if the version of the XSLT processor is not an XSLT 1.1 processor (which it finds out by using the system-property function):

```
<xsl:stylesheet version="1.1"

xmlns:xsl="http://www.w3.org/1999/XSL/Transform">
  <xsl:template match="/">
    <xsl:choose>
      <xsl:when test="system-property('xsl:version') >= 1.1">
        <xsl:exciting-new-1.1-feature/>
      </xsl:when>
      <xsl:otherwise>
        <html>
        <head>
          <title>XSLT 1.1 required</title>
        </head>
        <body>
          <p>Sorry, this stylesheet requires XSLT 1.1.</p>
        </body>
        </html>
      </xsl:otherwise>
    </xsl:choose>
  </xsl:template>
</xsl:stylesheet>
```

Another way of doing the same thing is by using xsl:message with the attribute terminate="yes", which means that processors that do not implement XSLT 1.1 simply ignore the top-level element that comes from XSLT 1.1. It would look like this:

```
<xsl:stylesheet version="1.5"
xmlns:xsl="http://www.w3.org/1999/XSL/Transform">
  <xsl:important-new-1.1-declaration/>
  <xsl:template match="/">
    <xsl:choose>
      <xsl:when test="system-property('xsl:version') &lt; 1.1">
        <xsl:message terminate="yes">
          <xsl:text>Sorry, this stylesheet requires XSLT 1.1.</xsl:text>
        </xsl:message>
      </xsl:when>
      <xsl:otherwise>
        ...
      </xsl:otherwise>
    </xsl:choose>
  </xsl:template>
</xsl:stylesheet>
```

Another way to use this function is to produce different markup languages as output by checking what the root node is (remember, in XHTML the root node of a document is HTML, and in WML it is WML). The following example will output HTML if the method selected is HTML. You use a parameter to determine whether the method has been selected, and if it is, you apply the HTML mode to the templates:

```
<xsl:template match="/">
   <xsl:choose>
      <xsl:when test="$method = 'html'">
         <xsl:apply-templates mode="html" />
      </xsl:when>
      <xsl:otherwise><xsl:apply-templates /></xsl:otherwise>
   </xsl:choose>
</xsl:template>
```

Similarly, if you want to pre-process the data to filter out something, you can use the same method:

```
<xsl:template match="/">
   <xsl:variable name="processed">
      <xsl:apply-templates mode="filter" />
   </xsl:variable>
   <xsl:apply-templates select="$processed/*" />
</xsl:template>
```

Using Attributes and Variables

XSLT has a function to handle variables in transformation sheets and also has a way of handling attributes. The mechanisms are similar, and there is a function by which you can insert a variable as an attribute in the result tree.

Variables

`xsl:variable` enables you to associate a variable with a string, a node list, or a result tree fragment. Variables are "single assignment" (no side effects), and they are lexically scoped. Variables that are assigned inside a conditional only apply inside that conditional. A variable is a name that can be bound to a value. The value of the variable can be an object of any of the types that an expression can return.

There are two elements in XSLT that can be used to bind variables: `xsl:variable` and `xsl:param`. The difference is that the value specified on the `xsl:param` variable is only a default value for the current binding and can be overridden by later variable bindings (in the templates). Both `xsl:variable` and `xsl:param` must have a name attribute that specifies the name of the variable. The value of the name attribute is a QName.

A variable-binding element can specify the value of the variable in three alternative ways:

- If the variable-binding element has a select attribute, then the value of the attribute must be an expression, and the value of the variable is the object that results from evaluating the expression. In this case, the content must be empty.

- If the variable-binding element does not have a select attribute and has non-empty content (in other words, the variable-binding element has one or more child nodes), then the content of the variable-binding element specifies the value. The content of the variable-binding element is a template, which is instantiated to give the value of the variable. The resulting value is a result tree fragment (and that is equivalent to a node set containing just a single root node having as children the sequence of nodes produced by instantiating the template). The base URI of the nodes in the result tree fragment is the base URI of the element that binds the variable. The node set cannot have an attribute node or a namespace node among its members, because a root node cannot have an attribute node or a namespace node as a child. An XSLT processor can signal the error. If it does not signal the error, it must recover by not adding the attribute node or namespace node.

- If the variable-binding element has empty content and does not have a select attribute, then the value of the variable is an empty string. So, `xsl:variable name="x"` is equivalent to `xsl:variable_ name="x" select="''"`.

XSLT variables are similar to variables in other programming languages with the major exception that they can only be assigned a value once, at the time they are declared. Variables in XSLT are not used in the same way as in other programming languages, however, but are instead used to aid readability and to avoid repeating lengthy Xpath expressions. This goal is accomplished by declaring variables by using the xsl:variable instruction and assigning them Xpath expressions as values. The variable is then used in other XSLT instructions in place of using a full Xpath expression. When a variable is used, it is prefixed with the $ symbol to distinguish it from regular Xpath expressions.

The following example creates a variable called `generalizations` which represent a general type for a class:

```
<!-- Example of variable) -->
<xsl:template name="variable_example">

    <!-- Generalizations variable set -->
    <xsl:variable name="generalizations"
        select="general_types/
                general_type_element"/>
```

Here, we see the declaration of an `xsl:variable` with the name "generalizations". It is assigned a value through the `select` attribute, which contains an Xpath expression that finds generalization relationships within the current context of the document.

There are several ways to use variables. We will use them extensively in the following chapters, so here are just a couple of examples. For instance, in conjunction with the `count()` function to determine whether any general types exist for the class or interface:

```
<xsl:if test="count($generalizations) > 0">
```

If generalizations are found, we proceed to output the list of names by using the `xsl:for-each` instruction to produce the node list for the iteration:

```
<xsl:for-each select="$generalizations">
```

As you can see, the use of variables aids significantly in creating more concise, readable code.

Be careful when creating variable names, however. If you are trying to resolve a relative path according to the base URI of the input XML document that you are using, you need to make sure the path that is relative to the style sheet really points to the document (which implies that you have to know the file structure of the system with which you are working, of course). It is (perhaps unfortunately) perfectly legal for an XSLT processor not to complain if it cannot find the file when the `document()` function is used, in which case it gets an empty node list.

As well as being allowed at the top level, both `xsl:variable` and `xsl:param` are also allowed inside templates. `xsl:variable` is allowed anywhere within an instruction. The variable binding is visible to the siblings of the element and their descendants but not to the `xsl:variable` element itself. `xsl:param` is allowed as a child at the beginning of an `xsl:template` element. The binding is visible for all following siblings and their descendants but not for the `xsl:param` element itself.

If the bindings have the same name and they occur at the same point, the bindings shadow each other. If a binding is established by an `xsl:variable` or `xsl:param` element within a template and shadows another binding established within the template, it is an error (but there is no error if it shadows a binding that is done in a different element).

The following is allowed:

```
<xsl:param name="x" select="1"/>
<xsl:template name="foo">
<xsl:variable name="x" select="2"/>
</xsl:template>
```

The nearest equivalent in Java to an `xsl:variable` element in a template is a final local variable declaration with an initializer. For example,

```
<xsl:variable name="x" select="'value'"/>
```

has similar semantics to

```
final Object x = "value";
```

XSLT does not provide an equivalent to the Java assignment operator x = "value", because it would be harder to create an implementation that processes a document other than in a batch-like way, starting at the beginning and continuing through to the end.

Parameters are passed to templates by using the `xsl:with-param` element inside the template. The name attribute specifies the name of the parameter (the variable value whose binding is to be replaced). The value of the name attribute is a QName.

`xsl:with-param` is allowed within both `xsl:call-template` and `xsl:apply-templates`. The value of the parameter is specified in the same way as for `xsl:variable` and `xsl:param`. The current node and current node list used for computing the value specified by the `xsl:with-param` element is the same as that used for the `xsl:apply-templates` or `xsl:call-template` element within which it occurs. It is not an error to pass a parameter x to a template that does not have an xsl:param element for x; rather, the parameter is simply ignored.

This example defines a named template for a numbered block with an argument to control the format of the number:

```
    <xsl:template name="numbered-block">
  <xsl:param name="format">1. </xsl:param>
  <fo:block>
    <xsl:number format="{$format}"/>
    <xsl:apply-templates/>
  </fo:block>
</xsl:template>
<xsl:template match="ol//ol/li">
  <xsl:call-template name="numbered-block">
    <xsl:with-param name="format">a. </xsl:with-param>
  </xsl:call-template>
    </xsl:template>
```

Within a template, the `xsl:value-of` element can be used to compute generated text (for example, by extracting text from the source tree or by inserting the value of a variable). The `xsl:value-of` element performs this function with an expression that is specified as the value of the select attribute. Expressions can also be used inside attribute values of literal result elements by enclosing the expression in curly braces, {}.

The `xsl:value-of` element is instantiated to create a text node in the result tree. The required select attribute is an expression. This expression is evaluated, and the resulting object is converted to a string as if by a call to the string function. The string specifies the string value of the created text node. If the string is empty, no text node will be created. The created text node will be merged with any adjacent text nodes. If you want to copy something to the result tree without converting it to a string, you should use `xsl:copy`.

For example, the following code creates an HTML paragraph from a person element with given-name and family-name attributes. The paragraph will contain the value of the given-name attribute of the current node, followed by a space and the value of the family-name attribute of the current node:

```
<xsl:template match="person">
  <p>
   <xsl:value-of select="@given-name"/>
   <xsl:text> </xsl:text>
   <xsl:value-of select="@family-name"/>
  </p>
</xsl:template>
```

Attributes

An *attribute value template* (AVT) is, simply put, an expression inside curly brackets {} that can only be used when adding an attribute to an element that is to go into the output tree:

```
<xsl:template match ="x">
  <elem attrib="{some-value}">
```

some-value can be an Xpath expression, such as `path/to/sought/element`, or it can be a variable.

It can not be used in `xsl:template match="..... "`, `xsl:value-of select="...."`, or `xsl:variable select="....."`. Rather, it can only be used in an attribute that is declared an attribute value template in the XSLT recommendation. The list of which elements take AVT arguments and which do not is somewhat arbitrary. You just have to check in each case. But attributes (select, test, and so on) that take Xpath expressions are never interpreted as AVT. It does not make sense to put an AVT in something that will already be evaluated as an expression.

- To test whether the attribute ID exists, use `xsl:if test="@id">`.

- To test whether the attribute ID exists and is not zero length, use `xsl:if_test="string(@id)">`.

You can get the name of an attribute by using the following expression:

```
<xsl:for-each select="@*">
   <xsl:text>Value of </xsl:text>
           <xsl:value-of select="name(.)"/>
   <xsl:text> is </xsl:text><xsl:value-of select="."/>
 </xsl:for-each>
```

It is also possible to use `xsl:attribute` to generate element values, such as a Mailto reference. Use the `xsl:attribute` call in your style sheet and then treat it like a normal `<A href=.../>` tag, like the following:

```
<xsl:attribute name="href">mailto:<xsl:value-of select="email"/>
</xsl:attribute>
    Mail us!
```

Or, if you want the e-mail address to be printed on the screen as well, use the following:

```
    <xsl:attribute name="href">mailto:<xsl:value-of
select="email"/></xsl:attribute>:<xsl:value-of select="email"/>
```

Even simpler is the following, which will give the same result:

```
<A href="mailto:{email}"><xsl:value-of select="email"/>
```

To match all elements `<x>` (that might have attributes) and to add new attributes, use the following:

```
<x>                     --> <x              b="b" c="c">
<x a="a">               --> <x a="a"         b="b" c="c">
<x a="a" d="d">         --> <x a="a" d="d" b="b" c="c">
```

You will use:

```
<xsl:template match="x">
<x b="b" c="c">
<xsl:copy-of select="@*"/>
</x>
</xsl:template>
```

Attributes can be used to create values that are then used in processing. Not all attributes are interpreted as AVTs, however. Attributes whose value is an expression or pattern, attributes of top-level elements, and attributes that refer to named XSLT objects are not interpreted as AVTs. In addition, xmlns attributes are not interpreted as AVTs (it would not conform to the XML Namespaces Recommendation).

If the attribute value is interpreted as an AVT (attributes of a literal result element), you can have an expression in the attribute. You can use this function by surrounding the expression with curly braces, {}. The AVT is instantiated by replacing the expression—together with the surrounding curly braces—by the result of the expression and converting the resulting object to a string as if by a call to the string function. Curly braces are not recognized in an attribute value in an XSLT style sheet unless the attribute is specifically stated as interpreted as an attribute value template. In an element syntax summary, curly braces surround the value of such attributes.

Attribute value expressions work if the element is a literal element (in other words, if there is no computation of the result but it is copied straight to the result tree). Any element in a template rule that is not in the XSL (or other extension) namespace is copied literally to the result tree. In other words, we are talking about xsl:text, xsl:copy-of, and xsl:copy.

The content of <xsl:text> elements is copied directly to the result tree. White space is preserved by default:

```
<xsl:text>Literal result text</xsl:text>
<xsl:value-of>
```

The coding below inserts the value of an expression into the result tree, converting it to a string first if necessary.

```
<xsl:value-of select="$count + 1"/>
```

Since xsl:copy and xsl:copy-of copies the current node, or in the case of xsl:copy-of, the selected nodes, into the result tree without first converting them to a string, they are also literal elements.

```
<xsl:copy-of select="title"/>
<xsl:element>
```

In XSL, element attributes that expect an expression can be used to set variables. These element attributes are summarized in Table 5.2.

Table 5.2 Attributes of XSLT Elements

XSLT ELEMENT	ATTRIBUTE
xsl:apply-templates	select
xsl:value-of	select
xsl:number	value
xsl:for-each	select
xsl:if	test
xsl:when	test
xsl:sort	select

Table 5.3 Allowed Attributes in XSLT

ELEMENT	ATTRIBUTE
Literal result elements	any attribute
xsl:element	name
	namespace
xsl:attribute	name
	namespace
xsl:number	level
	count
	from
	format
	lang
	grouping-separator
	grouping-size
xsl:sort	order
	lang
	data-type
	case-order
xsl:processing-instruction	name

AVTs have the form {$variable} and are allowed in the following places (Table 5.3):

Filtering Documents Using XSLT

The following example creates an `<img>` result element from a photograph element in the source. The value of the src attribute of the `<img>` element is computed from the value of the image-dir variable and the string value of the href child of the photograph element. The value of the width attribute of the `<img>` element is computed from the value of the width attribute of the size child of the photograph element:

```
<xsl:variable name="image-dir">/images</xsl:variable>
<xsl:template match="photograph">
<img src="{$image-dir}/{href}" width="{size/@width}"/>
</xsl:template>
```

With this source,

```
<photograph>
  <href>headquarters.jpg</href>
  <size width="300"/>
</photograph>
```

the result would be as follows:

```
<img src="/images/headquarters.jpg" width="300"/>
```

Curly braces are not recognized recursively inside expressions. For example,

```
<a href="#{id({@ref})/title}">
```

is not allowed. Instead, simply use the following:

```
<a href="#{id(@ref)/title}">
```

XSLT literal elements can not only be used to copy text straight through to the result tree, they can also be used to create messages if a condition evaluates to true. For instance, to report errors, use xsl:message>:

```
<xsl:message>
  <xsl:text>Error: no ID found for linkend: </xsl:text>
  <xsl:value-of select="@linkend"/>
  <xsl:text>.</xsl:text>
</xsl:message>
```

It is also possible to filter the source document using XSLT, just like you would apply a query to a database. You would do this with the xsl:for-each element, and use the select attribute. The result is pretty much the same as if you were making an SQL query on the document. Take the following XML source document:

```
<?xml version="1.0"?>
<catalog>
<cd>
<title>Exile On Main Street</title>
<artist>Rolling Stones</artist>
<country>USA</country>
<year>1972</year>
</cd>
</catalog>
```

To apply a filter to the XML file, simply add a filter to the select attribute in your `xsl:for-each` element in your XSL file as follows:

```
<xsl:for-each select="catalog/cd[artist='Rolling Stones']">***
```

The legal filter operators in XSLT expressions are the following:

- `=` (equal)
- `!=` (not equal)
- `&lt;` (less than)
- `&gt;` (greater than)

Now, look at your slightly adjusted XSL style sheet:

```
<?xml version='1.0'?>
<xsl:stylesheet
xmlns:xsl="http://www.w3.org/1999/XSL/Transform">
<xsl:template match="/">
 <html>
 <body>
  <table border="2" bgcolor="yellow">
   <tr>
    <th>Title</th>
    <th>Artist</th>
   </tr>
   <xsl:for-each select="catalog/cd[artist='Rolling Stones']">
   <tr>
    <td><xsl:value-of select="title"/></td>
    <td><xsl:value-of select="artist"/></td>
   </tr>
   </xsl:for-each>
  </table>
 </body>
 </html>
</xsl:template>
</xsl:stylesheet>
```

The distinction between element values and attribute values is actually somewhat arbitrary. You can convert elements to attributes in XSLT. For instance, with the following source tree

```
<atom  phase="gas">
   <name>Hydrogen</name>
   <symbol>H</symbol>
   <boiling_point units="Kelvin">20.28</boiling_point>
</atom>
```

and the following result tree,

```
<atom phase="gas" name="Hydrogen" symbol="H">
    <boiling_point units="Kelvin">20.28</boiling_point>
</atom>
```

you can use the following style sheet where the first select picks up attributes and elements that do not have element children or attributes and makes attributes of them. The second select picks up elements with element children or attributes and text nodes. Comments, processing instructions, and so on are thrown away but could be added to the second select:

```
<xsl:stylesheet
  xmlns:xsl="http://www.w3.org/1999/XSL/Transform" version="1.0"
default-space="strip">
<xsl:template match="*">
<xsl:copy>
<xsl:for-each select="@*|*[not(* or @*)]">
<xsl:attribute name="{name(.)}"><xsl:value-of select="."/>
</xsl:attribute>
</xsl:for-each>
<xsl:apply-templates select="*[* or @*]|text()"/>
</xsl:copy>
</xsl:template>
</xsl:stylesheet>
```

The creation of an attribute can be made conditional by using test attributes.

```
<element xmlns:xsl="http://www.w3.org/1999/XSL/Transform"
xsl:version="1.0">
<element>
 <xsl:if test="true()">
  <xsl:attribute name="name">value</xsl:attribute>
 </xsl:if>
 foobar
</element>
```

Attributes can also be set in the XSLT transformation sheet by taking attribute values from the source document. For instance,

```
<INPUT>
        <xsl:attribute name="Name">
                <xsl:value-of select="Name"/>
            </xsl:attribute>
```

takes the value of the node selected by "Name," which would be a child element of the current node.

```
<INPUT>
        <xsl:attribute name="Name">
                <xsl:value-of select="@Name"/>
        </xsl:attribute>
```

would always produce a Name attribute and would give Name=" " if the input did not supply an attribute. It is equivalent to the simpler coding,

```
<INPUT Name="{@Name}">
```

If you do not want the input to have a Name attribute if the source does not have one, you can use the following code:

```
<INPUT>
 <xsl:copy-of select="@Name"/>
```

If you want all attributes copied, you can add more such lines or use the following code,

```
<INPUT>
 <xsl:copy-of select="@*"/>_
```

where the Xpath expression selects all of the elements for which there are attributes in the source.

If you want to go through each file and copy those nodes to the result tree that *either* have no lang attribute set or that *do not* have lang="german" or lang="french" set, you could use

```
xsl:copy-of select="selection[not(@lang]"/>
```

or

```
[not(@lang='german' or @lang='french')]"/>
```

Note that a!=b in XSLT does not mean the same as not(a=b). If @a does not exist, then @a=b and @a!=b are both false.

It is possible to create an implied attribute. For instance, if you write

```
<table border="{@border}">
```

in a template, you can hope to copy the border attribute from some input table to an output table that will work only if the input attribute is always there. Otherwise, you get border="". If you want to supply a default, then

```
<table border border="1001" >
  <xsl:copy-of select="@border"/>
```

makes an element node with a name table and one attribute node with the name border

```
<xsl:copy-of select="@border"/>
```

Either it does nothing, in which case you get what you have above, or it generates an attribute node with the name border. XSLT specifies that if you add two attribute nodes of the same name to an element, the first one is discarded. So, in this case the original attribute node with value 1,001 is replaced by the border attribute copied from the source tree.

You can also use this code to create a default attribute so that it works even if the DTD or schema is not read. If you want

```
<xxx>
```

to act the same as

```
<xxx yyy="yes">
```

but are not sure whether the DTD or schema supplying that default will be acted upon, then write your XSLT as such:

```
<xsl:template match="xxx">
 <xsl:variable name="yyy">
  <xsl:value-of select="@yyy"/>
  <xsl:if test="not(@yyy)">yes</xsl:if>
 <xsl:variable>
```

And, in the rest of template, write it the same way but use $yyy instead of @yyy:

```
<!-- A default rule for processing link attributes -->
<xsl:template match="Link/@*" priority="-1">
    <xsl:copy/>
</xsl:template>

<!-- To change a name of an attribute -->
<xsl:template match="Link/@linkid">
    <xsl:attribute name="name">
```

```
            <xsl:value-of select="."/>
        </xsl:attribute>
    </xsl:template>

    <!-- To prevent an attribute from being copied -->
    <xsl:template match="Link/@unused-attribute"/>
```

If you only want to select a unique value of an attribute, the problem is the same as when you want to create an index from entries in the text. You want a list where words do not repeat themselves. The example here uses empty tags with entry as attributes, but you can use the same algorithms if you use enclosing tags.

To copy all attributes of an element, write:

```
    <xsl:copy-of select="@*" />
```

To copy only attributes of the type type and language, write:

```
    <xsl:copy-of select="@type|@language" />
```

To select *all* attributes except a specific one, if it is unprefixed (in other words, it is in the null namespace), then you can use

```
    <xsl:copy-of select="@*[local-name() != 'type']" />
```

to copy all but the type attribute. It selects all attributes (@*) and then filters out all those whose local name equals type.

If the attribute has a prefix (in other words, it is in a namespace), then you should use:

```
    <xsl:copy-of select="@*[count(.|../@xml:lang) !=
                         count(../@xml:lang)]" />
```

to copy all but the xml:lang attribute. Alternatively, you can use

```
    <xsl:copy-of select="@*[generate-id() !=
                         generate-id(../@xml:lang)]" />
```

which does exactly the same thing. It selects all attributes and then filters out those that *are* the xml:lang attribute. Or, if you want to, you can use

```
    <xsl:copy-of select="@*[not(local-name() = 'lang' and
                         namespace-uri() =

    'http://www.w3.org/XML/1998/namespace')]" />
```

This coding selects all attributes and filters out those whose local name is lang in the XML namespace.

The value of an attribute is given as its string value. The xsl:value-of instruction gives the string value of whatever Xpath is specified within the select expression. So, if you want the value of an attribute within the xsl:value-of, then use an Xpath that points to that attribute:

```
<xsl:value-of select="@*[name() = $attname]" />
```

If this result is what you wanted, then to prevent the same attribute being searched for twice (once in the xsl:if test and once in the xsl:value-of select), then you could assign the attribute to a variable and query that:

```
<xsl:variable name="att" select="@*[name() = $attname]" />
<xsl:if test="$att">
  <foo>
    <attribute name="width"><xsl:value-of
        select="$att" /></attribute>
  </foo>
</xsl:if>
```

xsl:if tests whether the attribute is present, rather than whether the attribute has a value. In other words, if $attname is bar, then

```
<foo bar="" />
```

would have the test return true. If you want to test whether the attribute is present and has a value, then use the following instead:

```
test="string($att)"
```

Another question is what you want your output to look like. If it should be a closed element (<foo width="value" />), then you need to prefix your attribute elements with xsl: to put them in the XSLT namespace and have the XSLT processor recognize them as instructions. Alternatively, you can use an AVT to achieve the same effect:

```
<foo width="{$att}" />
```

If you have a template for an attribute and you want to specify a choice based on the name of the element in which the attribute occurs (in other words, test="IF THE NAME OF YOUR ASSOCIATED ELEMENT IS 'FOO'").

To go from an attribute to its element involves using `parent::` axis. So, if the context node is an attribute (as it is in a template that matches attribute nodes), then you can identify the element that attribute is on with the following expression:

```
parent::*
```

(the element that is the parent of this node), or

```
parent::node()
```

(the node (which actually must be an element in this context) that is the parent of this node) or the abbreviation of the above.

To get the name of the parent, you can use the `name()` function, taking one of the above expressions as an argument:

```
name(..)
```

So, to test whether the name of the parent element is FOO, you could then use:

```
name(..) = 'FOO'
```

This answer will work perfectly well in most cases, but a better solution becomes apparent if you turn around the phrasing of what you are after. You want to know whether this attribute has a FOO element as a parent: is there a parent of this attribute that is a FOO element? The expression to reach such a parent is:

```
parent::FOO
```

(the FOO element that is the parent of this node). If the parent element is a FOO element, then that node will be returned. If the parent element is *not* a FOO element, then no node will be returned because there is no parent FOO element. Within a test expression, if a node is returned, the test returns true; if no node is returned, the test returns false. So, in most situations, the following is equivalent:

```
parent::FOO
```

is equivalent to

```
name(..) = 'FOO'
```

The situation where they are not equivalent is where namespaces are involved. The name() of a node gives the exact name for the node within the XML source. Look at the following XML:

```
<foo:FOO xmlns:foo="http://www.foo.com" />
```

In this code, the FOO element is in the http://www.foo.com namespace. The name() of that element is

```
foo:FOO
```

So, if you are using name() to test the identity of the element, then you need to use

```
name(..) = 'foo:FOO'
```

It might be, however, that in another document (or even in the same document) you have an element such as the following:

```
<bar:FOO xmlns:bar="http://www.foo.com" />
```

The FOO element here is in the same namespace (http://www.foo.com) but has a different prefix. Its name is

```
bar:FOO
```

and it would have to be tested with

```
name(..) = 'bar:FOO'
```

despite the fact that actually the two FOO elements in the two documents are meant to be precisely the same.

Fortunately, when you use parent::FOO instead, it takes into account the fact that the prefix of a namespace is not important. It is the URI at which you have to look. If within your XSLT you have declared the foo prefix to be associated with the http://www.foo.com URI by using

```
xmlns:baz="http://www.foo.com"
```

then the Xpath

```
parent::baz:FOO
```

will match both the foo:FOO and the bar:FOO elements. It looks for the equivalence in the namespace URI rather than in the namespace prefix. For this reason, it is worth getting into the habit of testing for nodes called a particular name by testing for whether the node called that name exists, rather than testing whether the node is called that name.Within a template, the `xsl:value-of` element can be used to compute generated text (for example, by extracting text from the source tree or by inserting the value of a variable). The `xsl:value-of` element performs this task with an expression that is specified as the value of the select attribute. Expressions can also be used inside attribute values of literal result elements by enclosing the expression in curly braces, {}.

If the expression is true, the resulting object is converted to a string as if by a call to the string function. The string specifies the string value of the created text node. If the string is empty, no text node will be created.

The xsl:copy-of element can be used to copy a node set over to the result tree without converting it to a string.

For example, the following code creates an HTML paragraph from a person element with given-name and family-name attributes. The paragraph will contain the value of the given-name attribute of the current node, followed by a space, and the value of the family-name attribute of the current node:

```
<xsl:template match="person">
  <p>
   <xsl:value-of select="@given-name"/>
   <xsl:text> </xsl:text>
   <xsl:value-of select="@family-name"/>
  </p>
</xsl:template>
```

For another example, the following code creates an HTML paragraph from a person element with given-name and family-name children elements. The paragraph will contain the string value of the first given-name child element of the current node, followed by a space, and the string value of the first family-name child element of the current node:

```
<xsl:template match="person">
  <p>
   <xsl:value-of select="given-name"/>
   <xsl:text> </xsl:text>
   <xsl:value-of select="family-name"/>
```

```
  </p>
 </xsl:template>
```

The following code precedes each procedure element with a paragraph containing the security level of the procedure. It assumes that the security level that applies to a procedure is determined by a security attribute on the procedure element or on an ancestor element of the procedure. It also assumes that if more than one such element has a security attribute, then the security level is determined by the element that is closest to the procedure.

```
<xsl:template match="procedure">
  <fo:block>
    <xsl:value-of select="ancestor-or-
self::*[@security][1]/@security"/>
  </fo:block>
  <xsl:apply-templates/>
</xsl:template>
```

Handling individual attributes is relatively straightforward. But to copy groups of attributes, you could use XML entities to give the attribute names. Define the entities in the DTD for the style sheet

```
<![DOCTYPE xsl:stylesheet [
<!ENTITY coreattrs '@id|@class|@style|@title'>
]>
```

and then use the entity name within the xsl:copy-of in the main code:

```
<xsl:template match="p">
  <p>
    <xsl:copy-of select="&coreattrs;" />
  </p>
</xsl:template>
```

Or, you could store the relevant attribute names in a separate XML structure somewhere, for example:

```
- --- definitions.xml ---
<attgroup name="coreattrs">
  <attribute name="id" />
  <attribute name="class" />
  <attribute name="style" />
  <attribute name="title" />
</attgroup>
```

This concept is actually similar to an XML Schema (or other schema), and you can either use one of the existing schema languages to create it or invent your own.

With this structure, you could retrieve the list of coreattrs through something like:

```
document('definitions.xml')//attgroup[@name = 'coreattrs']/attribute
```

Of course, you could probably do this task more efficiently with keys or IDs. Perhaps store that in a variable:

```
<xsl:variable name="coreattrs"
select="document('definitions.xml')//attgroup[@name
= 'coreattrs']/attribute/@name" />
```

Then, you can copy all of those attributes whose name is equal to one of the @names of the attribute elements stored in the $coreattrs variable:

```
<xsl:template match="p">
  <p>
    <xsl:copy-of select="@*[name() = $coreattrs/@name]" />
  </p>
</xsl:template>
```

This coding separates the information that you want from how you use it. You can easily edit definitions.xml if the membership of coreattrs changes (without having to touch the XSLT code).

Note that `xsl:copy-of` gives an exact copy of a node, including its name and value, and obviously it only copies a node if it is there to be copied—so you do not need the `xsl:if`'s testing for its presence. If you ever change the name of one of these attributes—changing `lang` to `xml:lang`, for example—then you cannot use `xsl:copy-of`. Using a separate named or "moded" template gives you a lot more flexibility and extensibility.

XSLT processors do not know whether an attribute is declared as #REQUIRED or #IMPLIED in the DTD or whether it has a default value (or anything in that regard). That is a matter for the XML processor. It can look in the DTD and fill in the gaps accordingly (for instance, adding #FIXED or defaulted attributes to elements), but the contents of the DTD are not available to the XSLT processor. In other words, the XSLT processor cannot tell the difference between a defaulted attribute and an attribute that has been declared with the same value as the default value.

If you were using an XML Schema rather than a DTD, then it would be possible to access that schema and check whether an attribute is (the equivalent of) #REQUIRED or #IMPLIED from there.

Given that an attribute has a value, you can copy the value. If there is no value, there will not be any copy. Use the `xsl:if` element to test whether there is an attribute:

```
<xsl:template match="Link">
  <h2>
    <xsl:attribute name="name">
      <xsl:value-of select="./@linkid"/>
    </xsl:attribute>
    <xsl:if test="@date">
      <xsl:attribute name="date">
        <xsl:value-of select="./@date"/>
      </xsl:attribute>
    </xsl:if>
    <xsl:apply-templates/>
  </h2>
</xsl:template>
```

Written in the abbreviated Xpath syntax, this code could instead be as follows:

```
<xsl:template match="Link">
  <h2 name="{@linkid}">                    <!-- changed for brevity -->
    <xsl:if test="@date">
      <xsl:copy-of select="@date" /> <!-- changed for brevity -->
    </xsl:if>
    <xsl:value-of select="." />        <!-- changed for performance -->
  </h2>
</xsl:template>
```

For a more generic solution, you can cycle through the attributes that are present and make copies of them. Naturally, this action will capture all #REQUIRED attributes (because they must be present) and any #IMPLIED attributes in the document.

```
<xsl:template match="Link">
  <h2>
    <xsl:for-each select="@*">
      <xsl:copy />
    </xsl:for-each>
    <xsl:value-of select="." />
  </h2>
</xsl:template>
```

The problem with this approach is that you cannot change the names of the attributes. This process involves using extra knowledge about the mapping between the old names and the new names, which you have to either embed in the template itself or make explicit elsewhere and reference from within the template. For another example, the following code creates an HTML paragraph from a person element with given-name and family-name children elements. The paragraph will contain the string value of the first given-name child element of the current node, followed by a space, and the string value of the first family-name child element of the current node:

```
<xsl:template match="person">
  <p>
   <xsl:value-of select="given-name"/>
   <xsl:text> </xsl:text>
   <xsl:value-of select="family-name"/>
  </p>
</xsl:template>
```

The following code precedes each procedure element with a paragraph containing the security level of the procedure. It assumes that the security level that applies to a procedure is determined by a security attribute on the procedure element or on an ancestor element of the procedure. It also assumes that if more than one such element has a security attribute, then the security level is determined by the element that is closest to the procedure.

```
<xsl:template match="procedure">
  <fo:block>
    <xsl:value-of select="ancestor-or-
self::*[@security][1]/@security"/>
  </fo:block>
  <xsl:apply-templates/>
</xsl:template>
```

Sorting, Counting, and Comparing XSLT Elements

Once you have a node set, you want to compare the nodes to each other. You also want to change their ordering (sorting). And numbering and counting them is a step in that direction.

Numbering

The xsl:number element is used to insert a formatted number into the result tree. The number to be inserted can be specified by an Xpath expression (for example, to count elements). The element can have a value attribute, which contains an expression. If so, the expression is evaluated and the resulting object is converted to a number as if by a call to the number function. The number is rounded to an integer and then converted to a string. After conversion, the resulting string is inserted into the result tree. For example, the following example numbers a sorted list:

```
<xsl:template match="items">
  <xsl:for-each select="item">
    <xsl:sort select="."/>
    <p>
      <xsl:number value="position()" format="1. "/>
      <xsl:value-of select="."/>
    </p>
  </xsl:for-each>
</xsl:template>
```

If no value attribute is specified, then the xsl:number element inserts a number based on the position of the current node in the source tree. The following attributes control how the current node is to be numbered:

level—Specifies how deep into the source tree the numbering should go. It can have the values single, multiple, or any. The default is single.

count—A pattern that specifies what nodes should be counted at the levels specified by the level attribute. If count attribute is not specified, then it defaults to the pattern that matches any node with the same node type as the current node, and if the current node has an expanded name, with the same expanded name as the current node.

from—A pattern that specifies where counting starts.

In addition, the attributes for number to string conversion are used for number to string conversion, as in the case when the value attribute is specified.

The xsl:number element first constructs a list of positive integers by using the level, count, and from attributes.

When level="single", it goes up to the first node in the ancestor-or-self axis that matches the count pattern and constructs a list of length one containing one plus the number of preceding siblings of that ancestor that match the count pattern. If there is no such ancestor, it constructs an empty list. If the from attribute is specified, then the only ancestors that are searched are those that are descendants of the nearest ancestor that matches the from pattern. Preceding siblings has the same meaning here as with the preceding-sibling axis.

When level="multiple", it constructs a list of all ancestors of the current node in document order followed by the element itself, then selects from the list those nodes that match the count pattern. It then maps each node in the list to one plus the number of preceding siblings of that node that match the count pattern. If the from attribute is specified, then the only ancestors that are searched are those that are descendants of the nearest ancestor that matches the from pattern. Preceding siblings has the same meaning here as with the preceding-sibling axis.

When level="any", it constructs a list of length one containing the number of nodes that match the count pattern and that belong to the set containing the current node and all nodes at any level of the document that are before the current node in document order, excluding any namespace and attribute nodes (in other words, the union of the members of the preceding and ancestor-or-self axes). If the from attribute is specified, then only nodes after the first node before the current node that match the from pattern are considered.

The list of numbers is then converted into a string by using the attributes. In this context, the value of each of these attributes is interpreted as an attribute value template. After conversion, the resulting string is inserted into the result tree.

The following code would number the items in an ordered list:

```
<xsl:template match="ol/item">
    <xsl:number/><xsl:text>. </xsl:text><xsl:apply-templates/>
<xsl:template>
```

The following two rules would number title elements. This function is intended for a document that contains a sequence of chapters followed by a sequence of appendices, where both chapters and appendices contain sections (which in turn contain subsections). Chapters are numbered 1, 2, and 3, and appendices are numbered A, B, and C. Sections in chapters are numbered 1.1, 1.2, and 1.3, and sections in appendices are numbered A.1, A.2, and A.3.

```
<xsl:template match="title">
    <xsl:number level="multiple"
                count="chapter|section|subsection"
                format="1.1 "/>
    <xsl:apply-templates/>
</xsl:template>
<xsl:template match="appendix//title" priority="1">
  <fo:block>
    <xsl:number level="multiple"
                count="appendix|section|subsection"
                format="A.1 "/>
    <xsl:apply-templates/>
  </fo:block>
</xsl:template>
```

The following example numbers notes sequentially within a chapter:

```
<xsl:template match="note">
  <fo:block>
    <xsl:number level="any" from="chapter" format=" (1)"/>
    <xsl:apply-templates/>
  </fo:block>
</xsl:template>
```

The following example would number H4 elements in HTML with a three-part label:

```
<xsl:template match="H4">
 <fo:block>
   <xsl:number level="any" from="H1" count="H2"/>
   <xsl:text>.</xsl:text>
   <xsl:number level="any" from="H2" count="H3"/>
   <xsl:text>.</xsl:text>
   <xsl:number level="any" from="H3" count="H4"/>
   <xsl:text> </xsl:text>
   <xsl:apply-templates/>
 </fo:block>
</xsl:template>
```

You can also convert the numbers (which, of course, are of the type number) into a string (for instance, if you want to use them in an HTML document or as text in some other context). The following attributes are used to control conversion of a list of numbers into a string. The numbers are integers greater than 0. These attributes are all optional.

format—The default value is 1. The format attribute is split into a sequence of tokens where each token is a maximal sequence of alphanumeric characters or a maximal sequence of non-alphanumeric characters. Alphanumeric means any character that has a Unicode category of Nd, Nl, No, Lu, Ll, Lt, Lm, or Lo. The alphanumeric tokens (format tokens) specify the format to be used for each number in the list.

If the first token is a non-alphanumeric token, then the constructed string will start with that token; if the last token is a non-alphanumeric token, then the constructed string will end with that token. Non-alphanumeric tokens that occur between two format tokens are separator tokens that are used to join numbers in the list. The nth format token will be used to format the nth number in the list. If there are more numbers than format tokens, then the last format token will be used to format remaining numbers. If there are no format tokens, then a format token of 1 is used to format all numbers. The format token specifies the string to be used to represent the number 1. Each number after the first will be separated from the preceding number by the separator token preceding the format token used to format that number, or if there are no separator tokens, then a period character (.) will be used. Format tokens are a superset of the allowed values for the type attribute for the OL element in HTML 4.0 and are interpreted as follows.

Any token where the last character has a decimal digit value of 1 (as specified in the Unicode character property database) and the Unicode value of preceding characters is one less than the Unicode value of the last character generates a decimal representation of the number where each number is at least as long as the format token. Thus, a format token 1 generates the sequence 1 2 . . . 10 11 12 . . . , and a format token 01 generates the sequence 01 02 . . . 09 10 11 12 . . . 99 100 101.

- A format token A generates the sequence A B C . . . Z AA AB AC . . .
- A format token a generates the sequence a b c . . . z aa ab ac . . .

- A format token i generates the sequence
  i ii iii iv v vi vii viii ix x . . .

- A format token I generates the sequence
  I II III IV V VI VII VIII IX X . . .

Any other format token indicates a numbering sequence that starts with that token. If an implementation does not support a numbering sequence that starts with that token, it must use a format token of 1.

When numbering with an alphabetic sequence, the lang attribute specifies which alphabet (or character set and ordering system) is to be used. It has the same range of values as xml:lang [XML]. If no lang value is specified, the language should be determined from the system environment. Implementers should document for which languages they support numbering.

You should not make any assumptions about how numbering works in particular languages and should properly research the languages that you wish to support. For instance, Japanese Kana ordering is very different from the Latin alphabetical order, as is Russian Cyrillic ordering. Of course, XSLT can be used to convert between these different ordering systems. But mind the value of your xml:lang attribute. The number of people who speak English is a small minority of the world population, after all.

letter-value—Separates different numbering sequences that use letters. In many languages, there are two commonly used numbering sequences that use letters or the corresponding character set (for instance, Japanese Kana ordering). One numbering sequence assigns numeric values to letters in alphabetic sequence, and the other assigns numeric values to each letter in some other manner that is traditional in that language.

In English, these would correspond to the numbering sequences specified by the format tokens a and i. In some languages, the first member of each sequence is the same, and so the format token alone would be ambiguous. A value of alphabetic specifies the alphabetic sequence; a value of traditional specifies the other sequence. If the letter-value attribute is not specified, then it is implementation-dependent how any ambiguity is resolved.

Two XSLT processors that conform to the specification might still not convert a number to exactly the same string. Some XSLT processors might not support some languages. Furthermore, there might be variations possible in the way conversions are performed for any particular languages that are not specifiable by the attributes on `xsl:number`. Future versions of XSLT might provide additional attributes to provide control over these variations. Implementations can also use implementation-specific, namespaced attributes on `xsl:number` for this task.

`grouping-separator`—Determines which separator should be used in grouping (for example, thousands) in decimal numbering sequences, and the optional grouping size specifies the size (normally 3 in Western languages, 4 in Japanese) of the grouping. For example, grouping-separator="," and grouping-size="3" would produce numbers of the form 1,000,000. If only one of the grouping separator and grouping size attributes is specified, then it is ignored.

Here are some examples of conversion specifications:

- `format="&#x30A2;"` specifies Katakana numbering.
- `format="&#x30A4;"` specifies Katakana numbering in the "iroha" order.
- `format="&#x0E51;"` specifies numbering with Thai digits.
- `format="&#x05D0;" letter-value="traditional"` specifies traditional Hebrew numbering.
- `format="&#x10D0;" letter-value="traditional"` specifies Georgian numbering.
- `format="&#x03B1;" letter-value="traditional"` specifies "classical" Greek numbering.
- `format="&#x0430;" letter-value="traditional"` specifies Old Slavic numbering.

The `xsl:number` element performs two functions:

It evaluates a numeric expression and converts the result into a formatted string:

```
<xsl:number value="3" format="A. "/>
<xsl:number value="count(listitem)" format="01"/>
```

It also counts elements in the source tree and converts the result into a formatted string:

```
<xsl:number count="listitem" format="i. "/>
<xsl:number count="chapter" from="book" level="any" format="1. "/>
<xsl:number count="h1|h2|h3" level="multiple"
from="chapter|appendix" format="1."/>
```

The `format-number` function converts its first argument to a string by using the format pattern string specified by the second argument and the decimal-format named by the third argument or the default decimal-format if there is no third argument. The format pattern string is in the syntax specified by the JDK 1.1 DecimalFormat class. The format pattern string is in a localized notation: the decimal-format determines what characters have a special meaning in the pattern (with the exception of the quote character, which is not localized). The format pattern must not contain the currency sign (#x00A4). Support for this feature was added after the initial release of JDK 1.1. The decimal-format name must be an expanded QName. It is an error if the style sheet does not contain a declaration of the decimal-format with the specified expanded-name.

The `xsl:decimal-format` element declares a decimal format, which controls the interpretation of a format pattern used by the `format-number` function. If there is a name attribute, then the element declares a named decimal-format; otherwise, it declares the default decimal-format. The value of the name attribute is a QName, which is expanded. It is an error to declare either the default decimal-format or a decimal-format with a given name more than once (even with different import precedence) unless it is declared every time with the same value for all attributes (taking into account any default values).

The other attributes on `xsl:decimal-format` correspond to the methods on the JDK 1.1 DecimalFormatSymbols class. For each get/set method pair there is an attribute defined for the `xsl:decimal-format` element.

The following attributes control both the interpretation of characters in the format pattern and specify characters that might appear in the result of formatting the number:

- `decimal-separator` specifies the character used for the decimal sign; the default value is the period character (.).

- `grouping-separator` specifies the character used as a grouping separator (for example, thousands); the default value is the comma character (,).

- percent specifies the character that is used as a percent sign; the default value is the percent character (%).

- per-mille specifies the character that is used as a per mille sign; the default value is the Unicode per-mille character (#x2030).

- zero-digit specifies the character used as the digit zero; the default value is the digit zero (0).

The following attributes control the interpretation of characters in the format pattern:

- digit specifies the character that is used for a digit in the format pattern; the default value is the number sign character (#).

- pattern-separator specifies the character that is used to separate positive and negative subpatterns in a pattern; the default value is the semi-colon character (;).

The following attributes specify characters or strings that might appear in the result of formatting the number:

- infinity specifies the string that is used to represent infinity; the default value is the string Infinity.

- NaN specifies the string used to represent the NaN value; the default value is the string NaN.

- minus-sign specifies the character used as the default minus sign; the default value is the hyphen-minus character (-, #x2D).

Sorting

Once you know how things are ordered, you can sort them. Adding xsl:sort elements as children of an -xsl:apply-templates or _-xsl:for-each element specifies sorting. The first xsl:sort child specifies the primary sort key; the second xsl:sort child specifies the secondary sort key; and so on. When an xsl:apply-templates or xsl:for-each element has one or more xsl:sort children, then instead of processing the selected nodes in document order, it sorts the nodes according to the specified sort keys and then processes them in sorted order. When used in xsl:for-each, xsl:sort elements must occur first. When a template is instantiated by xsl:apply-templates and xsl:for-each, the current node list consists of the complete list of nodes being processed in sorted order.

`xsl:sort` has a select attribute whose value is an expression. For each node to be processed, the expression is evaluated with that node as the current node and with the complete list of nodes being processed in unsorted order as the current node list. The resulting object is converted to a string as if by a call to the `string` function. This string is used as the sort key for that node. The default value of the select attribute is the period sign (.), which will cause the string value of the current node to be used as the sort key.

This string serves as a sort key for the node. The following optional attributes on `xsl:sort` control how the list of sort keys is sorted. The values of all of these attributes are interpreted as attribute value templates.

- `order` specifies whether the strings should be sorted in ascending or descending order; ascending specifies ascending order; and descending specifies descending order; the default is ascending.

- `lang` specifies the language of the sort keys; it has the same range of values as `xml:lang`. If no `lang` value is specified, the language should be determined from the system environment.

- `data-type` specifies the data type of the strings; the following values are allowed:

  - `text` specifies that the sort keys should be sorted lexicographically in the culturally correct manner for the language specified by lang.

  - `number` specifies that the sort keys should be converted to numbers and then sorted according to the numeric value; the sort key is converted to a number as if by a call to the number function; the lang attribute is ignored.

  - `QName` (with prefix) is expanded into an expanded name; the expanded name identifies the data type; the behavior in this case is not specified by the XSLT specification. The default value is text. In the future, there will probably be more data types based on XML Schema.

- `case-order` has the values `upper-first` or `lower-first`; this value applies when the `data-type="text"` and specifies that upper-case letters should sort before lower-case letters (or vice-versa, respectively). For example, if `lang="en"`, then A a B b are sorted with `case-order="upper-first"` and a A b B are sorted with `case-order="lower-first"`. The default value is language dependent.

It is possible for two XSLT processors to conform to the XSLT specification and still not give the same result from the sort. Some XSLT processors might not support some languages. Furthermore, there might be variations possible in the sorting of any particular languages that are not specified by the attributes on `xsl:sort` (for example, whether Hiragana or Katakana is sorted first in Japanese). Future versions of XSLT might provide additional attributes to provide control over these variations. Implementations might also use implementation-specific, namespaced attributes on xsl:sort for this task.

The sort must be stable. In the sorted list of nodes, any sublist that has sort keys that all compare equally must be in document order.

For example, suppose an employee database has the form

```
<employees>
  <employee>
    <name>
      <given>James</given>
      <family>Clark</family>
    </name>
    ...
  </employee>
</employees>
```

Then, a list of employees sorted by name could be generated by using:

```
<xsl:template match="employees">
  <ul>
    <xsl:apply-templates select="employee">
      <xsl:sort select="name/family"/>
      <xsl:sort select="name/given"/>
    </xsl:apply-templates>
  </ul>
</xsl:template>
<xsl:template match="employee">
  <li>
    <xsl:value-of select="name/given"/>
    <xsl:text> </xsl:text>
    <xsl:value-of select="name/family"/>
  </li>
</xsl:template>
```

The `xsl:sort` element sorts a set of nodes according to the criteria specified:

```
<xsl:apply-templates select="row">
  <xsl:sort data-type="number" select="entry[2]"/>
</xsl:apply-templates>
```

It can appear as a child of `xsl:apply-templates` or `xsl:for-each`. It can also be nested:

```
<doc>
<para>Table of stock trades</para>
<table>
<row><cell>3000</cell><cell>Ericsson</cell></row>
<row><cell>2400</cell><cell>Nokia</cell></row>
<row><cell>10000</cell><cell>Lucent</cell></row>
<row><cell>101</cell><cell>Nortel</cell></row>
</table>
</doc>
```

The sorting style sheet looks like the following:

```
<?xml version='1.0'?>
<xsl:stylesheet xmlns:xsl="http://www.w3.org/1999/XSL/Transform"
                version="1.0">
<xsl:import href="element.xsl"/>
<xsl:template match="table">
  <xsl:if test="@id"><a name="{@id}"/></xsl:if>
  <table>
    <xsl:apply-templates select="row">
      <xsl:sort data-type="number" select="./cell[1]"/>
    </xsl:apply-templates>
  </table>
</xsl:template>
</xsl:stylesheet>
```

And here is what the sorted result looks like:

```
<p>Table of stock trades</p>
<table>
<tr>
<td>101</td><td>Nortel</td>
</tr>
<tr>
<td>2400</td><td>Nokia</td>
</tr>
<tr>
<td>3000</td><td>Ericsson</td>
</tr>
<tr>
```

```
<td>10000</td><td>Lucent</td>
</tr>
</table>
```

The `count` attribute gives a match expression against which the ancestors and their preceding siblings are matched in order to create the numbering scheme. In the `count` attribute, the first term is '`//part`', which matches any `part` element that is a descendant of the root node. This term will match any `part` elements that it comes across, as will simply `part`. There is never any point in having '`//`' at the beginning of a match pattern if the only constraint it adds is that the node is a descendant of the root node, which is true for all nodes. It is therefore no constraint at all and completely superfluous.

Take a look at the following XML document.

```
<?xml version="1.0"?>
<catalog>
<cd>
<title>Exile On Main Street</title>
<artist>Rolling Stones</artist>
<country>USA</country>
<year>1972</year>
</cd>
</catalog>
```

To output this XML file as an ordinary HTML file and sort it at the same time, simply add an `order-by` attribute to your for-each element in your XSL file as such:

```
<xsl:for-each select="CATALOG/CD" order-by="+ ARTIST">
```

The order-by attribute takes a plus (+) or minus (–) sign to define an ascending or descending sort order and an element name to define the sort element.

Now, look at your slightly adjusted XSL style sheet:

```
<?xml version='1.0'?>
<xsl:stylesheet
xmlns:xsl="http://www.w3.org/1999/XSL/Transform">
<xsl:template match="/">
  <html>
  <body>
    <table border="2" bgcolor="yellow">
      <tr>
        <th>Title</th>
```

```
      <th>Artist</th>
    </tr>
    <xsl:for-each select="catalog/cd"
     order-by="+ artist">
    <tr>
      <td><xsl:value-of select="title"/></td>
      <td><xsl:value-of select="title"/></td>
    </tr>
    </xsl:for-each>
  </table>
 </body>
 </html>
</xsl:template>
</xsl:stylesheet>
```

The result is a table which is sorted at the same time.

Comparing Strings in XSLT

How do we compare strings with Xpath/XSLT? Is there some function like strcmp() in C or compareTo() in Java? There is no Xpath function or operator for comparing strings. Depending on the context of the problem, you might be able to use xsl:sort to order strings alphabetically. If you cannot, then you have to use a named template to do the comparison for you.

Apply templates to the term that either is the input term or the term immediately following the input term in alphabetical order with a template that operates on the term by outputting it and the next nine terms. In other words,

```
<xsl:template match="term">
  <xsl:for-each select=". |
                      following-sibling::term[position() &lt; 10]">
    <!-- display in some appropriate way -->
  </xsl:for-each>
</xsl:template>
```

So, the problem is in identifying the element that has a value that is the same as or follows alphabetically the input term. If you were allowing XSLT 1.1, then you could use xsl:sort to list the terms, including the input term, and select the one that you are after:

```
<xsl:template match="longman">
  <!-- create a list of terms that includes the input term -->
  <xsl:variable name="terms">
```

```
      <input><xsl:value-of select="$input" /></input>
      <xsl:copy-of select="term" />
   </xsl:variable>
   <xsl:for-each select="$terms">
      <!-- sort the terms (including the input term) alphabetically -->
      <xsl:sort select="." />
      <!-- select the term that immediately following the input term
           within the list -->
      <xsl:apply-templates select="input/following-sibling::term" />
   </xsl:for-each>
</xsl:template>
```

If you are not allowing XSLT 1.1, you have to use a named template to carry out the comparison. Here is a rough-and-ready one that takes two parameters ($first and $second) and returns true if $first comes before $second and false if not (if they are the same, it returns true):

```
<xsl:variable name="charorder"
select="'abcdefghijklmnopqrstuvwxyz'" />
<xsl:template name="strcmp">
   <xsl:param name="first" />
   <xsl:param name="second" />
   <xsl:variable name="nFirstFirst"
                 select="string-length(
                           substring-before($charorder,
                                        substring($first, 1, 1)))"
/>
   <xsl:variable name="nFirstSecond"
                 select="string-length(
                           substring-before($charorder,
                                        substring($second, 1, 1)))"
/>
   <xsl:variable name="restFirst" select="substring($first, 2)" />
   <xsl:variable name="restSecond" select="substring($second, 2)" />
   <xsl:choose>
      <xsl:when test="$nFirstFirst &lt;
$nFirstSecond">true</xsl:when>
      <xsl:when test="$nFirstFirst &gt;
$nFirstSecond">false</xsl:when>
      <xsl:when test="not($restFirst)">true</xsl:when>
      <xsl:when test="not($restSecond)">false</xsl:when>
      <xsl:otherwise>
         <xsl:call-template name="strcmp">
            <xsl:with-param name="first" select="$restFirst" />
            <xsl:with-param name="second" select="$restSecond" />
         </xsl:call-template>
      </xsl:otherwise>
   </xsl:choose>
</xsl:template>
```

The `$charorder` variable is particularly important because it forms the basis for comparison of the two strings. This solution lacks support for case-insensitive comparison and will not deal with hyphens and so on, but it is a start. We supplement with the following templates:

```
<xsl:template match="longman">
   <terms>
     <!-- apply templates to only the first term in compare mode -->
     <xsl:apply-templates select="term[1]" mode="compare" />
   </terms>
</xsl:template>
<xsl:template match="term" mode="compare">
   <!-- $comparison holds true if the input term is alphabetically
        before the current term -->
   <xsl:variable name="comparison">
      <xsl:call-template name="strcmp">
         <xsl:with-param name="first" select="$inputTerm" />
         <xsl:with-param name="second" select="." />
      </xsl:call-template>
   </xsl:variable>
   <xsl:choose>
      <xsl:when test="$comparison = 'false'">
         <!-- apply templates to the next term in the list in
              compare mode -->
         <xsl:apply-templates select="following-sibling::*[1]"
                              mode="compare" />
      </xsl:when>
      <xsl:otherwise>
         <!-- apply templates to this term, in the default mode, to
              get output -->
         <xsl:apply-templates select="." />
      </xsl:otherwise>
   </xsl:choose>
</xsl:template>
```

Determining the maximum number of cells in the rows and using it as the value for the "columns" attribute, you could use `xsl:key` (more about that in Chapter 6):

```
<xsl:key name="numCells" match="tr" use="count(td)"/>
 <xsl:template name="maxCols">
   <xsl:for-each select="//tr[not(key('numCells', count(td) + 1))]">
            <xsl:value-of select="count(td)"/>
   </xsl:for-each>
 </xsl:template>
```

This method only works if there are now rows that have one more one cell than the others. In these cases, the key will not return any nodes for some of the shorter rows, and therefore the number of cells in these rows will be given. For example:

```
<table>
  <tr><td>(1,1)</td></tr>
  <tr><td>(2,1)</td><td>(2,2)</td><td>(2,3)</td></tr>
  <tr><td>(3,1)</td><td>(3,2)</td></tr>

<tr><td>(4,1)</td><td>(4,2)</td><td>(4,3)</td><td>(4,4)</td><td>(4,5)</t
d></tr>
</table>
```

means that the maxCols template returns 35—a 3 from the length of the second row and a 5 from the length of the fourth. It would probably be better to use the following:

```
<xsl:template name="maxCols">
  <xsl:for-each select="//tr">
    <xsl:sort select="count(td)" order="descending" />
    <xsl:if test="position() = 1">
      <xsl:value-of select="." />
    </xsl:if>
  </xsl:for-each>
</xsl:template>
```

This template sorts all of the rows by the number of cells they have in them, in descending order, and then selects the first from that list (the one with the most cells) and tells you how many cells there are in it.

Alternatively, you can step through the rows recursively. This method is more efficient if you have a long table. There are many ways to step through recursively.

Here is a technique that applies templates to the first row in a maxCols mode. Within the template, if a row finds a following row that has more cells in it, it applies templates to that row in maxCols mode. If it cannot find one with more cells, then it knows it has reached the maximum and tells you how many cells it has.

```
<xsl:template name="maxCols">
  <xsl:apply-templates select="//tr[1]" mode="maxCols" />
</xsl:template>
<xsl:template match="tr" mode="maxCols">
  <xsl:variable
    name="next"
    select="following-sibling::tr[count(td) &gt;
                        count(current()/td)][1]" />
```

```
<xsl:choose>
  <xsl:when test="$next">
    <xsl:apply-templates select="$next" mode="maxCols" />
  </xsl:when>
  <xsl:otherwise><xsl:value-of select="count(td)"
/></xsl:otherwise>
  </xsl:choose>
</xsl:template>
```

In this version, again the templates are applied to only the first row in the table. Each row works out the maximum of the rest of the rows by applying templates to the next row in the table. If this maximum is more than the number of cells in it, then it tells you the maximum from the rest of the rows; if it has more cells itself, then it tells you how many cells it has.

```
<xsl:template name="maxCols">
  <xsl:apply-templates select="//tr[1]" mode="maxCols" />
</xsl:template>
<xsl:template match="tr" mode="maxCols">
  <xsl:variable name="max">
     <xsl:apply-templates select="following-sibling::tr[1]"
mode="maxCols" />
  </xsl:variable>
  <xsl:choose>
    <xsl:when test="$max &gt; count(td)">
       <xsl:value-of select="$max" />
    </xsl:when>
    <xsl:otherwise><xsl:value-of select="count(td)"
/></xsl:otherwise>
  </xsl:choose>
</xsl:template>
```

This version uses a parameter to store the rows that have to be looked at. This parameter is set to all the rows at the beginning. If there is only one row, it tells you how many cells there are in that row. If there are more, it works out the maximum number of cells in all the rows aside from the first one (by calling itself with a parameter with all the rows aside from the first) and then compares that number with the number of cells in the first row in the list. If the first row in the list has more cells, it tells you that number. If the maximum from the rest of the rows was more, it tells you that.

```
<xsl:template name="maxCols">
  <xsl:param name="rows" select="//tr" />
  <xsl:choose>
     <xsl:when test="count($rows) = 1">
        <xsl:value-of select="count(td)" />
```

```
            </xsl:when>
            <xsl:otherwise>
                <xsl:variable name="max">
                    <xsl:call-template name="maxCols">
                        <xsl:with-param name="rows"
    select="$rows[position() &gt; 1]" />
                    </xsl:call-template>
                </xsl:variable>
                <xsl:choose>
                    <xsl:when test="$max &gt; count($rows[1]/td)">
                        <xsl:value-of select="$max" />
                    </xsl:when>
                    <xsl:otherwise>
                        <xsl:value-of select="count($rows[1]/td)" />
                    </xsl:otherwise>
                </xsl:choose>
            </xsl:otherwise>
        </xsl:choose>
    </xsl:template>
```

Which of these is best depends quite a lot on the optimizations that are built into your XSLT processor.

Result Tree Fragments

Variables introduce an additional data-type into the Xpath expression language. This additional data type is called result tree fragment. A variable might be bound to a result tree fragment instead of one of the four basic Xpath data-types (string, number, Boolean, and node set). A result tree fragment represents a fragment of the result tree. A result tree fragment is treated equivalently to a node-set that contains just a single root node. The operations permitted on a result tree fragment, however, are a subset of those permitted on a node set. An operation is permitted on a result tree fragment only if that operation would be permitted on a string (the operation on the string might involve first converting the string to a number or Boolean). In particular, it is not permitted to use the /, //, and [] operators on result tree fragments. When a permitted operation is performed on a result tree fragment, it is performed exactly as it would be on the equivalent node set.

There are two possible meanings for the order in which nodes are added to the result tree.

One is the spatial order—in other words, which node becomes the first child, which the second, and so on. This ordering is determined in XSLT by the document order in the input and the templates used. Different processors only produce different results because the input nodes can be ordered differently (attributes and nodes from different document() calls are in system-dependent order) but once the input is determined, then the output for a given style sheet is specified.

There is also a chronological order in which nodes are added to the result tree. That is when the actual templates are fired. This situation might happen in any order, or all at the same time. For a pure XSL style sheet the result does not depend on this processing order as there are no side effects (that is the point about having no side effects), but if you use extensions, then they typically do (unfortunately), and so then you might get very different results on different systems.

There is one XSLT instruction that creates a side effect: xsl:message writing to the terminal lets you see the chronological order of template execution, and whether variables are evaluated at the point of definition or the point of use and several other things that might and do differ between systems. But note that this does not affect the result tree.

One of the features that the XSLT 1.0 spec provides to cater to the first-time-HTML-savvy user is the verbosely named "literal-result element as style sheet" capability. Style sheets that use this capability are often called "single-root-template" style sheets or style sheets written in the "simple form."

When a result tree fragment is copied into the result tree, then all the nodes that are children of the root node in the equivalent node set are added in sequence to the result tree.

Expressions can only return values of type result tree fragment by referencing variables of type result tree fragment or calling extension functions that return a result tree fragment or getting a system property whose value is a result tree fragment. Whenever an `xsl:variable` element is not empty, it will always return a value of type Result Tree Fragment. More to the point, `xsl:value-of` always copies the string-value of the designated Xpath expression, Boolean or otherwise.

Try hard-coding the true() value, first as a child of <xsl:variable> and then as the value of the select attribute.

This coding returns a Result Tree Fragment:

```
<xsl:variable name="units_gt_300">
  <xsl:value-of select="true()"/>
</xsl:variable>
```

This coding returns an Xpath Boolean:

```
<xsl:variable name="units_gt_300" select="true()"/>
```

Your if test will evaluate differently depending on the variable's type. In the first case, the comparison is between a result tree fragment and a string. The processor first converts the result tree fragment to a string and subsequently performs a string comparison. Thus, you are effectively comparing 'true' with 'true' or 'false' with 'true'. If you changed the if test to "$units_gt_300" or "$units_gt_300=true()" (same thing), it would not work correctly because 'true' and 'false' will always evaluate to true (being non-empty strings).

In the second case, the comparison is between a Boolean and a string. The string is first converted to a Boolean and then the comparison is made. If the string you include is not empty, then it will always convert to true, which effectively gives you the same result as "$units_gt_300" or "$units_gt_300='anything'."

For all practical purposes, a Result Tree Fragment containing just text will look and act the same as an Xpath string containing that text, except that an RTF with an empty string value will still convert to Boolean true, just like a node-set containing one root, which is what it will be in the future after XSLT 1.1 rids itself of the confusing RTF data type.

The `xsl:value-of` converts the Booleans to strings; and the use of `xsl:variable` with content creates a result tree fragment containing this string as a child node. So test="$units_gt_300" would always succeed, because it is testing whether the node-set equivalent to the result tree fragment contains any nodes: converting a result tree fragment to a Boolean always returns true.

More XSLT Programming: Import, Include, and Extensions to XSLT

T he xsl:stylesheet element, which is the top-level element in the XSLT document, can contain the following types of elements:

- xsl:import
- xsl:include
- xsl:strip-space
- xsl:preserve-space
- xsl:output
- xsl:key
- xsl:decimal-format
- xsl:namespace-alias
- xsl:attribute-set
- xsl:variable
- xsl:param
- xsl:template

These elements can, in turn, have the other elements in XSLT as children. In addition, the xsl:stylesheet element can contain any element not from the XSLT namespace if the expanded name of the element has a valid namespace URI. The presence of such top-level elements must not change the behavior of XSLT elements and functions. An XSLT processor is always free to ignore such top-level elements and must ignore a top-level element without giving an error if it does not recognize the namespace URI. Such elements can provide, for example,

- Information used by extension elements or extension functions
- Information about what to do with the result tree
- Information about how to obtain the source tree
- Metadata about the style sheet
- Structured documentation for the style sheet

xsl:include

When developing style sheets, you will probably find yourself writing the same code several times—for example, to display the same data in separate browsers. Each style sheet uses the same basic logic on a class of documents, for instance to traverse the document tree and transform each document instance into HTML. Because various browsers handle HTML differently, you can create several versions of a style sheet—each of which is tuned for a specific version of one of the major browsers (that is, Navigator and Internet Explorer for PCs, Ericsson and Nokia for WML, and so on). In addition, it is easy to create a generic style sheet that outputs a set of minimal HTML for any browser that it does not specifically recognize.

The formatting details typically vary only slightly. It would be useful to write the "static" code once and have a mechanism that enables you to use different pieces for each browser type. Then, each style sheet would simply include the code that handles browser variances. One obvious benefit is that you could make general changes to the user interface from one single file, rather than having to modify every style sheet.

The current XSLT standard has the `xsl:include` element for just such a purpose. That is, you can use the `xsl:include` element in a style sheet to perform a roughly textual inclusion of the referenced style sheet. Unfortunately, the XSL parser that comes with Internet Explorer 5 does not support the `xsl:include` element.

You can, however, not do conditional includes. The nearest you can get is to use modes. Alternatively, consider generating the style sheet dynamically before applying it. `xsl:include` is a compile-time facility, like #include in C.

It is not possible to parameterize `xsl:import` or `xsl:include` elements. Because they are top-level elements, *Attribute Value Templates* (AVTs) are not allowed. You cannot, say, pass the href attribute value in as a parameter, because the run-time assignment of that value is not allowed.

xsl:import

`xsl:import` is different from `xsl:include` in that the importing style sheet "extends" the imported style sheet. `xsl:import` can be used to import common, general-purpose rules into a style sheet that is designed to handle the specific transformation, but not the other way around. You can make summary-view and detailed-view the principal style sheet for the transformation and import the shared components into each of these.

Because `xsl:import` works by importing the other style sheets into the master, the order in which different parts are done in the different components can become an issue for xsl:import elements and for error recovery. Users are free to order the elements in style sheets as they prefer, and style sheet creation tools need not provide control over the order in which the elements occur.

If template A overrides template B, but you still want template B to be executed although it starts at the root, it never is—and only the matching template originally in template A is executed, overriding template B. Only import template B and not actually explicitly call any templates; it should just encounter matches (and does) as it progresses, and the tree can be done by using xsl:apply-imports within template A. To perform this task, you first have to import the style sheet that you want to apply to the current style sheet and then use xsl:apply-imports to actually have it execute:

```
--- in A.xsl ---
<xsl:import href="B.xsl" />
<xsl:template match="/">
  <!-- do something -->
  <xsl:apply-imports />
</xsl:template>
```

```
--- in B.xsl ---
<xsl:template match="/">
  <!-- do something more -->
</xsl:template>
```

The imported template in B.xsl should then be called.

Both `xsl:include` and `xsl:import` are compile-time facilities (they work when the processor takes the style sheet and starts working with it). Imagine, for instance, that you are trying to create a style sheet that uses a default style sheet for a portion of an HTML document but want to be able to replace that portion by a user simply specifying an alternate style sheet source in the source XML of the translation.

Instead of A conditionally importing style sheet B1, B2, or B3, each of which replaces part of A, the user should select style sheet B1, B2, or B3, each of which imports the fixed style sheet A and replaces or overrides parts of it. The special-case style sheet should import the general-case style sheet, not the other way around.

One model for applying style sheets is to allow the process to run recursively, driven primarily by the document. A series of templates is created such that there is a template to match each context, and then these templates are recursively applied starting at the root of the document:

```
<xsl:template>
<xsl:template match="section/title">
  <h2><xsl:apply-templates/></h2>
</xsl:template>
<xsl:apply-templates>
<xsl:apply-templates select="th|td"/>
```

There are two obstacles to overcome when using the recursive model: how to arbitrate between multiple patterns that match and how to process the same nodes in different contexts. When you import a style sheet into the current style sheet, it can happen that two template rules will match the same node in the source tree at the same time and contain conflicting instructions.

Here is the source document:

```
<doc>
<para>This is a <emphasis>test</emphasis>.
<emphasis>Nested <emphasis>emphasis</emphasis></emphasis>.</para>
</doc>
```

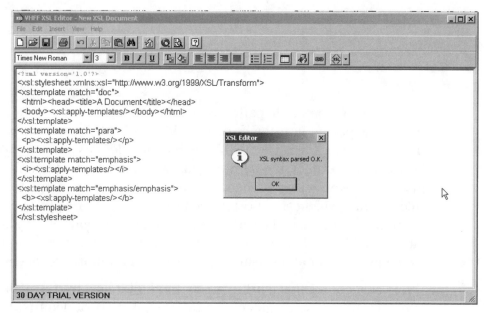

Figure 6.1 The transformation sheet after parsing.

The style sheet looks as such:

```
<xsl:stylesheet xmlns:xsl="http://www.w3.org/1999/XSL/Transform">
<xsl:template match="doc">
  <html><head><title>A Document</title></head>
  <body><xsl:apply-templates/></body></html>
</xsl:template>
<xsl:template match="para">
  <p><xsl:apply-templates/></p>
</xsl:template>
<xsl:template match="emphasis">
  <i><xsl:apply-templates/></i>
</xsl:template>
<xsl:template match="emphasis/emphasis">
  <b><xsl:apply-templates/></b>
</xsl:template>
</xsl:stylesheet>
```

In Figure 6.1, you can see what it looks like in an XSLT editor (after having parsed the document).

The result document will look like the following:

```
<html>
<head>
<title>A Document</title>
```

```
</head>
<body>
<p>This is a <i>test</i>.
<i>Nested <b>emphasis</b></i>.</p>
</body>
</html>
```

The problem of multiple patterns that match parts of the document and that are imported into the document is handled by the conflict-resolution function in XSLT. The XSLT specification defines a number of ways in which the conflict can be resolved. First, all matching template rules that have lower import precedence than the matching template rule (or rules) with the highest import precedence are eliminated from consideration. Import precedence is defined by looking at which style sheet element would be visited first, after all of the imports are done. The elements that would be visited first have lower import precedence.

If this concept sounds hard to grasp, think of it as a tree. The branches expand as imports are added, and the ones that are added first have the lowest precedence. For example, suppose that style sheet A imports style sheets B and C in that order; style sheet B imports style sheet D; and style sheet C imports style sheet E. The order of import precedence (lowest first) is D, B, E, C, and A, because D was imported first when the XSLT processor traverses the tree.

`xsl:import` elements must occur before any definitions or template rules, so that is why the ordering is done this way. A definition or template rule with higher import precedence takes precedence over a definition or template rule with lower import precedence. A style sheet cannot import itself, either directly or indirectly. Also, the case where a style sheet with a particular URI is imported in multiple places is not treated specially. The import tree will have a separate xsl:stylesheet for each place that it is imported. Confusingly, though, `xsl:apply-imports` can create different behavior than if the style sheet had been imported only at the place with the highest import precedence.

Next, only the template rule with the highest priority is considered (all others are eliminated from consideration). You can set the priority of a template rule by using the priority attribute. The value of this attribute must be a real number (positive or negative), with an optional leading minus sign (−) to determine whether it is negative.

Matching templates from imported modules are not considered if there is a matching template in the current module. Matching templates with a lower priority are not considered. The default priority is determined as follows: Unqualified child or attribute names have a priority of 0. Processing-instructions with a target have a priority of 0. A namespace-qualified "*" child or attribute name has a priority of -0.25. An unqualified "*" has a priority of -0.5. Any other template has a default priority of 0.5. Template priority can be specified explicitly with the priority attribute on xsl:template. In this case, "emphasis", "html:p", and "@foo" have a priority of 0. "html:*" has a priority of -0.25. "*" has a priority of -0.5. "para/emphasis" has a priority of 0.5. "emphasis/emphasis" has a priority of 0.5. "emphasis[@role]" has a priority of 0.5.

It is technically an error if the conflict-resolution process yields more than one template; however, XSLT processors can (silently) recover from this error by selecting the template that occurs last in the style sheet. Effectively, the style sheet template order is the final arbiter. If no priority attribute is set, the default priority is computed as follows:

If the pattern contains multiple alternatives separated by |, then it is treated equivalently to a set of template rules—one for each alternative.

If the pattern is a QName preceded by a ChildOrAttributeAxisSpecifier (see Chapter 4, "Xpath") or is a literal, which will create a processing instruction preceded by a ChildOrAttributeAxisSpecifier, then the priority is 0. If the pattern has the form NCName:* preceded by a ChildOrAttributeAxisSpecifier, then the priority is -0.25. Otherwise, if the pattern consists of just a NodeTest preceded by a ChildOrAttributeAxisSpecifier, then the priority is -0.5. Otherwise, the priority is 0.5.

A rule that tests for a node with a particular type and a particular expanded name will have priority 0. A pattern that tests for a node with a particular type and an expanded name with a particular namespace URI will have priority -0.25. Patterns that are less specific than this one (patterns that just tests for nodes with particular types) have priority -0.5. Patterns that are more specific than the most common kind of pattern have priority 0.5.

This scenario should leave only one matching template rule. If it does not, the XSLT processor can either stop and signal an error or select the template that occurs last in the style sheet and continue processing.

If you override a template rule in an imported style sheet, you can use xsl:apply-imports to invoke the rule that you had overridden. xsl:apply-imports processes the current node by using only template rules that were imported into the style sheet element containing the current template rule. The node is processed in the current template rule's mode (more about modes later). The current template rule is the one that was selected by matching a pattern. It is an error if xsl:apply-imports is instantiated when the current template rule is null, which it is for the instantiation of the content of the xsl:for-each element.

For example, suppose the style sheet doc.xsl contains a template rule for example elements:

```
<xsl:template match="example">
  <pre><xsl:apply-templates/></pre>
</xsl:template>
```

Another style sheet could import doc.xsl and modify the treatment of example elements as follows:

```
<xsl:import href="doc.xsl"/>
<xsl:template match="example">
  <div style="border: solid red">
     <xsl:apply-imports/>
  </div>
</xsl:template>
```

The combined effect would be to transform an example into an element of the form:

```
<div style="border: solid red"><pre>...</pre></div>
```

xsl:for-each

One way of using `xsl:for-each` is to iterate over a list. An Xpath expression must be present as the value of the select attribute of an `xsl:for-each` instruction and is used to find the set of nodes over which the iteration will be applied.

The other model for applying a style sheet is to select each action procedurally. A series of templates is created such that each template explicitly selects and processes the necessary elements.

Here is an example that iterates over the document:

```
<xsl:for-each>
<xsl:for-each select="row">
```

```
    <tr><xsl:apply-templates/></tr>
  </xsl:for-each>
```

You can do the same by using named templates; for instance, using `xsl:param`:

```
<xsl:param>
<xsl:param name="type">warning</xsl:param>
or xsl:call-template:
<xsl:call-template>
<xsl:call-template name="admonition"/>
or xsl: with-param:
<xsl:with-param>
<xsl:call-template name="admonition">
  <xsl:with-param name="type">caution</xsl:with-param>
</xsl:call-template>
```

The source document is:

```
<?xml version='1.0'?>
<table>
  <row><entry>a1</entry><entry>a2</entry></row>
  <row><entry>b1</entry><entry>b2</entry></row>
  <row><entry>c1</entry><entry>c2</entry></row>
</table>
```

And using the following style sheet:

```
<?xml version='1.0'?>
<xsl:stylesheet xmlns:xsl="http://www.w3.org/1999/XSL/Transform">
<xsl:output method="html"/>
<xsl:template match="table">
  <table>
    <xsl:for-each select="row">
      <tr>
        <xsl:for-each select="entry">
          <td><xsl:apply-templates/></td>
        </xsl:for-each>
      </tr>
    </xsl:for-each>
  </table>
</xsl:template>
</xsl:stylesheet>
```

you get the following HTML document:

```
<table>
<tr>
<td>a1</td><td>a2</td>
```

```
</tr>
<tr>
<td>b1</td><td>b2</td>
</tr>
<tr>
<td>c1</td><td>c2</td>
</tr>
</table>
```

If you want to rewrite this style sheet in recursive terms and you have the following document,

```
<chapter>
<warning>
<para>Using a damaged extension cord may cause a fire.</para>
</warning>
<caution>
<para>Freshly brewed coffee is hot.</para>
</caution>
</chapter>
```

then, a transformation sheet:

```
<xsl:stylesheet xmlns:xsl="http://www.w3.org/1999/XSL/Transform">
<xsl:output method="html"/>
<xsl:template name="admonition">
  <xsl:param name="type">Warning</xsl:param>
  <table border="1">
    <tr><th><xsl:value-of select="$type"/>:</th></tr>
    <tr><td><xsl:apply-templates/></td></tr>
  </table>
</xsl:template>
<xsl:template match="warning">
  <xsl:call-template name="admonition"/>
</xsl:template>
<xsl:template match="caution">
  <xsl:call-template name="admonition">
    <xsl:with-param name="type">Caution</xsl:with-param>
  </xsl:call-template>
</xsl:template>
<xsl:template match="para">
  <p><xsl:apply-templates/></p>
</xsl:template>
<xsl:template match="emphasis">
  <i><xsl:apply-templates/></i>
</xsl:template>
</xsl:stylesheet>
```

and finally, this code generates an HTML document:

```
<table border="1">
<tr>
<th>Warning:</th>
</tr>
<tr>
<td>
<p>Using a damaged extension cord may cause a fire.</p>
</td>
</tr>
</table>
<table border="1">
<tr>
<th>Caution:</th>
</tr>
<tr>
<td>
<p>Freshly brewed coffee is hot.</p>
</td>
</tr>
</table>
```

XSL Key

Keys provide a way to work with documents that contain an implicit cross-reference structure. The ID, IDREF, and IDREFS attribute types in XML provide a mechanism to enable XML documents to make their cross-reference explicit. XSLT supports this function through the Xpath ID function. This mechanism has a number of limitations, however. ID attributes must be declared as such in the DTD. If an ID attribute is declared as an ID attribute only in the external DTD subset, then it will be recognized as an ID attribute only if the XML processor reads the external DTD subset. XML does not require XML processors to read the external DTD, however, and they might well choose not to do so—especially if the document is declared standalone="yes".

A document can contain only a single set of unique IDs. There cannot be separate, independent sets of unique IDs. The ID of an element can only be specified in an attribute; it cannot be specified by the content of the element or by a child element. An ID is constrained to be an XML name. For example, it cannot contain spaces. An element can have at most one ID. At most, one element can have a particular ID.

Because of these limitations, XML documents sometimes contain a cross-reference structure that is not explicitly declared by ID/IDREF/IDREFS attributes: xsl:key. A key is a triple containing the node that has the key, the name of the key (an expanded-name), and the value of the key (a string). A style sheet declares a set of keys for each document by using the `xsl:key` element. When this set of keys contains a member with node x, name y, and value z, we say that node x has a key with name y and value z.

In other words, a key is a kind of generalized ID that is not subject to the same limitations as an XML ID. Keys are declared in the style sheet by using `xsl:key` elements. A key can have a name as well as a value, and there can be a use and match attribute on the key element. The value of the name attribute is a QName, which is expanded. The match attribute is an Xpath pattern; an `xsl:key` element gives information about the keys of any node that matches the pattern that is specified in the match attribute. The use attribute is an expression specifying the values of the key, and the expression is evaluated once for each node that matches the pattern. Each key name can be thought of as distinguishing a separate, independent space of identifiers. An Xpath expression is used to specify where to find the value for a particular named key. The value of a key can be an arbitrary string; it is not constrained to be a name. There can be multiple keys in a document with the same node and the same key name but with different key values. There can be multiple keys in a document that have the same key name and same key value but different nodes.

Also note that there might be more than one `xsl:key` element that matches a given node. All of the matching `xsl:key` elements are used even if they do not have the same import precedence. Also, note that neither the use attribute nor the match attribute can contain a VariableReference.

When the second argument to the key function is of type node set, then the result is the union of the result of applying the key function to the string value of each of the nodes in the argument node set. When the second argument to key is of any other type, the argument is converted to a string as if by a call to the string function. It returns a node set containing the nodes in the same document as the context node that have a value for the named key that is equal to this string. In order to speed up processing, a good XSLT processor will create an index for each key declaration. The index is analogous to an index that is created for a column in a relational database (also used to speed up searching).

Keys can be used for sorting and structuring information, as in the following example. Using a key, you group all identical entries and take only the first of them. Define a key for every @entry of the index:

```
<xsl:key name="paul" match="index" use="@entry" />
```

Then, walk through your index elements and choose only the first of each group (in other words, each key):

```
<xsl:for-each select="index[generate-id()=generate-
id(key('paul',@entry)[1])]">
```

Now you have unique entries that need to be sorted, which you do with the following function:

```
<xsl:sort select="@entry" />
```

Then, you need to output the list:

```
<xsl:value-of select="@entry" />
```

The complete template is as follows:

```
<xsl:template match="paul">
    <xsl:for-each
        select="index[generate-id()=generate-
id(key('paul',@entry)[1])]">
        <xsl:sort select="@entry" />
        <xsl:value-of select="@entry" />
        <xsl:text>&#xA;</xsl:text>
    </xsl:for-each>
</xsl:template>
```

If you have a declaration

```
<xsl:key name="idkey" match="div" use="@id"/>
```

an expression key (idkey and @ref) will return the same node set as id(@ref), assuming that the only ID attribute declared in the XML sou document is:

```
<!ATTLIST div id ID #IMPLIED>
```

and that the ref attribute of the current node contains no white space. Suppose that a document describing a function library uses a prototype element to define functions:

```
<prototype name="key" return-type="node-set">
<arg type="string"/>
<arg type="object"/>
</prototype>
```

and a function element to refer to function names:

```
<function>key</function>
```

Then, the style sheet could generate hyperlinks between the references and definitions as follows:

```
<xsl:key name="func" match="prototype" use="@name"/>
<xsl:template match="function">
<b>
  <a href="#{generate-id(key('func',.))}">
    <xsl:apply-templates/>
  </a>
</b>
</xsl:template>
<xsl:template match="prototype">
<p><a name="{generate-id()}">
<b>Function: </b>
</a></p>
</xsl:template>
```

The key can be used to retrieve a key from a document other than the document containing the context node. For example, suppose a document contains bibliographic references in the form <bibref>XSLT </bibref>, and there is a separate XML document bib.xml that contains a bibliographic database with entries in the form:

```
<entry name="XSLT">...</entry>
```

Then, the style sheet could use the following to transform the bibref elements:

```
<xsl:key name="bib" match="entry" use="@name"/>
<xsl:template match="bibref">
  <xsl:variable name="name" select="."/>
  <xsl:for-each select="document('bib.xml')">
    <xsl:apply-templates select="key('bib',$name)"/>
  </xsl:for-each>
</xsl:template>
```

You can also use the XSLT processor to create an index where the values are taken from the keys. The result of a lookup on this index is to return the associated node in the document.

Remember that within the xsl:for-each, the current node is the document root node; therefore, if you use an expression in the key value, then it will be resolved relative to that document's root node. Usually, you will want to use a variable. Remember also that it is an `xsl:for-each`, but actually you are just using it to change the current node. (Do not have a select expression that contains more than one node or it will repeat output left, right, and center.)

There are occasions where this limitation on `key()` causes real problems, particularly when you are using `key()` within a sort select expression.

It is also possible to use `xsl:key` to sort elements. If your input XML looks like:

```
<sales>
  <projects>
    <id>1</id><name>Customer 1</name><project_name>Project
1</project_name>
  </projects>
  <projects>
    <id>2</id><name>Customer 1</name><project_name>Project
2</project_name>
  </projects>
  <projects>
    <id>3</id><name>Customer 2</name><project_name>Project
1</project_name>
  </projects>
</sales>
```

and you are trying to group the rows according to the customer name, you can define a key to group the rows according to customer name. You define a key by using the xsl:key element, which has to go at the top level in the style sheet (right under `xsl:stylesheet`). The use attribute will be the key that you want to use to group the nodes that are expressed as an Xpath from the item you are matching to the key that you want to use to access those nodes (here, the value of the name element child of the projects). So, the `xsl:key` element should look something like:

```
<xsl:key name="rows" match="projects" use="name" />
```

The key indexes each of the rows according to the customer. You can use the `key()` function to get the list of rows relating to a customer, so `key('rows', 'Customer 1')` gives you a list of the projects elements with IDs 1 and 2, whereas `key('rows', 'Customer 2')` gives you the projects element with ID 3. This function makes it easy to get to your rows once you know the name of the customer.

Next, you have to arrange it so that you can get a list of the customers in which each customer only appears once. You have grouped the rows within the key, and you know that each group relates to one particular customer—so it is a matter of identifying one row from each group. The way you perform this task is through an Xpath expression that identifies all of the rows that appear first in their group:

```
projects[generate-id(.) = generate-id(key('rows', name)[1])]
```

This says:

Find a `projects` element such that

  A unique ID generated for that element is the same as

  A unique ID generated for

    The first node in the node list returned by

    Indexing the 'rows' key on the value of

      The 'name' child element of that element

If you apply templates only to those projects elements, then you know that you are applying templates to one `projects` element per customer:

```
<xsl:template match="sales">
  <xsl:apply-templates
    select="projects[generate-id(.) = generate-id(key('rows',
name)[1])]" />
</xsl:template>
```

Your projects-matching template should now output information about all of the rows relating to the customer named in that `projects` element. You can access them through the `key()` function as described earlier and cycle through them by using `xsl:for-each` (or through calling `xsl:apply-templates`, if you want).

```
<xsl:template match="projects">
  <b><xsl:value-of select="name" /></b>
```

```
<ul>
  <xsl:for-each select="key('rows', name)">
    <li>
      <a href="projects_results.xml?project={id}">
        <xsl:value-of select="project_name" />
      </a>
    </li>
  </xsl:for-each>
</ul>
</xsl:template>
```

Whenever a list of similar items is produced, it is helpful to the reader if the items in the list are sorted. A sorted list enables the reader to quickly locate an item of interest.

Calling Templates

There is no mechanism in XSLT for calling a template whose name is not known and fixed at the time you write the style sheet, other than generating a style sheet dynamically and executing that.

But there is a function in XSLT to call a template that has been given a name. `xsl:call-template`, unlike `xsl:apply-templates`, does not change the context node. Also, a select attribute is only meaningful on apply-templates, not on call-templates. An `xsl:template` element that has a name attribute specifies a named template. The value of the name attribute must be a QName, not an Xpath expression. If an `xsl:template` element has a name attribute, it might (but does not need to) also have a match attribute. An `xsl:call-template` element invokes a template by name; it has a required name attribute that identifies the template to be invoked. Unlike `xsl:apply-templates`, however, `xsl:call-template` does not change the current node or the current node list.

The match, mode, and priority attributes on an `xsl:template` element do not affect whether the template is invoked by an `xsl:call-template` element. Similarly, the name attribute on an `xsl:template` element does not affect whether the template is invoked by an `xsl:apply-templates` element. It is, however, an error if a style sheet contains more than one template with the same name and same import precedence (see the section about `xsl:import`).

Passing Parameters to Templates

When invoking a template for processing, it is often a requirement to pass some piece of information to the template, similar to a parameter in a method invocation for an object-oriented language. XSLT does provide a mechanism for this function: the `xsl:with-param` element. It can be used to give a named template variable values as attributes. The following is an example:

```
<xsl:call-template name="classify">
    <xsl:with-param name="target" select="$target" />
</xsl:call-template>
```

This calls the template "classify." The parameter that is passed to the classify template is the variable "target." The `xsl:with-param` instruction is used to pass the variable by name with the value determined by the 'select' attribute.

The called template must also declare the parameter in order to provide a way to reference the parameter within the template. This task is performed with the `xsl:param` instruction, which must immediately follow the xsl:template instruction:

```
<!-- Classification -->
<xsl:template name="classify">
    <xsl:param name="target"/>
```

The parameter can be used within the template in the same way that XSLT variables are used.

If you are used to procedural programming languages, you will realize that these functions feel familiar. You are probably used to testing whether the current object is the first in a list in order to decide whether to put a start tag and testing whether it is the last in the list to decide where to put an end tag.

That is not how XSLT works. It is a declarative programming language, and you are building a node tree rather than outputting start and end tags. You can build functions, however, which work in much the same way. The following style sheet creates a loop that creates rows in a formatted data table:

```
<xsl:for-each
    select="departure/duration/fee
               [count(. |
                       key('DepartureByMonthAndFee',
                           concat(substring(
                                     normalize-space(../../text()), 1, 6),
                                   '::', normalize-space()))[1]) = 1]">
  <!-- for each fee with a unique departure month and fee -->
  <xsl:sort select="../../text()" data-type="number" />
  <xsl:sort select="." data-type="number" />
  <tr>
    <td><xsl:apply-templates select="../.." mode="month" /></td>
    <td><xsl:apply-templates select="../.." mode="day" /></td>
    <td><xsl:apply-templates select="." /></td>
  </tr>
</xsl:for-each>
```

The select expression identifies unique, month-fee combinations. The days are output by using the following template:

```
<xsl:template match="departure" mode="day">
   <xsl:variable name="days"
                 select="key('DepartureByMonthAndFee',
                             concat(
                               substring(normalize-space(text()), 1, 6),
                               '::', normalize-space(duration/fee)))" />
   <xsl:choose>
      <xsl:when test="$days[2]">
         <xsl:for-each select="$days">
            <xsl:sort select="substring(normalize-space(../../text()),
7, 2)"
                      data-type="number" />
            <xsl:choose>
               <xsl:when test="position() = 1">
                  <xsl:apply-templates select="../.." mode="format-day" />
               </xsl:when>
               <xsl:when test="position() = last()">
                  <xsl:text>-</xsl:text>
                  <xsl:apply-templates select="../.." mode="format-day" />
               </xsl:when>
            </xsl:choose>
         </xsl:for-each>
      </xsl:when>
      <xsl:otherwise>
         <xsl:apply-templates select="." mode="format-day" />
      </xsl:otherwise>
   </xsl:choose>
</xsl:template>
```

If you are in charge of the DTD, you might consider changing it to make it easier for XSLT to handle. XSLT does not handle getting data out of mixed content very well. If you separate the data into subelements, you can just use the value of those nodes rather than go to their `text()` children. Also, with one of these formats, white space is not as much of a problem, so you do not have to `normalize-space()` everywhere.

Repeating XSLT Transformation Templates Conditionally: Mode

In these examples, we have been using the `mode` attribute on the `xsl:template` and `xsl:apply-templates`. Modes enable an element to be processed multiple times—each time producing a different result. The `mode` attribute is optional on those elements (which are the only ones that can have it). The `mode` attribute is required to be a QName. If `xsl:template` does not have a `match` attribute, it must not have a `mode` attribute. If an `xsl:apply-templates` element has a `mode` attribute, then it applies only to those template rules from `xsl:template` elements that have a `mode` attribute with the same value. If an `xsl:apply-templates` element does not have a mode attribute, then it applies only to those template rules from `xsl:template` elements that do not have a `mode` attribute.

Modes have to be declared in the style sheet and cannot be set dynamically. The only real workaround is an `xsl:choose` instruction that lists the possible options.

The same elements can be processed in multiple contexts when, for example, dealing with cross references, automatic tables of contents, and multiple views of the same data.

Consider the following example:

```
<?xml version='1.0'?>
<chapter id="foo"><title>Chapter Title</title>
<para>This chapter is self-referential:
<xref linkend="foo"/>.</para>
</chapter>
```

And a style sheet that produces the following:

```
<h2>Chapter Title</h2>
<p>This chapter is self-referential:
<i>Chapter Title</i>.</p>
```

The chapter title must be processed twice—once to produce the title and once to produce the cross-reference. There is no dynamic mechanism for adjusting template priority, but we can use modes to select specific sets of templates.

```xml
<?xml version='1.0'?>
<xsl:stylesheet xmlns:xsl="http://www.w3.org/1999/XSL/Transform"
                version="1.0">
<xsl:output method="html"/>
<xsl:template match="chapter/title">
  <h2><xsl:apply-templates/></h2>
</xsl:template>
<xsl:template match="chapter/title" mode="crossref">
  <i><xsl:apply-templates/></i>
</xsl:template>
<xsl:template match="xref">
  <xsl:variable name="linkend" select="@linkend"/>
  <xsl:apply-templates select="//*[@id=$linkend]/title"
                       mode="crossref"/>
</xsl:template>
<xsl:template match="para">
  <p><xsl:apply-templates/></p>
</xsl:template>
<xsl:template match="emphasis">
  <i><xsl:apply-templates/></i>
</xsl:template>
</xsl:stylesheet>
```

It will result in the following:

```
<h2>Chapter Title</h2>
<p>This chapter is self-referential:
<i>Chapter Title</i>.</p>
```

xsl:for-each

If the result tree has a known regular structure and the source tree follows a known and regular structure, you can think in terms of components and apply templates directly to selected nodes. To perform this task, you use `xsl:for-each`. The `xsl:for-each` instruction contains a template that is instantiated for each node selected by the expression specified by the select attribute. The select attribute is required. The expression must evaluate to a node set. The template is instantiated with the selected node as the current node and with a list of all of the selected nodes as the current node list. The nodes are processed in document order unless a sorting specification is present.

For example, given an XML document with this structure,

```
<customers>
  <customer>
    <name>...</name>
    <order>...</order>
    <order>...</order>
  </customer>
  <customer>
    <name>...</name>
    <order>...</order>
    <order>...</order>
  </customer>
</customers>
```

the following would create an HTML document containing a table with a row for each customer element:

```
<xsl:template match="/">
  <html>
    <head>
      <title>Customers</title>
    </head>
    <body>
      <table>
      <tbody>
        <xsl:for-each select="customers/customer">
          <tr>
            <th>
            <xsl:apply-templates select="name"/>
            </th>
            <xsl:for-each select="order">
            <td>
              <xsl:apply-templates/>
            </td>
            </xsl:for-each>
          </tr>
        </xsl:for-each>
      </tbody>
      </table>
    </body>
  </html>
</xsl:template>
```

Selecting Data in Other Documents: Using the document( ) Function

XSLT adds a few functions to Xpath. One of them is document(), which can be used to identify nodes in different documents and include them in the source tree. One important reason to perform this action is when the nodes are the same in the two different documents. There are two main ways of saying that two nodes in different documents are the same node:

1. They are in the same position (relative to other nodes).

2. They have the same identifier.

How you go about merging and reporting on differences between the two XML documents really depends on which of these can be used.

If it is the first (same position), then you have to keep track of the context node in the two documents. One of the context nodes will be tracked by using the XSLT processor, but the other will have to be passed from template to template. You have to make sure it is not lost through the use of built-in templates. With document1.xml and document2.xml as the two documents and document1.xml being the input, something like the following will fulfill the requirement:

```
<xsl:template match="/">
  <xsl:variable name="doc2node" select="document('document2.xml')" />
  <xsl:for-each select="*">
    <xsl:variable name="index" select="position()" />
    <xsl:apply-templates select=".">
      <xsl:with-param name="doc2node" select="$doc2node/*[position() =
$index]" />
    </xsl:apply-templates>
  </xsl:for-each>
</xsl:template>
<xsl:template match="*">
  <xsl:param name="doc2node" />
  <!-- do your element comparison here -->
  <xsl:for-each select="@*">
    <xsl:variable name="name" select="name()" />
    <xsl:apply-templates select=".">
      <xsl:with-param name="doc2node" select="$doc2node/@*[name() =
$name]" />
    </xsl:apply-templates>
  </xsl:for-each>
  <xsl:for-each select="*">
    <xsl:variable name="index" select="position()" />
    <xsl:apply-templates select=".">
      <xsl:with-param name="doc2node" select="$doc2node/*[position() =
$index]" />
    </xsl:apply-templates>
  </xsl:for-each>
</xsl:template>
```

```
<xsl:template match="@*">
  <xsl:param name="doc2node" />
  <!-- do your attribute comparison here -->
</xsl:template>
```

If, on the other hand, you have a structure in which elements can be individually identified somehow (for example, by using ID), then you do not have to keep track of where you are in the second document all of the time. You can just index into it in order to get the node to compare. So, say that you had two documents, each of which had a load of elements with @id attributes on them. You could have something like the following:

```
<xsl:key name="ided-nodes" match="*[@id]" use="@id" />
<xsl:template match="*[@id]">
  <xsl:variable name="doc1node" select="." />
  <xsl:for-each select="document('document2.xml')">
    <xsl:variable name="doc2node" select="key('ided-nodes',
$doc1node/@id)" />
    <!-- do your comparison between $doc1node and $doc2node here -->
  </xsl:for-each>
</xsl:template>
```

Both of these approaches take document1.xml as the primary document, which is specified as the input and is used as the basis of the comparison. You would have to do something a bit more complicated if you wanted to do the comparison the other way as well (for example, identify the elements that exist in document2 but not in document1).

XSLT Extensions

XSLT is XML, and one of the main functions of XML is the capability to extend the functions in the current namespace by using other namespaces. In XSLT, the element extension mechanism has this function. When a namespace is designated as an extension namespace and an element with a name from that namespace occurs in a template, the element is treated as an instruction rather than as a literal result element. The namespace determines the semantics of the instruction.

Because an element that is a child of an xsl:stylesheet element is not occurring in a template, non-XSLT, top-level elements are not extension elements as defined here, and nothing in this section applies to them.

A namespace is designated as an extension namespace by using an extension-element-prefixes attribute on an `xsl:stylesheet` element or an `xsl:extension-element-prefixes` attribute on a literal result element or extension element. The value of both of these attributes is a white space-separated list of namespace prefixes. The namespace that is bound to each of the prefixes is designated as an extension namespace. It is an error if there is no namespace bound to the prefix on the element bearing the extension-element-prefixes or `xsl:extension-element-prefixes` attribute.

The default namespace (as declared by xmlns) can be an extension namespace by including #default in the list of namespace prefixes. The designation of a namespace as an extension namespace is effective within the subtree of the style sheet rooted at the element bearing the extension-element-prefixes or `xsl:extension-element-prefixes` attribute; a subtree rooted at an `xsl:stylesheet` element does not include any style sheets imported or included by children of that `xsl:stylesheet` element.

If the XSLT processor does not have an implementation of a particular extension element available, then the element-available function must return false for the name of the element. When such an extension element is instantiated, then the XSLT processor must perform fallback. An XSLT processor must not signal an error merely because a template contains an extension element for which no implementation is available. If the XSLT processor has an implementation of a particular extension element available, then the element-available function must return true for the name of the element.

If the XSLT processor has an implementation of an extension function of a particular name available, then the function-available function must return true for that name. If such an extension is called, then the XSLT processor must call the implementation—passing it the function call arguments. The result returned by the implementation is returned as the result of the function call.

Which extension namespaces are supported depends on the processor. The most frequent seems to be the ECMAscript namespace (formerly Javascript). We will not cover the specifics about it in this book, however, because there are many good ECMAscript books.

XSL Fallback

Normally, instantiating an `xsl:fallback` element does nothing. When an XSLT processor performs fallback for an instruction element, however, if the instruction element has one or more `xsl:fallback` children, then the content of each of the `xsl:fallback` children must be instantiated in sequence; otherwise, an error must be signaled. The content of an `xsl:fallback` element is a template.

The following functions can be used with the `xsl:choose` and `xsl:if` instructions to explicitly control how a style sheet should behave if particular elements or functions are not available.

`Function: element-available(string)`

The argument must evaluate to a string that is a QName. The QName is expanded into an expanded name by using the namespace declarations in scope for the expression. The element-available function returns true if and only if the expanded name is the name of an instruction. If the expanded name has a namespace URI equal to the XSLT namespace URI, then it refers to an element defined by XSLT. Otherwise, it refers to an extension element. If the expanded name has a null namespace URI, the element-available function will return false.

`Function: boolean function-available(string)`

The argument must evaluate to a string that is a QName. The QName is expanded into an expanded name by using the namespace declarations in scope for the expression. The function-available function returns true if and only if the expanded name is the name of a function in the function library. If the expanded name has a non-null namespace URI, then it refers to an extension function; otherwise, it refers to a function defined by Xpath or XSLT.

XSL Output

An XSLT processor can output the result tree as a sequence of bytes, although it is not required to have this capability. The `xsl:output` element enables style sheet authors to specify how they wish the result tree to be outputted. If an XSLT processor outputs the result tree, it should do so as specified by the `xsl:output` element; however, it is not required to do so.

The `xsl:output` element is only allowed as a top-level element. The method attribute on `xsl:output` identifies the overall method that should be used for outputting the result tree. The value must be a QName. If the QName does not have a prefix, then it identifies a method specified in this document and must be one of XML, HTML, or text. If the QName has a prefix, then the QName is expanded; the expanded name identifies the output method, and the behavior in this case is not specified by this document.

The default for the method attribute is chosen as follows:

- The root node of the result tree has an element child.
- The expanded name of the first element child of the root node (in other words, the document element) of the result tree has local part html (in any combination of upper and lower case) and a null namespace URI.
- Any text nodes preceding the first element child of the root node of the result tree contain only white space characters.

If all of the preceding applies, then the default output method is html; otherwise, the default output method is XML. The default output method should be used if there are no `xsl:output` elements or if none of the `xsl:output` elements specifies a value for the method attribute.

The other attributes of `xsl:output` provide parameters for the output method. The following attributes are allowed:

`version` Specifies the version of the output method.

`indent` Specifies whether the XSLT processor can add additional white space when outputting the result tree; the value must be yes orno.

`encoding` Specifies the preferred character encoding that the XSLT processor should use to encode sequences of characters as sequences of bytes. The value of the attribute should be treated case-insensitively; the value must contain only characters in the range #x21 to #x7E (in other words, printable ASCII characters). The value should either be a character set registered with the *Internet Assigned Numbers Authority* (IANA) or start with X-.

media-type   Specifies the media type (MIME content type) of the data that results from outputting the result tree; the charset parameter should not be specified explicitly; instead, when the top-level media type is text, a charset parameter should be added according to the character encoding actually used by the output method.

doctype-system   Specifies the system identifier to be used in the DTD.

doctype-public   Specifies the public identifier to be used in the DTD.

omit-xml-declaration   Specifies whether the XSLT processor should output an XML declaration; the value must be yes or no.

standalone   Specifies whether the XSLT processor should output a standalone document declaration; the value must be yes or no.

cdata-section-elements   Specifies a list of the names of elements whose text-node children should be output by using CDATA sections.

The detailed semantics of each attribute will be described separately for each output method for which it is applicable. If the semantics of an attribute are not described for an output method, then it is not applicable to that output method.

A style sheet can contain multiple xsl:output elements and can include or import style sheets that also contain xsl:output elements. All of the xsl:output elements occurring in a style sheet are merged into a single effective xsl:output element. For the cdata-section-elements attribute, the effective value is the union of the specified values. For other attributes, the effective value is the specified value with the highest import precedence. It is an error if there is more than one such value for an attribute. An XSLT processor can signal the error. If it does not signal the error, however, it should recover by using the value that occurs last in the style sheet. The values of attributes are defaulted after the xsl:output elements have been merged. Different output methods might have different default values for an attribute.

The XML output method outputs the result tree as a well-formed XML external general parsed entity. If the root node of the result tree has a single element node child and no text-node children, then the entity should also be a well-formed XML document entity. When the entity is referenced within a trivial XML document wrapper like this one,

```
<!DOCTYPE doc [
<!ENTITY e SYSTEM "entity-URI">
]>
<doc>&e;</doc>
```

where entity-URI is a URI for the entity, then the wrapper document as a whole should be a well-formed XML document conforming to the XML namespaces recommendation. In addition, the output should be such that if a new tree were constructed by parsing the wrapper as an XML document and then removing the document element, making its children instead be children of the root node, then the new tree would be the same as the result tree with the following possible exceptions:

- The order of attributes in the two trees might be different.

- The new tree might contain namespace nodes that were not present in the result tree.

An XSLT processor might need to add namespace declarations in the course of outputting the result tree as XML.

If the XSLT processor generated a DTD because of the doctype-system attribute, then these requirements apply to the entity with the generated DTD removed.

The version attribute specifies the version of XML to be used for outputting the result tree. If the XSLT processor does not support this version of XML, it should use a version of XML that it does support. The version output in the XML declaration (if an XML declaration is output) should correspond to the version of XML that the processor used for outputting the result tree. The value of the version attribute should match the VersionNum production of the XML recommendation. The default value is 1.0.

The encoding attribute specifies the preferred encoding to use for outputting the result tree. XSLT processors are required to respect values of UTF-8 and UTF-16. For other values, if the XSLT processor does not support the specified encoding, it might signal an error. If it does *not* signal an error, it should use UTF-8 or UTF-16 instead. The XSLT processor must not use an encoding whose name does not match the EncName production of the XML recommendation.

If no encoding attribute is specified, then the XSLT processor should use either UTF-8 or UTF-16. It is possible that the result tree will contain a character that cannot be represented in the encoding that the XSLT processor is using for output. In this case, if the character occurs in a context where XML recognizes character references (for example, in the value of an attribute node or text node), then the character should be outputted as a character reference. Otherwise (for example, if the character occurs in the name of an element), the XSLT processor should signal an error.

If the indent attribute has the value yes, then the XML output method might output white space in addition to the white space in the result tree (possibly based on white space that is stripped from either the source document or the style sheet) in order to indent the result nicely. If the indent attribute has the value no, it should not output any additional white space. The default value is no. The XML output method should use an algorithm to output additional white space that ensures that the result if white space were to be stripped from the output by using the white space stripping process, with the set of preserving-preserving elements consisting of just xsl:text, would be the same when additional preserving is output as when additional preserving is not output. It is usually not safe to use indent="yes" with document types that include element types with mixed content.

The cdata-section-elements attribute contains a whitespace-separated list of QNames. Each QName is expanded into an expanded name by using the namespace declarations in effect on the xsl:output element in which the QName occurs. If there is a default namespace, it is used for QNames that do not have a prefix. The expansion is performed before the merging of multiple xsl:output elements into a single effective xsl:output element. If the expanded name of the parent of a text node is a member of the list, then the text node should be output as a CDATA section. For example,

```
<xsl:output cdata-section-elements="example"/>
```

would cause a literal result element written in the style sheet as

```
<example>&lt;foo></example>
```

or as

```
<example><![CDATA[<foo>]]></example>
```

to be output as

```
<example><![CDATA[<foo>]]></example>
```

If the text node contains the sequence of characters]]>, then the currently open CDATA section should be closed following the]] and a new CDATA section opened before the >. For example, a literal result element written in the style sheet as

```
<example>]]&gt;</example>
```

would be output as

```
<example><![CDATA[]]]]><![CDATA[>]]></example>
```

If the text node contains a character that is not representable in the character encoding that is being used to output the result tree, then the currently open CDATA section should be closed before the character. The character should be output by using a character reference or entity reference, and a new CDATA section should be opened for any further characters in the text node.

CDATA sections should not be used except for text nodes that the cdata-section-elements attribute explicitly specifies should be output by using CDATA sections.

The XML output method should output an XML declaration unless the omit-xml-declaration attribute has the value yes. The XML declaration should include both version information and an encoding declaration. If the standalone attribute is specified, it should include a standalone document declaration with the same value as the value of the standalone attribute. Otherwise, it should not include a standalone document declaration. This action ensures that it is both an XML declaration (allowed at the beginning of a document entity) and a text declaration (allowed at the beginning of an external general parsed entity).

If the doctype-system attribute is specified, the XML output method should output a DTD immediately before the first element. The name following <!DOCTYPE should be the name of the first element. If the doctype-public attribute is also specified, then the XML output method should output PUBLIC followed by the public identifier and then the

system identifier; otherwise, it should output SYSTEM followed by the system identifier. The internal subset should be empty. The doctype-public attribute should be ignored unless the doctype-system attribute is specified.

The media-type attribute is applicable for the XML output method. The default value for the media-type attribute is text/xml.

The html output method outputs the result tree as HTML. For example,

```
<xsl:stylesheet version="1.0"
        xmlns:xsl="http://www.w3.org/1999/XSL/Transform">
<xsl:output method="html"/>
<xsl:template match="/">
  <html>
   <xsl:apply-templates/>
  </html>
</xsl:template>
...
</xsl:stylesheet>
```

The version attribute indicates the version of the HTML. The default value is 4.0, which specifies that the result should be output as HTML conforming to the HTML 4.0 recommendation.

The html output method should not output an element differently from the XML output method unless the expanded name of the element has a null namespace URI. An element whose expanded name has a non-null namespace URI should be output as XML. If the expanded name of the element has a null namespace URI but the local part of the expanded name is not recognized as the name of an HTML element, the element should output in the same way as a non-empty, inline element (such as span).

The html output method should not output an end tag for empty elements. For HTML 4.0, the empty elements are area, base, basefont, br, col, frame, hr, img, input, isindex, link, meta, and param. For example, an element written as <br/> or
</br> in the style sheet should be output as <br>.

The html output method should recognize the names of HTML elements regardless of case. For example, elements named br, BR, or Br should all be recognized as the HTML br element and output without an end tag.

The html output method should not perform escaping for the content of the script and style elements. For example, a literal result element written in the style sheet as

```
<script>if (a &lt; b) foo()</script>
```

or

```
<script><![CDATA[if (a < b) foo()]]></script>
```

should be output as

```
<script>if (a < b) foo()</script>
```

The html output method should not escape < characters occurring in attribute values.

If the indent attribute has the value yes, then the html output method can add or remove white space as it outputs the result tree as long as it does not change how an HTML user agent would render the output. The default value is yes.

The html output method should escape non-ASCII characters in URI attribute values by using the method recommended in Section B.2.1 of the HTML 4.0 recommendation.

The html output method might output a character by using a character entity reference if one is defined for it in the version of HTML that the output method is using.

The html output method should terminate processing instructions with > rather than ?>.

The html output method should output Boolean attributes (that is, attributes with only a single allowed value that is equal to the name of the attribute) in minimized form. For example, a start tag written in the style sheet as

```
<OPTION selected="selected">
```

should be output as

```
<OPTION selected>
```

The html output method should not escape an ampersand (&) character occurring in an attribute value immediately followed by a { character (see Section B.7.1 of the HTML 4.0 recommendation). For example, a start tag written in the style sheet as

```
<BODY bgcolor='&amp;{{randomrbg}};'>
```

should be output as

```
<BODY bgcolor='&{randomrbg};'>
```

The encoding attribute specifies the preferred encoding to be used. If there is a HEAD element, then the html output method should add a META element immediately after the start tag of the HEAD element specifying the character encoding actually used. For example,

```
<HEAD>
<META http-equiv="Content-Type" content="text/html; charset=EUC-JP">
```

It is possible that the result tree will contain a character that cannot be represented in the encoding that the XSLT processor is using for output. In this case, if the character occurs in a context where HTML recognizes character references, then the character should be output as a character entity reference or a decimal numeric character reference. Otherwise (for example, in a script or style element or in a comment), the XSLT processor should signal an error.

If the doctype-public or doctype-system attributes are specified, then the html output method should output a DTD immediately before the first element. The name following <!DOCTYPE should be HTML or html. If the doctype-public attribute is specified, then the output method should output PUBLIC followed by the specified public identifier. If the doctype-system attribute is also specified, it should also output the specified system identifier following the public identifier. If the doctype-system attribute is specified but the doctype-public attribute is not specified, then the output method should output SYSTEM followed by the specified system identifier.

The media-type attribute is applicable for the html output method. The default value is text/html.

The text output method outputs the result tree by outputting the string value of every text node in the result tree in document order without any escaping.

The media-type attribute is applicable to the text output method. The default value for the media-type attribute is text/plain.

The encoding attribute identifies the encoding that the text output method should use to convert sequences of characters to sequences of bytes. The default is system-dependent. If the result tree contains a character that cannot be represented in the encoding that the XSLT processor is using for output, the XSLT processor should signal an error.

Normally, the XML output method escapes & and < (and possibly other characters) when outputting text nodes. This function ensures that the output is well-formed XML. It is sometimes convenient to be able to produce output that is almost, but not quite, well-formed XML, however. For example, the output can include ill-formed sections that are intended to be transformed into well-formed XML by a subsequent non-XML aware process. For this reason, XSLT provides a mechanism for disabling output escaping. An xsl:value-of or xsl:text element might have a disable-output-escaping attribute. The allowed values are yes or no, and the default is no. If the value is yes, then a text node generated by instantiating the xsl:value-of or xsl:text element should be output without any escaping. For example,

```
<xsl:text disable-output-escaping="yes">&lt;</xsl:text>
```

should generate the single character <.

It is an error for output escaping to be disabled for a text node that is used for something other than a text node in the result tree. Thus, it is an error to disable output escaping for an `xsl:value-of` or `xsl:text` element that is used to generate the string value of a comment, processing instruction, or attribute node. It is also an error to convert a result-tree fragment to a number or a string if the result-tree fragment contains a text node for which escaping was disabled. In both cases, an XSLT processor can signal the error. If it does not signal the error, it must recover by ignoring the disable-output-escaping attribute.

The disable-output-escaping attribute can be used with the html output method as well as with the XML output method. The text output method ignores the disable-output-escaping attribute because it does not perform any output escaping.

An XSLT processor will only be capable of disabling output escaping if it controls how the result tree is output. This situation might not always be the case, however. For example, the result tree might be used as the source tree for another XSLT transformation instead of being output. An XSLT processor is not required to support disabling output escaping. If an `xsl:value-of` or `xsl:text` specifies that output escaping should be disabled and the XSLT processor does not support this function, the

XSLT processor might signal an error. If it does not signal an error, it must recover by not disabling output escaping.

If output escaping is disabled for a character that is not representable in the encoding that the XSLT processor is using for output, then the XSLT processor might signal an error. If it does not signal an error, it must recover by not disabling output escaping.

Because disabling output escaping might not work with all XSLT processors and can result in XML that is not well formed, it should be used only when there is no alternative.

Documenting Your XSLT

Even if XSLT is a declarative programming language, it is not transparent. Understanding what the programmer meant with a section in the code is hard. Documenting your work becomes as important as writing it if you want it to be used more than once and by someone else. This situation is especially important in the production of large Web sites by using XSLT, because the person who wrote the transformation sheet might no longer even be with the company. Documenting the work makes it easier for everyone. And, for the lone consultant, of course, it saves money by reusing sections of transformation sheets if he or she knows where to find them.

The easiest way is to insert comments into the code. XSLT, being XML, supports the comment mechanism of XML, which means anything surrounded by the comment marks `<!--  -->`. Note that there has to be a white space between the - and the comment.

You can also use extension elements in a separate namespace, such as the doc namespace, to hold documentation that would be ignored by the processor with an empty `xsl:fallback` element being used to stop processors from complaining that they do not recognize the extension element. You can easily imagine having structured documentation within the documentation on a template, commenting on each of the parameters that it takes. Here is an example of including documentation within a template:

```
<xsl:template match="...">
  <doc:template><xsl:fallback />
```

```
      <!-- documentation on the template -->
    </doc:template>
    <!-- body of the template -->
  </xsl:template>
```

The point, of course, of using XML to represent the documentation within the style sheet is that you can get at it with things that understand XML (most importantly, XSLT). So, you can then have another XSLT style sheet that takes our documented XSLT style sheet as input and produces an HTML frameset that explains what the style sheet does and how it works.

There are also tools for creating documentation for XSLT files. Xsldoc is a tool for generating documentation of your XSLT files. The output is similar to Javadoc output for Java source files. The same commenting tags are used, as well.

XSLT and Document Structure: Databases, DOM, and XML Schema

Transformation sheets embed application logic for transformations in much the same way as stored procedures do for a *database management system* (DBMS). In other words, each transformation sheet in principle is unique to the site and to the format to which it transforms. It is also possible to transform different markup elements in different ways. You can also actually use XSLT to perform database searches (by generating a *Structured Query Language* [SQL] query from a transformation sheet, for instance). But a more usual way to use XSLT is probably to transform the results of searches in a database to HTML or XML formats.

To generate queries, of course, you generate a text file that contains the SQL query. If the database can put out XML, the results can also be transformed by using XSLT. When you have XML documents that represent the result sets of database queries, you can combine DOM and XSL techniques to search for them, to filter the result sets, to perform refinements, and to present the results. In the case of database queries, the client application might see XML, HTML, or even raw data. What you get depends upon both the database format and how data is processed on the server.

In a low-tech solution, the data could be stored on the server in a flat XML file format. If the client is capable of handling XML data, the server simply redirects the client to the file. In this case, the client must provide all of the database features (including the capability of searching the database and filtering and displaying records). In this case, there is little or no server-side processing.

The other end of the spectrum is when the data is stored in a proprietary database and the server processes queries and returns an XML-ized data stream. In this situation, the client application makes a query (most likely, a SQL query) and receives in return an XML stream representing the result set.

XSLT style sheets can be used to extract data from databases, which is one main use of ASP, Active Server Pages (for instance, where almost all of the page is static and you just want to "fill in the blanks"). In those cases, you would create a style sheet in the same way as a program for receiving data from any other database extraction.

Some database management systems enable you to query the database directly through a URL. By using a FOR XML clause in your SQL query, you can have the resulting record set back as an XML string (in database management systems that support it). Another more typical method is to invoke a server-side script that receives the query, posts it to a back-end database, converts the result set to XML, and returns it to the client.

The middle of the road is similar to the previous scenario. The client application invokes a server-side script that receives the query, posts it to a back-end database, and converts the result set to XML. Rather than returning XML to the client, however, the server script can perform the XML processing on the server and ship out an XML transformation (for example, HTML) instead.

The bottom line is that you might not always have control over where your XML data is processed—especially as database vendors add the capability to output XML directly to the browser. The good news is that using XSL and the DOM will work equally well in all three situations, whether you are working with flat files, XML data that has been streamed to the browser, or server-side XML.

As a developer, you must have knowledge of the structure and organization, or "schema," of the data that are being transformed. That knowledge is important, because style sheet transformations often use simple step patterns (or even full-blown Xpath expressions) to locate a given element or attribute in the document tree, then use <xsl:value-of> to retrieve the item's content. So, XSL style sheets are highly reliant on a document's structure.

By moving from statically created style sheets to dynamically generated transformations, you shift responsibility from the style-sheet author to the DOM developer. If you can generalize the process, however, you can realize significant benefits from generating your XSL dynamically.

If you are converting a document format of any complexity down to HTML (for example), using template rules is more natural and easier to code in XSLT because the output is driven by the input. Define some templates for the transforms that you want, and recurse down with apply-templates. Then, your table of contents automatically grows to fit the document. This process only works, however, if the input is in some sense already a document. XSLT, at its best, is about pipes and filters. Its weakest points are where this model breaks down.

Instead of writing

```xml
<?xml version="1.0"?>
<xsl:stylesheet xmlns:xsl="http://www.w3.org/1999/XSL/Transform"
                version="1.0">
  <xsl:template match="/">
    <HTML>
      <HEAD>
        <TITLE>Welcome</TITLE>
      </HEAD>
      <BODY>
        <FONT bgcolor="{member/favoriteColor}">
          Welcome <xsl:value-of select="member/name"/>!
        </FONT>
        <TABLE>
          <TR><TH>Type</TH><TH>Number</TH></TR>
          <xsl:for-each select="member/phone">
            <TR>
              <TD><xsl:value-of select="@type"/></TD>
              <TD><xsl:value-of select="."/></TD>
            </TR>
          </xsl:for-each>
        </TABLE>
      </BODY>
    </HTML>
  </xsl:template>
</xsl:stylesheet>
```

You can write

```
<HTML xsl:version="1.0"
xmlns:xsl="http://www.w3.org/1999/XSL/Transform">
  <HEAD>
    <TITLE>Welcome</TITLE>
  </HEAD>
  <BODY>
    <FONT bgcolor="{member/favoriteColor}">
      Welcome <xsl:value-of select="member/name"/>!
    </FONT>
    <TABLE>
      <TR><TH>Type</TH><TH>Number</TH></TR>
      <xsl:for-each select="member/phone">
        <TR>
          <TD><xsl:value-of select="@type"/></TD>
          <TD><xsl:value-of select="."/></TD>
        </TR>
      </xsl:for-each>
    </TABLE>
  </BODY>
</HTML>
```

You can teach people that to get started, you first get an HTML template from the Web designers and then use Tidy (a piece of free software that enables you to turn HTML into XHTML) with the -asxml option to convert the HTML to well-formed HTML and add an xsl:version to the <HTML> root element. Then, you can fill in with the different XSLT templates.

The key to generalizing this process lies in the schema. If you have a formal schema, such as a DTD or an XML Schema document, you should be able to discover enough about the organization and structure of the document to generate a reasonable XSL style sheet document.

While XML documents separate data from presentation and program logic, XSL style sheets do not. Depending on how you write them, your style sheets can rely heavily on the structure of the XML document itself. A simple change, like adding a new element type for a particular class of XML documents, could affect 24 or more style sheets—making the system quite fragile. Generating style sheets dynamically eases this situation.

You can instruct the parser to apply a specific style sheet by including a <?stylesheet ...?> declaration in the XML document instance. Or, more typically, you can apply the style sheet dynamically by using the DOM's transformNode method.

In both cases, the style sheet is presumed to be static. One problem with static style sheets—all static documents, including scripts and programs—is that by modifying the original XML document, you risk breaking the application. At the least, document modifications require maintenance throughout the rest of your application.

You could use DOM, but then you would have to walk the document tree by using DOM methods and include an `if` statement to perform the filtering. You would lose a major benefit that XSL transformations offer: the capability to separate presentation from logic. For example, the DOM approach does not enable you to generate custom HTML documents based on browser type.

Because a style sheet is a well-formed (and in fact, valid) document, you can load one into the DOM just like any other XML document. You can use this feature to load a basic style sheet into a DOM object and then use DOM methods to construct a style sheet instance.

To begin working with the DOM, you must create a new DOM object and then load an XML document into that object. From that point, you can use DOM methods to walk the document tree, access nodes, query properties, modify nodes, create new ones, and so on. The parser that you use determines how your DOM object is created and loaded. If you are creating a DOM object on the server side (say, from an active server page), then you must instead use Server.CreateObject().

Stylesheet for XML Schema

The purpose of this chapter is to demonstrate how an XSLT stylesheet can be used to transform an XML Schema document into XHTML in order to make the schema easier to read.

A schema defines a class of XML documents. The schema defines rules for how elements and attributes in the document can be combined and what kind of data they can contain. An XML document that complies with the rules in the schema is said to be an *instance* of that schema. The W3C has specified an XML application for writing schema: the XML Schema definition language *XML Schema*.

NOTE

When we refer to any schema in general, we use the term *schema*. When we refer to a schema that is created with the W3C-recommended schema definition language, we use the term *XML Schema*.

If you have used XML for some time, you might have read or even developed a *document type definition* (DTD). Then, you have already used a kind of schema—only a very trivial one compared to a real schema language such as XML Schema.

XML Schema is a new technology on the Web. It will be used as part of *XForms*—the next generation of forms on the Web—and as a part of e-commerce applications. The ability to quickly look up information in the schema will become essential. Few content authors will actually write any schema themselves; rather, large corporations or organizations will create it for them. Many content authors will read and use an existing schema, however, without being XML Schema experts themselves. The problem now is that if developing and writing a schema is hard, then reading one might be even harder. The complexity of a schema increases with the number of elements, attributes, and data types that it defines. A schema that defines XHTML documents involves several hundred lines of XML. Typically, the number of readers exceeds the number of authors. Computer programs might read an XML Schema with ease, but a human being will not. At this point, we apply XSLT. We want to present the information that is in the schema in a human-readable form.

We will not develop a schema in this chapter. Instead, we will use one that already exists. We will show how you can use XSLT to transform a schema into a nice-looking XHTML document that is readable by a human being without much knowledge of the XML Schema syntax but with some basic knowledge of schemas in general. We can use any layout of the XHTML document we want, and we can use a *Cascading Style Sheet* (CSS) to fine-tune the presentation (for example, to highlight required attributes and elements).

NOTE

The XML Schema specifications are available at the W3C Web site at www.w3.org. There, you can also find an XML Schema for XHTML as well as information about XForms, one of many new Web technologies that are based on XML Schema.

The Expense Schema

First, we introduce an already-existing schema that we will use in the examples. Many *personal digital assistants* (PDAs) have an "expense" application where the user can enter receipts for later retrieval from a PC or laptop or from another PDA or mobile phone. The kind of data that can be entered into such an application is what we here call an *expense report*. An expense report is a collection of *receipts*.

Let's consider its usage. The information in the expense application should be viewable in a standard XML browser. Also, it should be possible to check that the information in the receipts is correct—that it complies with some specific business rules that we specify. Each receipt might have a category; for example, *Personal* or *Business*. The receipt must have a date and include the amount and currency. It can, in addition, indicate the payment method, the city, and in the event that the receipt was for a dinner, names of the attendees. In order to view the data in an XML browser we choose XML as the transfer syntax, and in order to validate the data we define an XML Schema.

Here is an example of an XML expense report with two receipts:

```xml
<expense>

    <receipt category="Personal">
        <date>2001-05-07</date>
        <type>Dinner</type>
        <amount>175</amount>
        <currency>SEK</currency>
        <payment>VISA</payment>
        <city>Malm?</city>
        <attendees>Johan Peter</attendees>
    </receipt>

    <receipt category="Business">
        <date>2001-05-07</date>
        <type>Hotel</type>
        <amount>250</amount>
        <currency>USD</currency>
        <payment>VISA</payment>
        <city>San Francisco</city>
    </receipt>

</expense>
```

With a schema for this expense report, we can check that the information in the receipts is correct. Is the data in the date element a correct date? Does each receipt contain the date, amount, and currency? Is the data in the payment element one of the payment methods that we accept? Using a schema, we can answer these questions with a program that checks that the data in the expense report complies with rules expressed in the schema. This program is great for finding errors in the receipt before they are sent to a server somewhere.

Here is the XML Schema for the expense reports:

```
<xsd:schema xmlns:xsd="http://www.w3.org/2001/XMLSchema">

    <xsd:element name="expense" >
        <xsd:complexType>
        <xsd:sequence minOccurs="0" maxOccurs="unbounded" >
            <xsd:element name="receipt" type="Receipt" />
        </xsd:sequence>
        </xsd:complexType>
    </xsd:element>

    <xsd:complexType name="Receipt">
        <xsd:sequence>
        <xsd:element name="date" type="xsd:date"  />
        <xsd:element name="type" type="xsd:string" minOccurs="0" />
        <xsd:element name="amount" type="xsd:positiveInteger" />
        <xsd:element name="currency" type="xsd:string" />
        <xsd:element name="payment" type="Cards" />
        <xsd:element name="city" type="xsd:string" minOccurs="0" />
        <xsd:element name="attendees" minOccurs="0">
            <xsd:simpleType>
                <xsd:list itemType="xsd:string" />
            </xsd:simpleType>
        </xsd:element>
        </xsd:sequence>
        <xsd:attribute ref="category" use="optional"/>
    </xsd:complexType>

    <xsd:attribute name="category">
        <xsd:simpleType>
            <xsd:restriction base="xsd:string">
                <xsd:enumeration value="Business" />
                <xsd:enumeration value="Personal" />
            </xsd:restriction>
        </xsd:simpleType>
    </xsd:attribute>

    <xsd:simpleType name="Cards">
```

```
          <xsd:restriction base="xsd:string" >
              <xsd:enumeration value="VISA" />
              <xsd:enumeration value="AMEX" />
              <xsd:enumeration value="MASTERCARD" />
          </xsd:restriction>
      </xsd:simpleType>

   </xsd:schema>
```

TIP

By downloading an XML Schema validating program from the Web, you can check that the expense report above really is correct (it should be). You will find free XML Schema tools and more information about XML Schema on the W3C Web site, in addition to many other sites about XML programming. Just follow the instructions for the tool that you choose to download, and validating that the expense report complies with the schema should be an easy task.

If you actually try to read the XML Schema above and you are not already an XML Schema expert, you will find out what many have found before you: making any sense of an XML Schema is hard. It is verbose, it is complex, it is designed to be read by machines (rather than humans), and it contains lots and lots of information.

What the XML Schema Defines

Here is a quick introduction to what you will find in the schema. The schema defines what elements, attributes, and data that the XML document might contain and how it can be combined. You already know that XML documents can contain elements and attributes, so the only new concept here is that of *data types*, which is not so new after all. Most programming languages have built-in data types; for example, integers, floats, structures, and strings. With XML Schema, XML gets data types, as well. You see some of them in the receipts: strings (xsd:string), dates (xsd:date), and positive integers (xsd:positiveInteger). The following definition means that the date element can contain only data that is a true *date* (as defined by XML Schema):

```
<xsd:element name="date" type="xsd:date"  />
```

Here is an example of a valid date element:

```
<date>2001-05-07</date>
```

When XML is used without XML Schema and has no data types, all we can specify in the DTD is that the date element must contain text. There is no way to specify exactly what kind of text. With XML Schema, however, rather than passing around plain "text" on the Web with some XML markup, we can now specify exactly what type of data is delivered. You realize how powerful XML Schema can become when used with e-commerce and other non-trivial Web applications. If only the schema did not become so hard to read as soon as it gets a little complex.

NOTE

In XML Schema, the XML Schema namespace is used on essentially any object that is defined in the XML Schema specification. Built-in datatypes such as strings, numbers, dates, and time are in the XML Schema namespace and are thus prefixed with the XML Schema namespace prefix ("xsd" in all of our examples). For a complete list of XML data types, see the "XML Schema Part 2: Datatypes" specification available at www.w3.org/TR/xmlschema-2/.

Dates, strings, time, and integers are *simple types*. An element that contains other elements and attributes is said to have a *complex type*. The expense element contains a complex type that is a sequence of zero or many receipt elements where each contains data of the Receipt complex type (defined elsewhere in the schema):

```
<xsd:element name="expense" >
    <xsd:complexType>
    <xsd:sequence minOccurs="0" maxOccurs="unbounded" >
        <xsd:element name="receipt" type="Receipt" />
    </xsd:sequence>
    </xsd:complexType>
</xsd:element>
```

Complex types are common. Whenever you define that an element can contain other elements and one or many attributes, you have a complex type.

A simple type (such as a string) can be further constrained. The category attribute contains a string—a simple type that is restricted to contain only two defined keywords ("Business" and "Personal"). It is still a string but is constrained to only two possible values:

```
<xsd:attribute name="category">
    <xsd:simpleType>
        <xsd:restriction base="xsd:string">
```

```
            <xsd:enumeration value="Business" />
            <xsd:enumeration value="Personal" />
        </xsd:restriction>
    </xsd:simpleType>
</xsd:attribute>
```

We will not explain XML Schema in more detail than what we already have. It is not necessary for what we will do in the chapter. But even for an XML Schema expert, it can become hard to grasp all of the information that a schema might contain. Rules about structure and data types are mixed with declarations and many cross references, and the syntax is verbose with deep hierarchies of elements in which the reader is quickly lost. It is hard. Now, we will show how XSLT can make it easier.

This issue is the topic for the rest of this chapter: an XSLT stylesheet that transforms the XML Schema for the expense report into a more readable form (so why not into an XHTML document?).

NOTE

The XSLT stylesheet created in this chapter transforms a subset of what an XML Schema can contain. It is, of course, possible to extend the stylesheet to present all of XML Schema. Such an exercise would, however, take up more space than what is available in this book. The goal of the XSLT stylesheet in this chapter is to transform only what is in the expense report schema, which are more XML Schema features than most schemas will ever need.

An XHTML Template for XML Schema

The first thing we need to do is to define the template for the resulting XHTML document. Knowing that an XML Schema contains much information, how can we best present it by using XHTML headers, paragraphs, tables, and, in addition, a CSS style sheet?

Here are some requirements of the resulting XHTML document:

- It must be easy to look up any element, attribute, and data type defined in the XML Schema. So, there probably should be an index at the beginning or at the end of the document.

- For each element and data type, it must be clearly shown what attributes it can have and what other elements and data it can contain. So, each element and data type should have its own section in the document.

- In case an element or attribute is required or there is a default or some other special constraint, it must be presented in a special way. We can perform this task by using a CSS to assign different style rules depending on the specified constraints.

Here is the XHTML template we will use:

```
<xsl:template match="xsd:schema">
    <html>
    <head>
        <title>XML Schema</title>
            <link rel="stylesheet" type="text/css" href="xsdhtml.css"
/>
    </head>
    <body>
    <h1>Quick Reference</h1>

    <h2>Index</h2>
    <table>
    <xsl:if test="xsd:element">
    <tr><th>Elements</th></tr>
    <xsl:apply-templates select="xsd:element[@name]" mode="toc" >
        <xsl:sort select="@name" />
    </xsl:apply-templates>
    </xsl:if>
    <xsl:if test="xsd:attribute">
    <tr><th>Attributes</th></tr>
    <xsl:apply-templates select="xsd:attribute[@name]" mode="toc" >
        <xsl:sort select="@name" />
    </xsl:apply-templates>
    </xsl:if>
    <xsl:if test="xsd:complexType | xsd:simpleType">
    <tr><th>Types</th></tr>
    <xsl:apply-templates select="xsd:complexType[@name] |
xsd:simpleType[@name]" mode="toc" >
        <xsl:sort select="@name" />
    </xsl:apply-templates>
    </xsl:if>
    </table>

    <legend>
    <h2>Legend</h2>
    <p>The following syntax is used to describe content models:</p>
    <dl>
        <dt>*</dt>
        <dd>Zero or many</dd>
        <dt>?</dt>
        <dd>Zero or one</dd>
        <dt>+</dt>
```

```
            <dd>One or many</dd>
            <dt>a , b</dt>
            <dd>a followed by b</dd>
            <dt>a | b</dt>
            <dd>a or b</dd>
      </dl>
      </legend>

      <xsl:if test="xsd:element[@name] | xsd:attribute[@name]">
      <h1>Element and Attribute Declarations</h1>

      <p>The following elements and attributes are declared.</p>

      <xsl:apply-templates select="xsd:element[@name] |
  xsd:attribute[@name]" mode="global" >
            <xsl:sort select="@name" />
      </xsl:apply-templates>
      </xsl:if>

      <xsl:if test="xsd:complexType[@name] | xsd:simpleType[@name]">
      <h1>Type Definitions</h1>

      <p>The following types are defined.</p>
                      <xsl:apply-templates
  select="xsd:complexType[@name] | xsd:simpleType[@name]" mode="global" >
            <xsl:sort select="@name" />
      </xsl:apply-templates>
      </xsl:if>

      </body>
      </html>
  </xsl:template>
```

The XHTML document template matches the xsd:schema element, the schema root element that contains all other definitions. In the head of the XHTML document, there is a reference to a CSS that we will return to later. The title of the document is "XML Schema."

First, in the resulting document is a table with the name of every named global element, attribute, and type defined in the schema and a link to the actual definition later in the document. The definitions are sorted in alphabetical order.

```
          <h2>Index</h2>
      <table>
      <xsl:if test="xsd:element">
      <tr><th>Elements</th></tr>
      <xsl:apply-templates select="xsd:element[@name]" mode="toc" >
```

```
              <xsl:sort select="@name" />
     </xsl:apply-templates>
     </xsl:if>
     <xsl:if test="xsd:attribute">
     <tr><th>Attributes</th></tr>
     <xsl:apply-templates select="xsd:attribute[@name]" mode="toc" >
          <xsl:sort select="@name" />
     </xsl:apply-templates>
     </xsl:if>
     <xsl:if test="xsd:complexType | xsd:simpleType">
     <tr><th>Types</th></tr>
     <xsl:apply-templates select="xsd:complexType[@name] |
  xsd:simpleType[@name]" mode="toc" >
          <xsl:sort select="@name" />
     </xsl:apply-templates>
     </xsl:if>
     </table>
```

The templates that are applied are actually only one template that operates in a special *table-of-contents* (toc) mode:

```
<xsl:template match="xsd:element | xsd:attribute| xsd:simpleType |
xsd:complexType" mode="toc">
     <tr>
     <td>
     <a href="#{@name}">
          <xsl:value-of select="@name" />
     </a>
     </td>
     </tr>
</xsl:template>
```

The template generates an XHTML table row with one cell that contains the name and a link to an element with a matching identity. We will see later how the id attribute is used for each definition in the schema.

The rest of the resulting XHTML document is the list of all named global declarations and definitions in the schema. It includes all elements, attributes, and types that are defined with a name to which we can refer:

```
     <xsl:if test="xsd:element[@name] | xsd:attribute[@name]">
     <h1>Element and Attribute Declarations</h1>

     <p>The following elements and attributes are declared.</p>

     <xsl:apply-templates select="xsd:element[@name] |
  xsd:attribute[@name]" mode="global" >
          <xsl:sort select="@name" />
```

```
    </xsl:apply-templates>
    </xsl:if>

    <xsl:if test="xsd:complexType[@name] | xsd:simpleType[@name]">
    <h1>Type Definitions</h1>

    <p>The following types are defined.</p>

    <xsl:apply-templates select="xsd:complexType[@name] |
xsd:simpleType[@name]" mode="global" >
        <xsl:sort select="@name" />
    </xsl:apply-templates>
    </xsl:if>
```

Note that the "global" mode selects special templates for presentation of global definitions and declarations.

When the xsd:element element is presented as part of the content model for another element, we use another less-verbose template than the "global" one and refer back to the original element definition with a link. The same thing happens for attributes and types. All of this information will become clearer as we move on to the description of these templates.

Attributes

In XML Schema, attributes are defined by using the xsd:attribute element. Here is how the category attribute is defined in the expense report:

```
<xsd:attribute name="category">
    <xsd:simpleType>
        <xsd:restriction base="xsd:string">
            <xsd:enumeration value="Business" />
            <xsd:enumeration value="Personal" />
        </xsd:restriction>
    </xsd:simpleType>
</xsd:attribute>
```

Attributes are simple. They have a name and a value that can be a simple type. In the case of the category attribute, the simple type is based on the built-in XML Schema string type and is further restricted to contain only two string keywords.

When an attribute is declared at the top level in the schema, under the xsd:schema element, it can be referred to later in an element declaration or complex type definition. In this case, the "ref" attribute is used instead of the "name" attribute, and the declared attribute gets all of its properties from the referred attribute. In the following example from the expense report schema, the "category" attribute of the receipt element refers to the global declaration:

```
<xsd:attribute ref="category" use="optional"/>
```

When presenting the global attribute declaration, we first write its name followed by a list of properties. Here is the template that does that:

```
<xsl:template match="xsd:attribute[@name]" mode="global">
<h2 id="{@name}">
<span class="attname">
    <xsl:value-of select="@name"/>
</span> Attribute
</h2>

<p>
This attribute has the following properties:
</p>

<xsl:call-template name="WriteAttributeProperties"/>
</xsl:template>
```

The *WriteAttributeProperties* is a named template that generates a list of attribute properties, starting with the attribute type followed by any value constraints.

```
<xsl:template name="WriteAttributeProperties">
    <dl>
        <dt>Type definition:</dt>
        <dd>
            <xsl:choose>
            <xsl:when test="xsd:simpleType">
                <xsl:apply-templates
select="xsd:simpleType"/>
            </xsl:when>
            <xsl:when test="@type">
            <span class="typename">
            <xsl:value-of select="@type"/></span>
            </xsl:when>
            <xsl:otherwise>
            <span class="typename">anySimpleType</span>
            </xsl:otherwise>
            </xsl:choose>
```

```
            </dd>
            <dt>Value constraint: </dt>
            <dd>
                <xsl:choose>
                    <xsl:when test="@default">
                        <xsl:text> #DEFAULT='</xsl:text>
                        <span class="default">
                            <xsl:value-of select="@default"/>
                        </span>
                        <xsl:text>'</xsl:text>
                    </xsl:when>
                    <xsl:when test="@fixed">
                        <xsl:text> #FIXED='</xsl:text>
                        <span class="fixed">
                            <xsl:value-of select="@fixed"/>
                        </span>
                        <xsl:text>'</xsl:text>
                    </xsl:when>
                    <xsl:otherwise>
                        <xsl:text>none</xsl:text>
                    </xsl:otherwise>
                </xsl:choose>
            </dd>
        </dl>
    </xsl:template>
```

The type is determined by the xsd:simpleType element (if present); otherwise, the "type" attribute determines the type. If none is present, the type defaults to the generic *anySimpleType* (a built-in XML Schema type without any restrictions).

After the type has been determined, the value constraints are generated. It is either *default* or *fixed*.

The element templates use the last template for attributes (see next section) in order to write out the name and to use an attribute on an element:

```
<xsl:template match="xsd:attribute" mode="local">
    <li>
    <p>
        <xsl:if test="@use = 'required'">
        <xsl:attribute name="class">required</xsl:attribute>
        </xsl:if>
        <xsl:if test="@name">
            <xsl:value-of select="@name"/>
        </xsl:if>
        <xsl:if test="@ref">
            <a href="#{@ref}">
```

```
                    <xsl:value-of select="@ref"/>
              </a>
         </xsl:if>
    </p>
    <xsl:if test="not(@ref)">
         <xsl:call-template name="WriteAttributeProperties"/>
    </xsl:if>
    </li>
</xsl:template>
```

The name of the attribute is written out. It is either the "name" attribute or a reference to a global attribute declaration. If the "ref" attribute is not used, the name is followed by the list of attribute properties for which the named template *WriteAttributeProperties* is used.

Attributes are not useful without elements. So, in the next section we will examine how to present element declarations.

Elements

The element declaration contains information about what attributes and other elements the element might contain. This information is essential for the content author, because attributes elements can be declared both as global and as local. In the expense report schema, the expense element is declared as a global element because the declaration is located right under the xsd:schema element:

```
<xsd:element name="expense" >
    <xsd:complexType>
    <xsd:sequence minOccurs="0" maxOccurs="unbounded" >
         <xsd:element name="receipt" type="Receipt" />
    </xsd:sequence>
    </xsd:complexType>
</xsd:element>
```

Contained inside the xsd:element element is the definition of the element type. In this case, the type is complex—a sequence of zero or many receipt elements.

The other way to declare an element is directly inside a complex type definition, as in the following example from the expense report schema:

```
<xsd:complexType name="Receipt">
    <xsd:sequence>
```

```
<xsd:element name="date" type="xsd:date"  />
<xsd:element name="type" type="xsd:string" minOccurs="0" />
<xsd:element name="amount" type="xsd:positiveInteger" />
<xsd:element name="currency" type="xsd:string" />
<xsd:element name="payment" type="Cards" />
<xsd:element name="city" type="xsd:string" minOccurs="0" />
<xsd:element name="attendees" minOccurs="0">
    <xsd:simpleType>
        <xsd:list itemType="xsd:string" />
    </xsd:simpleType>
</xsd:element>
</xsd:sequence>
<xsd:attribute ref="category" use="optional"/>
</xsd:complexType>
```

Global elements are presented by using the following template:

```
<xsl:template match="xsd:element[@name]" mode="global">
    <h2 id="{@name}">
    <span class="elmname">
            <xsl:value-of select="@name"/>
        </span> Element
    </h2>
    <p>
    This element has the following attributes and content model.
    </p>

    <h3>Attributes</h3>
    <xsl:call-template name="WriteAttributes"/>

    <h3>Content Model</h3>
    <xsl:call-template name="WriteContentModel"/>
    <xsl:if test=".//xsd:element[@name and not(@ref)]">

    <h3>Local Elements</h3>
    <div style="margin-left:2em; font-size: smaller; ">
    <xsl:apply-templates
        select=".//xsd:element[@name and not(@ref)]"
        mode="local"/>
    </div>
    </xsl:if>
</xsl:template>
```

There are three parts in this template. The name of the element is written out as a header and follows a list of attributes generated by the named template *WriteAttributes* and the content model. As we will see later, the list of attributes and the content model is similar for complex type.

The content model is written out by using the notation that is familiar to all XML DTD readers. Here is the content model for the receipt element of the expense report:

```
(date,type?,amount,currency,payment,city?,attendees?)
```

The "," separator indicates that the element must appear in sequence. A "|" would have indicated an OR relation. The "?" means that the element is optional and that other elements must appear exactly once.

NOTE
The notation for content models can be found in the XML specification, available at www.w3.org/TR/REC-xml. You will also find it explained in almost any book about XML.

In the case any elements are declared inside another element declaration, the template generates a list of local element declarations. These are the element declarations with a "ref" attribute. Here is the template to present local elements (it is almost the same as the one for global elements):

```
<xsl:template match="xsd:element" mode="local">
    <h4>
    <span class="elmname">
        <xsl:value-of select="@name"/>
    </span> Element
    </h4>
    <xsl:choose>
    <xsl:when test="@ref">
        <p>See <a href="#{@ref}">
            <xsl:value-of select="@ref"/>
        </a>.</p>
    </xsl:when>
    <xsl:otherwise>
        <p>
        This element has the following attributes
        and content model.</p>

        <h4>Attributes</h4>
        <xsl:call-template name="WriteAttributes"/>

        <h4>Content Model</h4>
        <xsl:call-template name="WriteContentModel"/>
    </xsl:otherwise>
    </xsl:choose>
</xsl:template>
```

The differences between the template for local elements and the template for global elements is that the local one is generating smaller headers, does not list locally declared elements (because that is already done by the global element declaration or complex type definition of which this local element is part), and if the "ref" attribute is present, it creates a link to the referred element declaration.

Two important components of an element declaration is the list of attributes and the content mode. The following two sections are devoted to this topic.

The Attribute List

For an element, you can declare an unordered list of attributes. If so, it is presented by using the named template *WriteAttributes*:

```
<xsl:template name="WriteAttributes">
    <xsl:param name="attlist" />

    <xsl:choose>
        <xsl:when test="$attlist">
            <ul>
            <xsl:apply-templates
                select="$attlist"
                mode="local"/>
            </ul>
        </xsl:when>
        <xsl:otherwise>
            <p>This element has no attributes.</p>
        </xsl:otherwise>
    </xsl:choose>
</xsl:template>
```

This template is simple and takes as an input parameter a list of attribute nodes. If the list is empty, it writes out a message that says that there are no attributes; in all other cases, it calls the template for local attributes with the list of attributes.

The Content Model

The content model of the element defines whether it is an empty element (no content), an element that can contain strings (simple types), or an element that can contain other elements and attributes (complex type). The templates for the global and local element declarations use the named template *WriteContentModel* to write out the element's content mode:

```
<xsl:template name="WriteContentModel">
    <xsl:choose>
    <xsl:when
test="xsd:complexType/xsd:sequence | xsd:complexType/xsd:choice">
    <xsl:apply-templates
select="xsd:complexType/xsd:sequence |
xsd:complexType/xsd:choice"
    mode="contentmodel"/>
    </xsl:when>
    <xsl:when test="xsd:simpleType">
        <xsl:apply-templates select="xsd:simpleType"/>
    </xsl:when>
    <xsl:when test="@type">
        <p>Data of type
        <span class="typename">
        <a href="#{@type}">
        <xsl:value-of select="@type"/></a></span>
        </p>
    </xsl:when>
    <xsl:otherwise>
    <p>EMPTY.</p>
    </xsl:otherwise>
    </xsl:choose>
</xsl:template>
```

As already mentioned, the content model of an element can be either a complex type, a simple type, or empty. When it is a simple type, the type is defined in either the xsd:simpleType element or the "type" attribute.

The following two sections take a closer look at complex and simple types (in particular, when the content model of the element is a complex type, how it is presented, what other elements it can contain, and how they can be combined). At this point, the templates for choices and sequences are used (xsd:sequence and xsd:choice).

Complex Types

Despite its name, the complex type is used often in most schemas. In the expense report schema, the Receipt type is a complex type:

```
<xsd:complexType name="Receipt">
    <xsd:sequence>
```

```
        <xsd:element name="date" type="xsd:date"   />
        <xsd:element name="type" type="xsd:string" minOccurs="0" />
        <xsd:element name="amount" type="xsd:positiveInteger" />
        <xsd:element name="currency" type="xsd:string" />
        <xsd:element name="payment" type="Cards" />
        <xsd:element name="city" type="xsd:string" minOccurs="0" />
        <xsd:element name="attendees" minOccurs="0">
            <xsd:simpleType>
                <xsd:list itemType="xsd:string" />
            </xsd:simpleType>
        </xsd:element>
        </xsd:sequence>
        <xsd:attribute ref="category" use="optional" />
    </xsd:complexType>
```

Complex types contain both element groups and attributes. Here, the complex type is a sequence of elements and one attribute.

Like element and attribute declarations, complex type definitions can appear at the top level of the schema, where they become global types (the Receipt complex type is a global type in the expense report schema).

The following template is used to present global complex types:

```
    <xsl:template match="xsd:complexType[@name]" mode="global">
<h2 id="{@name}">
    <span class="typename">
        <xsl:value-of select="@name"/>
    </span> Complex Type
</h2>
<h3>Attributes</h3>
<xsl:call-template name="WriteAttributes" >
    <xsl:with-param name="attlist" select="xsd:attribute" />
</xsl:call-template>

<h3>Content Model</h3>
<xsl:apply-templates
    select="xsd:choice | xsd:sequence" mode="contentmodel"/>

<xsl:if test=".//xsd:element[@name]">
    <h3>Local Elements</h3>
    <div style="margin-left:2em; font-size: smaller; ">
    <xsl:apply-templates
        select=".//xsd:element[@name]" mode="local"/>
    </div>
    </xsl:if>
  </xsl:template>
```

This template is not very different from the one for global element declarations. It is, for example, calling the same named template *WriteAttributes*. For the content model, it applies the templates for choices and sequences (xsd:choice and xsd:sequence). The two templates are similar:

```
<xsl:template match="xsd:choice" mode="contentmodel">
    <xsl:param name="separator"/>
    <xsl:text>(</xsl:text>
    <xsl:apply-templates
    select="xsd:element | xsd:choice | xsd:sequence"
    mode="contentmodel">
        <xsl:with-param name="separator"> | </xsl:with-param>
    </xsl:apply-templates>

    <xsl:text>)</xsl:text>
    <xsl:call-template name="ElementOccurrenceConstraints"/>
    <xsl:if test="position() != last()">
        <xsl:value-of select="$separator"/>
    </xsl:if>
</xsl:template>
<xsl:template match="xsd:sequence" mode="contentmodel">
    <xsl:param name="separator"/>
    <xsl:text>(</xsl:text>
    <xsl:apply-templates
select="xsd:element | xsd:choice | xsd:sequence" mode="contentmodel">
        <xsl:with-param name="separator">,</xsl:with-param>
    </xsl:apply-templates>
    <xsl:text>)</xsl:text>
    <xsl:call-template name="ElementOccurrenceConstraints"/>
    <xsl:if test="position() != last()">
        <xsl:value-of select="$separator"/>
    </xsl:if>
    <xsl:text/>
</xsl:template>
```

The difference between these two templates is that the template for choices generates a list of element names separated with "|" while the template for sequences generates a list separated with ",". Both templates call the template for presenting elements inside a content model:

```
<xsl:template match="xsd:element" mode="contentmodel">
    <xsl:param name="separator"/>
    <xsl:choose>
        <xsl:when test="@ref">
            <a href="#{@ref}">
                <xsl:value-of select="@ref"/>
            </a>
        </xsl:when>
```

```
            <xsl:otherwise>
                <xsl:value-of select="@name"/>
            </xsl:otherwise>
        </xsl:choose>
        <xsl:call-template name="ElementOccurrenceConstraints"/>
        <xsl:if test="position() != last()">
            <xsl:value-of select="$separator"/>
        </xsl:if>
        <xsl:text/>
    </xsl:template>
```

This template writes out the name of the element or the reference if the "ref" attribute is used.

The templates for generating the content mode, essentially a list of element names separated by either "," or "|", call the named template *ElementOccurrenceConstraints* in order to write out the occurrence of an individual element, sequence list, or choice list:

```
<xsl:template name="ElementOccurrenceConstraints">
    <xsl:choose>
    <xsl:when test="@minOccurs='0' and @maxOccurs='unbounded'">
        <xsl:text>*</xsl:text>
    </xsl:when>
    <xsl:when test="(@minOccurs='1' or not(@minOccurs)) and
@maxOccurs='unbounded'">
        <xsl:text>+</xsl:text>
    </xsl:when>
    <xsl:when test="@minOccurs='0' and (@maxOccurs='1' or
not(@maxOccurs))">
        <xsl:text>?</xsl:text>
    </xsl:when>
    </xsl:choose>
</xsl:template>
```

This template is straightforward and interprets the "maxOccurs" and "minOccurs" attributes and transforms into the shorter notation.

The next section is about simple types. When an element is not a complex type, unless it is empty it is a simple type. An attribute is always a simple type.

Simple Types

Simple types are strings that are defined with some restrictions or special structure. In the expense report schema, the Cards type was a simple type:

```
<xsd:simpleType name="Cards">
    <xsd:restriction base="xsd:string" >
        <xsd:enumeration value="VISA" />
        <xsd:enumeration value="AMEX" />
        <xsd:enumeration value="MASTERCARD" />
    </xsd:restriction>
</xsd:simpleType>
```

The definition says that the simple type Cards is based on the built-in XML Schema string data type but is restricted to the following three strings: "VISA", "AMEX", and "MASTERCARD".

Here is another example of a simple type from the expense report:

```
<xsd:element name="attendees" minOccurs="0">
    <xsd:simpleType>
        <xsd:list itemType="xsd:string" />
    </xsd:simpleType>
</xsd:element>
```

This definition says that the attendees element is a simple type that is a list of strings. This definition, by the way, is located inside the definition of the Receipt complex type.

The Cards type is a global simple type because the Receipt complex type and the "category" attribute are located at the top level under the xsd:schema element.

Here is the template for global simple types:

```
<xsl:template match="xsd:simpleType[@name]" mode="global">
<h2 id="{@name}">
        <span class="typename">
            <xsl:value-of select="@name"/>
        </span> Simple Type
</h2>
<xsl:apply-templates select="xsd:restriction | xsd:list | xsd:union" />
</xsl:template>
```

The template just writes out the name of the simple type and then goes on to apply templates for the type of constraints: restriction, list, and union.

In the case, as it often is, that the simple type definition is located inside another type definition, then the following template is used:

```
<xsl:template match="xsd:simpleType">
    <dl>
        <dt>
```

```
            <xsl:if test="@name">
                <span class="typename">
                    <xsl:value-of select="@name"/>
                </span>.
            </xsl:if>
            </dt>
            <dd>
            <xsl:apply-templates
            select="xsd:restriction | xsd:list | xsd:union" />
            </dd>
        </dl>
    </xsl:template>
```

As the template for global simple types, this template as well applies the templates for the different types of constraints. The following three sections will explain what these templates do.

Restriction

Restrictions specify, as the name suggests, restrictions on the simple type. It was used in the expense report to restrict the possible values of the "category" attribute:

```
<xsd:attribute name="category">
    <xsd:simpleType>
        <xsd:restriction base="xsd:string">
            <xsd:enumeration value="Business" />
            <xsd:enumeration value="Personal" />
        </xsd:restriction>
    </xsd:simpleType>
</xsd:attribute>
```

The base type, the type that gets restricted, is a string. The restriction is an enumeration, a set of possible values. In an XML Schema, there are other types of restrictions as well. A restriction has a name and a value. The value of the restriction is always in a "value" attribute. Typically, the name suggests what the restriction is.

Here is the template used to present restrictions:

```
<xsl:template match="xsd:restriction">
    <xsl:choose>
        <xsl:when test="@base">
            <p>Based on the <span class="typename">
                    <xsl:value-of select="@base"/>
                </span> type.</p>
```

```
            </xsl:when>
            <xsl:otherwise>
                <xsl:apply-templates select="xsd:simpleType"/>
            </xsl:otherwise>
        </xsl:choose>
        <dl>
            <xsl:for-each select="xsd:minExclusive | xsd:minInclusive |
xsd:maxExclusive | xsd:maxInclusive | xsd:totalDigits |
xsd:fractionDigits | xsd:length | xsd:minLength | xsd:maxLength |
xsd:enumeration | xsd:whiteSpace | xsd:pattern">
                <dt>
                    <xsl:value-of select="name(.)"/>
                </dt>
                <dd>
                    <xsl:value-of select="@value"/>
                </dd>
            </xsl:for-each>
        </dl>
    </xsl:template>
```

The template writes out the base type of the restriction, as indicated in the "base" attribute or the xsd:simpleType element.

Then, it follows a list of restrictions. For each restriction, its name and value are written out as an XHTML definition list.

Lists and Union

When you derive a simple type by using a *list*, the list can contain only a list of values of one type. Remember how the list was used to restrict the value of the attendees element in the expense report to a list of strings?

```
<xsd:element name="attendees" minOccurs="0">
    <xsd:simpleType>
        <xsd:list itemType="xsd:string" />
    </xsd:simpleType>
</xsd:element>
```

Here is the template that presents the list:

```
<xsl:template match="xsd:list">
    <p>A list of:</p>
    <xsl:choose>
        <xsl:when test="@itemType">
            <p>
                <span class="typename">
                    <xsl:value-of select="@itemType"/>
```

```
            </span>
        </p>
    </xsl:when>
    <xsl:otherwise>
        <xsl:apply-templates select="xsd:simpleType"/>
    </xsl:otherwise>
</xsl:choose>
</xsl:template>
```

The type of data that the list can contain is indicated in the "itemType" attribute or the xsd:simpleType element. The template presents the list with the words "A list of:" and the item type.

The template for *unions* is almost as simple as the one for lists, so it is not included here. The full stylesheet is available at the end of this chapter.

The Resulting XHTML Document

Now, it is time to generate the resulting XHTML document. As we saw in the template that matched the whole schema (the one with the template for the resulting XHTML document), it contains a link to a CSS that can be used to further style the document. For example, the CSS can contain the following style rules to highlight some of the components of the schema:

```
.default
    {font-style: italic;}
.required
    {font-style: italic;}
.elmname,
.typename,
.attname
    {color:blue; font-weight: bold;}
```

Here is the resulting XHTML document:

```
<?xml version="1.0" encoding="utf-8"?>
<html xmlns:xsd="http://www.w3.org/2001/XMLSchema"
xmlns="http://www.w3.org/1999/xhtml">
<head>
<title>XML Schema</title>
<link rel="stylesheet" type="text/css" href="xsdhtml.css"/>
</head>
<body>
<h1>Quick Reference</h1>
```

```
<h2>Index</h2>
<table>
<tr>
<th>Elements</th>
</tr>
<tr>
<td>
<a href="#expense">expense</a>
</td>
</tr>
<tr>
<th>Attributes</th>
</tr>
<tr>
<td>
<a href="#category">category</a>
</td>
</tr>
<tr>
<th>Types</th>
</tr>
<tr>
<td>
<a href="#Cards">Cards</a>
</td>
</tr>
<tr>
<td>
<a href="#Receipt">Receipt</a>
</td>
</tr>
</table>
<legend>
<h2>Legend</h2>
<p>The following syntax is used to describe content models:</p>
<dl>
<dt>*</dt>
<dd>Zero or many</dd>
<dt>?</dt>
<dd>Zero or one</dd>
<dt>+</dt>
<dd>One or many</dd>
<dt>a , b</dt>
<dd>a followed by b</dd>
<dt>a | b</dt>
<dd>a or b</dd>
</dl>
</legend>
<h1>Element and Attribute Declarations</h1>
<p>The following elements and attributes are declared.</p>
```

```
<h2 id="category">
<span class="attname">category</span> Attribute
</h2>
<p>
This attribute has the following properties:
</p>
<dl>
<dt>Type definition:</dt>
<dd>
<dl>
<dt/>
<dd>
<p>Based on the <span class="typename">xsd:string</span> type.</p>
<dl>
<dt>xsd:enumeration</dt>
<dd>Business</dd>
<dt>xsd:enumeration</dt>
<dd>Personal</dd>
</dl>
</dd>
</dl>
</dd>
<dt>Value constraint: </dt>
<dd>none</dd>
</dl>
<h2 id="expense">
<span class="elmname">expense</span> Element
</h2>
<p>This element has the following attributes and content model.</p>
<h3>Attributes</h3>
<p>This element has no attributes.</p>
<h3>Content Model</h3>(receipt)*<h3>Local Elements</h3>
<div style="margin-left:2em; font-size: smaller; ">
<h4>
<span class="elmname">receipt</span> Element
</h4>
<p>This element has the following attributes and content model.</p>
<h4>Attributes</h4>
<p>This element has no attributes.</p>
<h4>Content Model</h4>
<p>Data of type
    <span class="typename">
<a href="#Receipt">Receipt</a>
</span>
</p>
</div>
<h1>Type Definitions</h1>
<p>The following types are defined.</p>
<h2 id="Cards">
<span class="typename">Cards</span> Simple Type
```

```
</h2>
<p>Based on the <span class="typename">xsd:string</span> type.</p>
<dl>
<dt>xsd:enumeration</dt>
<dd>VISA</dd>
<dt>xsd:enumeration</dt>
<dd>AMEX</dd>
<dt>xsd:enumeration</dt>
<dd>MASTERCARD</dd>
</dl>
<h2 id="Receipt">
<span class="typename">Receipt</span> Complex Type
</h2>
<h3>Attributes</h3>
<ul>
<li>
<p>
<a href="#category">category</a>
</p>
</li>
</ul>
<h3>Content
Model</h3>(date,type?,amount,currency,payment,city?,attendees?)<h3>Local
Elements</h3>
<div style="margin-left:2em; font-size: smaller; ">
<h4>
<span class="elmname">date</span> Element
</h4>
<p>This element has the following attributes and content model.</p>
<h4>Attributes</h4>
<p>This element has no attributes.</p>
<h4>Content Model</h4>
<p>Data of type
    <span class="typename">
<a href="#xsd:date">xsd:date</a>
</span>
</p>
<h4>
<span class="elmname">type</span> Element
</h4>
<p>This element has the following attributes and content model.</p>
<h4>Attributes</h4>
<p>This element has no attributes.</p>
<h4>Content Model</h4>
<p>Data of type
    <span class="typename">
<a href="#xsd:string">xsd:string</a>
</span>
</p>
<h4>
```

```
<span class="elmname">amount</span> Element
</h4>
<p>This element has the following attributes and content model.</p>
<h4>Attributes</h4>
<p>This element has no attributes.</p>
<h4>Content Model</h4>
<p>Data of type
    <span class="typename">
<a href="#xsd:positiveInteger">xsd:positiveInteger</a>
</span>
</p>
<h4>
<span class="elmname">currency</span> Element
</h4>
<p>This element has the following attributes and content model.</p>
<h4>Attributes</h4>
<p>This element has no attributes.</p>
<h4>Content Model</h4>
<p>Data of type
    <span class="typename">
<a href="#xsd:string">xsd:string</a>
</span>
</p>
<h4>
<span class="elmname">payment</span> Element
</h4>
<p>This element has the following attributes and content model.</p>
<h4>Attributes</h4>
<p>This element has no attributes.</p>
<h4>Content Model</h4>
<p>Data of type
    <span class="typename">
<a href="#Cards">Cards</a>
</span>
</p>
<h4>
<span class="elmname">city</span> Element
</h4>
<p>This element has the following attributes and content model.</p>
<h4>Attributes</h4>
<p>This element has no attributes.</p>
<h4>Content Model</h4>
<p>Data of type
    <span class="typename">
<a href="#xsd:string">xsd:string</a>
</span>
</p>
<h4>
<span class="elmname">attendees</span> Element
</h4>
```

```
<p>This element has the following attributes and content model.</p>
<h4>Attributes</h4>
<p>This element has no attributes.</p>
<h4>Content Model</h4>
<dl>
<dt/>
<dd>
<p>A list of:</p>
<p>
<span class="typename">xsd:string</span>
</p>
</dd>
</dl>
</div>
</body>
</html>
```

The Complete Stylesheet

Here is the complete stylesheet for transforming from an XML Schema into an XTML document. You can copy and paste this stylesheet into your text editor and apply it on the expense report schema (or any other XML Schema), and an XHTML document will present itself as the result:

```
<?xml version="1.0" encoding="UTF-8"?>
<!--==========================================
Transforms a subset of XML Schema into an XHTML document.
==========================================-->
<xsl:stylesheet version="1.0"
xmlns:xsl="http://www.w3.org/1999/XSL/Transform"
xmlns:xsd="http://www.w3.org/2001/XMLSchema"
xmlns="http://www.w3.org/1999/xhtml">

<xsl:output method="xml" indent="yes"/>
<!--==========================================
ATTRIBUTE Component
==========================================-->
<!--
Transforms global attribute declarations.
-->
<xsl:template match="xsd:attribute[@name]" mode="global">
    <h2 id="{@name}">
        <span class="attname">
            <xsl:value-of select="@name"/>
        </span> Attribute
</h2>
    <p>
```

```
This attribute has the following properties:
</p>
     <xsl:call-template name="WriteAttributeProperties"/>
</xsl:template>
<!--
Transforms local attribute declarations into list items.
-->
<xsl:template match="xsd:attribute" mode="local">
     <li>
          <p>
               <xsl:if test="@use = 'required'">
                    <xsl:attribute
name="class">required</xsl:attribute>
               </xsl:if>
               <xsl:if test="@name">
                    <xsl:value-of select="@name"/>
               </xsl:if>
               <xsl:if test="@ref">
                    <a href="#{@ref}">
                         <xsl:value-of select="@ref"/>
                    </a>
               </xsl:if>
          </p>
          <xsl:if test="not(@ref)">
               <xsl:call-template name="WriteAttributeProperties"/>
          </xsl:if>
     </li>
</xsl:template>
<!--
Transforms attribute properties type and value constraint
into a dl list.
-->
<xsl:template name="WriteAttributeProperties">
     <dl>
          <dt>Type definition:</dt>
          <dd>
               <xsl:choose>
               <xsl:when test="xsd:simpleType">
                    <xsl:apply-templates select="xsd:simpleType"/>
               </xsl:when>
               <xsl:when test="@type">
               <span class="typename"><xsl:value-of
select="@type"/></span>
               </xsl:when>
               <xsl:otherwise>
               <span class="typename">anySimpleType</span>
               </xsl:otherwise>
               </xsl:choose>
          </dd>
          <dt>Value constraint: </dt>
          <dd>
```

```xml
                    <xsl:choose>
                        <xsl:when test="@default">
                            <xsl:text> #DEFAULT='</xsl:text>
                            <span class="default">
                                <xsl:value-of select="@default"/>
                            </span>
                            <xsl:text>'</xsl:text>
                        </xsl:when>
                        <xsl:when test="@fixed">
                            <xsl:text> #FIXED='</xsl:text>
                            <span class="fixed">
                                <xsl:value-of select="@fixed"/>
                            </span>
                            <xsl:text>'</xsl:text>
                        </xsl:when>
                        <xsl:otherwise>
                            <xsl:text>none</xsl:text>
                        </xsl:otherwise>
                    </xsl:choose>
            </dd>
        </dl>
</xsl:template>
<!--=========================================
ELEMENT Component
=========================================-->
<!--
Transforms global element declarations.
-->
<xsl:template match="xsd:element[@name]" mode="global">
        <h2 id="{@name}">
            <span class="elmname">
                <xsl:value-of select="@name"/>
            </span> Element
</h2>
        <p>This element has the following attributes and content model.</p>
        <h3>Attributes</h3>
        <xsl:call-template name="WriteAttributes" >
            <xsl:with-param name="attlist"
select="xsd:complexType/xsd:attribute" />
        </xsl:call-template>
        <h3>Content Model</h3>
        <xsl:call-template name="WriteContentModel"/>
        <xsl:if test=".//xsd:element[@name and not(@ref)]">
            <h3>Local Elements</h3>
            <div style="margin-left:2em; font-size: smaller; ">
                <xsl:apply-templates select=".//xsd:element[@name and
not(@ref)]" mode="local"/>
            </div>
        </xsl:if>
</xsl:template>
```

```xml
<!--
Transforms local element declarations.
-->
<xsl:template match="xsd:element" mode="local">
    <h4>
        <span class="elmname">
            <xsl:value-of select="@name"/>
        </span> Element
</h4>
    <xsl:choose>
        <xsl:when test="@ref">
            <p>See <a href="#{@ref}">
                    <xsl:value-of select="@ref"/>
                </a>.</p>
        </xsl:when>
        <xsl:otherwise>
            <p>This element has the following attributes and content
model.</p>
            <h4>Attributes</h4>
            <xsl:call-template name="WriteAttributes" >
                <xsl:with-param name="attlist"
select="xsd:complexType/xsd:attribute" />
            </xsl:call-template>
            <h4>Content Model</h4>
            <xsl:call-template name="WriteContentModel"/>
        </xsl:otherwise>
    </xsl:choose>
</xsl:template>
<!--
Transforms a list of attribute declarations
into a an unordered list (ul).
-->
<xsl:template name="WriteAttributes">

    <xsl:param name="attlist" />

    <xsl:choose>
        <xsl:when test="$attlist">
            <ul>
                <xsl:apply-templates select="$attlist"
mode="local"/>
            </ul>
        </xsl:when>
        <xsl:otherwise>
            <p>This element has no attributes.</p>
        </xsl:otherwise>
    </xsl:choose>
</xsl:template>
<!--
Transforms the content model of an element.
```

```xsl
-->
<xsl:template name="WriteContentModel">
    <xsl:choose>
        <xsl:when test="xsd:complexType/xsd:sequence |
xsd:complexType/xsd:choice">
            <xsl:apply-templates
select="xsd:complexType/xsd:sequence | xsd:complexType/xsd:choice"
mode="contentmodel"/>
        </xsl:when>
        <xsl:when test="xsd:simpleType">
            <xsl:apply-templates select="xsd:simpleType"/>
        </xsl:when>
        <xsl:when test="@type">
            <p>Data of type
    <span class="typename">
                        <a href="#{@type}">
                            <xsl:value-of select="@type"/>
                        </a>
                </span>
            </p>
        </xsl:when>
        <xsl:otherwise>
            <p>EMPTY.</p>
        </xsl:otherwise>
    </xsl:choose>
</xsl:template>
<!--=========================================
COMPLEX TYPE Component
=========================================-->
<!--
Transforms global complex type definitions.
-->
<xsl:template match="xsd:complexType[@name]" mode="global">
    <h2 id="{@name}">
        <span class="typename">
            <xsl:value-of select="@name"/>
        </span> Complex Type
</h2>
    <h3>Attributes</h3>
    <xsl:call-template name="WriteAttributes" >
            <xsl:with-param name="attlist" select="xsd:attribute" />
    </xsl:call-template>
    <h3>Content Model</h3>
    <xsl:apply-templates select="xsd:choice | xsd:sequence"
mode="contentmodel"/>
    <xsl:if test=".//xsd:element[@name]">
        <h3>Local Elements</h3>
        <div style="margin-left:2em; font-size: smaller; ">
            <xsl:apply-templates select=".//xsd:element[@name]"
mode="local"/>
        </div>
```

```
        </xsl:if>
    </xsl:template>
    <!--
Transforms a list of choices into a "|" separate list.
-->
    <xsl:template match="xsd:choice" mode="contentmodel">
        <xsl:param name="separator"/>
        <xsl:text>(</xsl:text>
        <xsl:apply-templates select="xsd:element | xsd:choice |
xsd:sequence" mode="contentmodel">
            <xsl:with-param name="separator"> | </xsl:with-param>
        </xsl:apply-templates>
        <xsl:text>)</xsl:text>
        <xsl:call-template name="ElementOccurrenceConstraints"/>
        <xsl:if test="position() != last()">
            <xsl:value-of select="$separator"/>
        </xsl:if>
        <xsl:text/>
    </xsl:template>
    <!--
Transforms a sequence into a "," separate list.
-->
    <xsl:template match="xsd:sequence" mode="contentmodel">
        <xsl:param name="separator"/>
        <xsl:text>(</xsl:text>
        <xsl:apply-templates select="xsd:element | xsd:choice |
xsd:sequence" mode="contentmodel">
            <xsl:with-param name="separator">,</xsl:with-param>
        </xsl:apply-templates>
        <xsl:text>)</xsl:text>
        <xsl:call-template name="ElementOccurrenceConstraints"/>
        <xsl:if test="position() != last()">
            <xsl:value-of select="$separator"/>
        </xsl:if>
        <xsl:text/>
    </xsl:template>
        <!--
Used by xsd:complexType to create content model.
-->
    <xsl:template match="xsd:element" mode="contentmodel">
    <xsl:param name="separator"/>
    <xsl:choose>
        <xsl:when test="@ref">
            <a href="#{@ref}">
                <xsl:value-of select="@ref"/>
            </a>
        </xsl:when>
        <xsl:otherwise>
            <xsl:value-of select="@name"/>
        </xsl:otherwise>
```

```
</xsl:choose>
<xsl:call-template name="ElementOccurrenceConstraints"/>
<xsl:if test="position() != last()">
     <xsl:value-of select="$separator"/>
</xsl:if>
<xsl:text/>
</xsl:template>
<!--
Transforms occurrence constraints for elements.

*      Zero or more
?      Zero or one
+      One or more
-->
<xsl:template name="ElementOccurrenceConstraints">
<xsl:choose>
     <xsl:when test="@minOccurs='0' and @maxOccurs='unbounded'">
          <xsl:text>*</xsl:text>
     </xsl:when>
     <xsl:when test="(@minOccurs='1' or not(@minOccurs)) and
@maxOccurs='unbounded'">
          <xsl:text>+</xsl:text>
     </xsl:when>
     <xsl:when test="@minOccurs='0' and (@maxOccurs='1' or
not(@maxOccurs))">
          <xsl:text>?</xsl:text>
     </xsl:when>
</xsl:choose>
</xsl:template>

<!--==========================================
SIMPLE TYPE Component
==========================================-->
<!--
Transforms global simple type definitions.
-->
<xsl:template match="xsd:simpleType[@name]" mode="global">
<h2 id="{@name}">
     <span class="typename">
          <xsl:value-of select="@name"/>
     </span> Simple Type
</h2>
<xsl:apply-templates select="xsd:restriction | xsd:list | xsd:union" />
</xsl:template>
<!--
Transforms local simple type definitions.
-->
<xsl:template match="xsd:simpleType">
<dl>
     <dt>
```

```xml
            <xsl:if test="@name">
                <span class="typename">
                    <xsl:value-of select="@name"/>
                </span>.
</xsl:if>
        </dt>
        <dd>
        <xsl:apply-templates select="xsd:restriction | xsd:list |
xsd:union" />
        </dd>
</dl>
</xsl:template>

<xsl:template match="xsd:restriction">
<xsl:choose>
    <xsl:when test="@base">
        <p>Based on the <span class="typename">
                    <xsl:value-of select="@base"/>
                </span> type.</p>
    </xsl:when>
    <xsl:otherwise>
        <xsl:apply-templates select="xsd:simpleType"/>
    </xsl:otherwise>
</xsl:choose>
<dl>
    <xsl:for-each select="xsd:minExclusive | xsd:minInclusive |
xsd:maxExclusive | xsd:maxInclusive | xsd:totalDigits |
xsd:fractionDigits | xsd:length | xsd:minLength | xsd:maxLength |
xsd:enumeration | xsd:whiteSpace | xsd:pattern">
        <dt>
            <xsl:value-of select="name(.)"/>
        </dt>
        <dd>
            <xsl:value-of select="@value"/>
        </dd>
    </xsl:for-each>
</dl>
</xsl:template>
<xsl:template match="xsd:list">
    <p>A list of:</p>
    <xsl:choose>
        <xsl:when test="@itemType">
            <p>
                <span class="typename">
                    <xsl:value-of select="@itemType"/>
                </span>
            </p>
        </xsl:when>
        <xsl:otherwise>
            <xsl:apply-templates select="xsd:simpleType"/>
```

```xml
            </xsl:otherwise>
        </xsl:choose>
    </xsl:template>
    <xsl:template match="xsd:union">
        <p>A union of:</p>
        <p>
            <span class="typename">
                <xsl:value-of select="@memberTypes"/>
            </span>
        </p>
        <xsl:apply-templates select="xsd:simpleType"/>
    </xsl:template>
    <!--=========================================
    Result XHTML document template
    =========================================-->
    <xsl:template match="xsd:schema">
        <html>
            <head>
                <title>XML Schema</title>
                <link rel="stylesheet" type="text/css"
href="xsdhtml.css"/>
            </head>
            <body>
                <h1>Quick Reference</h1>
                <h2>Index</h2>
                <table>
                    <xsl:if test="xsd:element">
                        <tr>
                            <th>Elements</th>
                        </tr>
                        <xsl:apply-templates
select="xsd:element[@name]" mode="toc">
                            <xsl:sort select="@name"/>
                        </xsl:apply-templates>
                    </xsl:if>
                    <xsl:if test="xsd:attribute">
                        <tr>
                            <th>Attributes</th>
                        </tr>
                        <xsl:apply-templates
select="xsd:attribute[@name]" mode="toc">
                            <xsl:sort select="@name"/>
                        </xsl:apply-templates>
                    </xsl:if>
                    <xsl:if test="xsd:complexType | xsd:simpleType">
                        <tr>
                            <th>Types</th>
                        </tr>
                        <xsl:apply-templates
select="xsd:complexType[@name] | xsd:simpleType[@name]" mode="toc">
```

```xslt
                                        <xsl:sort select="@name"/>
                                    </xsl:apply-templates>
                                </xsl:if>
                        </table>
                        <legend>
                            <h2>Legend</h2>
                            <p>The following syntax is used to describe content
models:</p>
                            <dl>
                                <dt>*</dt>
                                <dd>Zero or many</dd>
                                <dt>?</dt>
                                <dd>Zero or one</dd>
                                <dt>+</dt>
                                <dd>One or many</dd>
                                <dt>a , b</dt>
                                <dd>a followed by b</dd>
                                <dt>a | b</dt>
                                <dd>a or b</dd>
                            </dl>
                        </legend>
                        <xsl:if test="xsd:element[@name] |
 xsd:attribute[@name]">
                            <h1>Element and Attribute Declarations</h1>
                            <p>The following elements and attributes are
declared.</p>
                            <xsl:apply-templates select="xsd:element[@name] |
xsd:attribute[@name]" mode="global">
                                    <xsl:sort select="@name"/>
                            </xsl:apply-templates>
                        </xsl:if>
                        <xsl:if test="xsd:complexType[@name] |
xsd:simpleType[@name]">
                            <h1>Type Definitions</h1>
                            <p>The following types are defined.</p>
                            <xsl:apply-templates
select="xsd:complexType[@name] | xsd:simpleType[@name]" mode="global">
                                    <xsl:sort select="@name"/>
                            </xsl:apply-templates>
                        </xsl:if>
                </body>
        </html>
</xsl:template>
<!--
Table of Content (TOC)
Creates a table row for each named primary XML Schema component.
-->
<xsl:template match="xsd:element | xsd:attribute| xsd:simpleType |
xsd:complexType" mode="toc">
    <tr>
        <td>
```

```
                    <a href="#{@name}">
                        <xsl:value-of select="@name"/>
                    </a>
                </td>
            </tr>
        </xsl:template>
    </xsl:stylesheet>
```

CHAPTER 8

XSLT and Style

X SLT is about transformation, but its origin is in the W3C XML Style Language, XSL. Styling is the rendering of information into a form that is suitable for consumption by a target audience. Because the audience can change for a given set of information, we often need to apply different styling for that information in order to obtain dissimilar renderings in order to meet the needs of each audience. Perhaps some information needs to be rearranged to make more sense to the reader. Perhaps some information needs to be highlighted differently to bring focus to key content.

It does not matter if your target is a presentation-oriented structure, for example, or a structure that is appropriate for another markup-based system. Modeling practice should focus on both the business reasons and inherent relationships existing in the semantics behind the information being described (as such, the vocabularies are then content-oriented). For example, emphasized text is often confused with a particular format in which it is rendered. Where we could model information by using a <b> element type for eventual rendering in bold face, we would be better off modeling the information by using an <emph> element type. In this way, we capture the reason for marking up information (that it is emphasized from surrounding information), and we do not lock the downstream targets into only using a bold face for rendering.

Many times, the midstream or downstream processes need only rearrange, relabel, or synthesize the information for a target purpose and never apply any semantics of style for rendering purposes. Transformation tasks stand alone in such cases, meeting the processing needs without introducing rendering issues.

A Web user agent (typically known as a browser, although non-displaying user agents are becoming more common, such as search engines and translation engines) does not know how to render an element named <customer>. The HTML vocabulary used to render the customer information could be as follows:

```
<p>From: <i>(Customer Reference) <b>cust123</b></i>
</p>
```

This example illustrates these two distinct styling steps: transforming the instance of the XML vocabulary into a new instance according to a vocabulary of rendering semantics and formatting the instance of the rendering vocabulary in the user agent.

When using a formatting semantics vocabulary as the rendering language, the objective for a style sheet writer is to convert an XML instance of some arbitrary XML vocabulary into an instance of the formatting semantics vocabulary. The result of transformation cannot contain any user-defined vocabulary construct (for example, an address, customer identifier, or purchase order number construct) because the rendering agent would not know what to do with constructs labeled with these foreign, unknown identifiers.

Of course, a problem occurs when the presentation requires a change in the information. This situation can occur when a document needs to be summarized for mobile presentation, for instance, or when the same document should be presented to both marketing and engineering. As you have surmised by now, however, it is quite possible to create transformation sheets that can perform most of these adaptations.

An XML development team will probably consist of several people who have different skill sets. For example, an information architect, or what we might once have called a "knowledge engineer," possesses the background and aptitude for designing and implementing document structure. That is the DTD or schema developer. Distinctly different is the software engineer who uses *Application Programming Interfaces* (APIs) such as SAX or the *Document Object Model* (DOM) to access and process documents programmatically. And then, there is a transformation specialist. This position is held by someone who uses XSLT to convert, translate, and transform XML into other formats, often for the purpose of data exchange with other systems.

The problem arises because this last person, or more importantly his or her skill set, is not very well understood. Most managers push these responsibilities onto their user-interface designers. After all, these are style sheets, right? In fact, XSLT is a verbose language with far more complexity than the relatively straightforward CSS for style, or DOM for document manipulation. Though not a traditional programming language, XSLT includes features that enable you to walk document trees, create, access, and modify individual nodes, perform iterative and conditional processing, and much more. Thus, XSLT is more similar to a declarative programming language that uses XML syntax than a styling language used for layout.

It is this misconception that XSL is a formatting mechanism that causes XSL in general, and XSLT in particular, to be overlooked. Managers, often thinking that XSL is for formatting, decide that XSL should not be used because their applications are not displaying XML—they are using it for data exchange. In the end, you either wind up with resistant designers who are overwhelmed by the syntax or programmers who will not touch XSLT because "it's not a programming language."

You can solve this problem by dynamically generating XSLT style sheets by using the DOM. One benefit of this approach is that generating style sheets reduces the number of static style sheets that you must write to do all the transformations required. Also, you can use dynamic style-sheet generation to convert older style sheets into the newer XSL standards. Even if you are not developing style sheets, the techniques presented here will be instructive for anyone who is creating complex XML documents by using the DOM. Documents become more streamlined and manageable when designers effectively separate presentation from Web markup.

While style sheets have expanded to include detailed syntax for broad presentation options, support is often limited, buggy, or sometimes completely nonexistent within certain versions of popular Web browsers.

Part of the problem is that style sheets have gotten a bad reputation. While frustrating to most Web designers and developers, style sheets also suffer from poor marketing. This situation is typical of complex or emerging technologies, and it is a serious problem because it makes people leery of trying them. XHTML is a good example: Poor marketing equals a misunderstood tool. By being compared only with early versions of HTML (before version 4), it has come to be percieved as complex. However, XHTML Basic is actually simpler than HTML 4, and simpler to use.

Even the most sophisticated developer is hesitant to wade through convoluted W3C documents in order to unravel which markup technologies actually work. It is a challenge that only a very brave or very patient person is willing to tackle.

Having understood a little more about how XSLT is used in the Web development process, we can start to look at the differences between CSS and XSL.

A Style Sheet Briefing

XSL is a style language that is intended to format XML documents for output onto a number of various devices, such as printers, CD-ROMs, and computer screens. Just as one of its predecessors in the field, PostScript, it is better suited to present information when the processing can be done in a batch, such as for printing or for CD-ROMs. For onscreen presentation, the W3C has developed a different language, CSS. Unfortunately, CSS is not an XML language at present, and it therefore does not enable the transformations that are possible with XSL, for instance. For lightweight presentations such as presentations of HTML documents, however, CSS is better suited.

Another unfortunate point is that the implementations of CSS are quite spotty. The best, in the Norwegian Opera browser, is not a full implementation of CSS2 because there are two distinct versions of CSS: CSS1 and CSS2.

We said previously that the rendering of an element is no longer described in the document but rather in a style sheet that may be external to the document or inline. Style sheets are a method in which to apply a design to an information set. This design is usually a graphic design, but it might as well be a vocal design in the case of aural style sheets (where the formatting determines how the text is spoken—emphasis will be stressed, strong will be pronounced louder, and so forth).

Style instructions in HTML, as in XHTML and XML, can be referenced where the style sheet is applied to multiple documents. These instructions can be used to give a Web site a common look and feel, and they can also be used (when the style sheet is changed) to apply a different look and feel to a Web page that is to be shown on a client. So far, style sheets have not been applied to WML, but the WAP Forum is actively working on this issue, and the mechanisms in place in WML can easily be used to apply style sheets. When you have only a telephone with four lines of text, applying a style sheet is not a high priority, so this issue is not on the short-term roadmap of the WAP Forum. In XML, you create documents with tags that are semantic—they convey a meaning, either in themselves or about the content. They say nothing about the presentation. If they do, it becomes virtually impossible to create a presentation that works on more than one type of device. You describe how the tags are to be presented in a separate document—a stylesheet (where you can say that the content of the element <seminar> should always be bold, Times Roman, 20 points, for example). Style sheets are referenced by means of a special processing instruction as follows:

The advantages of defining the formatting in a separate document should be clear. It can be centrally maintained, and you do not have to define all of the formatting every time you create a document. You can also set formatting rules that apply to all corporate presentations or to all presentations that are done on a certain class of device. You can also nest one style sheet into another and let it take over for a set of objects inside a document. For instance, if you are quoting a section of another document, you can let the original style hold.

If you have problems understanding the concept of separation of content and presentation (which is what style sheets are about), try reading your document aloud. The formatting will, as you notice, be quite different from what it was on the printed page, but it is the same information. Surfing audibly is a big help to the blind and to those who are sitting with a mobile phone to their ear or driving.

The rendering rules become very different. If you are listening to a text, it does not matter if it is rendered in Zapf Antique or Arial Bold. The relevant concern is to render the inflections and intonations correctly. The CSS2 style sheet standard of the W3C has special functions that are built in to handle aural rendering. But just as you have to change your presentation to reflect the limited presentation properties of your screen, you have to change it when you want to present it audibly. How to do this restructuring is being worked out in the W3C Voice Browsing working group.

Style sheets cannot only be referenced, but you can also apply style sheet instructions inside a document, inline to a specific XML/XHTML element (as part of the content), or you can embed them in the document itself. They will then override each other (the most specific overriding the more general). An inline style will override an embedded style, which will override a referenced style.

Style instructions in CSS consist of rules for the formatting of the tag, which have two parts: selector and declaration. The selector designates the tag, and the declaration declares how it should be formatted. The following is a style sheet rule:

```
h1 {font-size: 18pt; font-style: bold}
```

You might ask what happened to the angle brackets. The answer is that the CSS language actually precedes much of the XML work, and so it has been developed by using its own conventions. There is a formatting language closer to XML called XSL, and work is going on in the W3C to normalize the formatting models in XSL and CSS. This work is for the future at this point, and the preferred way today is to apply CSS to XML documents.

In the preceding example, H1 is the selector and the part in { } is the declaration. It consists of two parts: the properties and their values. In this example, there are two properties: the font-size and the font-style; the values of these are 18 point and bold, respectively. As you understand, you cannot invent your own style properties and values. They are all regulated in the CSS specification.

Besides styling the text content, style sheets can be used to designate positions on a page for documents and positions within a grid of boxes for elements. They can also be used for floating images over the text and floating text in relation to other parts of the text (for instance, menus).

There are style sheet editors on the market that make it easy to modify and view style sheets. The easiest way to work with style sheets is to view them in an editor and then add or remove instructions as you work with them. Remember, though, that the rendering is still not intended to be pixel-perfect—there will inevitably be some differences in presentation. If you require the rendering to be the same in all different formats, you should avoid computer-based presentations as you have understood from the reasoning earlier in this chapter. Mobile phones simply do not have the presentation capabilities of a large computer.

Documents with the same content but different formatting using style sheets can be formatted differently by using the selector mechanisms in the style sheets. If you do not, they might look different in XML and HTML browsers. To minimize the problems of crossing over from HTML to XML, use lower-case names for all element and attribute names even in the style sheet and add the <tbody> element in tables (the XML user agent will not automatically infer it, but the HTML browser does).

CSS defines different conformance rules for HTML and XML documents. Be aware that the HTML rules apply to XHTML documents delivered as HTML, and the XML rules apply to XHTML documents delivered as XML (that is, the MIME type as set in the Web server is text/html or text/xml). You might need to make sure that the formats and the style sheets match.

CSS properties enable you to specify a wide range of display characteristics for an element. These properties are "decorations" on the source tree. In XSL, however, you must specify both the result object and its properties.

For example, the following CSS fragment formats a quote as an indented block with some font changes:

```
quote { display: block; font-size: 90%; margin-left: 0.5in; margin-
right: 0.5in; }
```

In XSL, the same formatting could be achieved with XSL formatting objects by using this template:

```
<xsl:template pattern="quote">
  <fo:block font-size="90%"
      indent-start="0.5in"
      indent-end="0.5in">
    <xsl:process-children/>
  </fo:block>
</xsl:template>
```

The advantage of both constructing a new object and applying properties to it can be seen when you consider the things that you cannot do with CSS properties alone:

- Change the order of elements for display.

- Process elements more than once.

- Suppress elements in one place and present them in another.

- Add generated text to the presentation (CSS2 introduced a simple form of pre- and post-element generated text but falls short of solving the general problem).

XSL and CSS have similar goals, and it is useful to compare them. XSL is more powerful than CSS in many ways, but it is also more complex. XSL and CSS are not competitors. For some common applications (such as HTML+ documents that use mostly HTML but have a few extra non-HTML tags thrown in), CSS will be the easiest solution. For others, the manipulative power of XSL will be required.

Although very different, XSL and CSS have two things in common: each provides a mechanism for selecting elements and for specifying how the selected elements are to be presented. CSS uses selectors and properties in this way:

```
selector { properties; }
```

XSL uses patterns and formatting objects that look very similar to the (by now) familiar XSLT syntax:

```
<xsl:template pattern="pattern">
<formatting objects/>
</xsl:template>_
```

CSS2 (which is considerably more complex than CSS1 with respect to selectors) and XSL each provide a rich set of features for selecting elements. In XSL, the formatting objects perform the same function as CSS. Formatting objects are a much more powerful way of styling documents, however, and are correspondingly both more complex and demanding in terms of processing power.

The *Extensible Stylesheet Language* (XSL) Working Draft describes a vocabulary that is recognized by a rendering agent to take abstract expressions and format the document into a form suited to a particular medium of presentation. The hierarchical vocabulary of XSL captures formatting semantics for rendering textual and graphic information in different media. The rendering agent, typically a browser (but it may also be a printing process) is responsible for interpreting an instance of the vocabulary for a given medium in order to create a presentable result.

Members of WSSSL, an association of researchers and developers who are passionate about the application of markup technologies in today's information technology infrastructure, endorse both XSLT and XSL.

The XSL format is no different in concept and architecture than using HTML and CSS as a hierarchical vocabulary for rendering a set of information in a Web browser. In essence, we are transforming our XML documents into their final display form by transforming instances of our XML vocabularies into instances of a particular rendering vocabulary.

Because XML does not use predefined tags (we can use any tags we want), the meanings of these tags are not understood: <table> could mean an HTML table or maybe a piece of furniture. Because of the nature of XML, there is no standard way to display an XML document.

Just as with HTML, a style sheet writer who is utilizing XSL for rendering must transform each user construct into a rendering construct in order to direct the rendering agent to produce the desired result. By learning and understanding the semantics behind the constructs of XSL formatting, the style sheet writer can create an instance of the formatting vocabulary expressing the desired layout of the final result (for example, area geometry, spacing, font metrics, and so on), with each piece of information in the result coming from either the source data or from the style sheet itself.

Most of the XSL formatting objects (so far, only available in working drafts) draw their semantics from a combination of the *Document Style Semantics and Specification Language* (DSSSL, defined by ISO/IEC 10179:1996) and CSS formatting models.

Here is an example of a set of formatting objects to describe how an element should be formatted (for example, <customer>). Note that although the styling is added to the content in the same way as with a CSS style sheet applied to an HTML document, the document maintains its inherent semantics (in other words, the <customer> element is still known as <customer> and is not transformed into <h1>):

```
<fo:block space-before.optimum="20pt" font-size="20pt">From:
<fo:inline-sequence font-style="italic">(Customer Reference)
<fo:inline-sequence font-weight="bold">cust123</fo:inline-sequence>
</fo:inline-sequence>
</fo:block>
```

The following list describes some common formatting objects defined by the first XSL working draft:

- page-sequence defines a sequence of pages. The page master describes the formatting of pages in a sequence. Currently, only a simple-page-master is defined, which is sufficient for simple, single-column Web or print publishing.

- Queue gathers content for later insertion into an area or set of areas.

- Sequence is a general wrapper for inline or block content. A sequence provides a wrapper on which shared, inherited properties can be hung.

- Block represents a block of text. Paragraphs, titles, and figure captions are all examples of blocks.

- List defines a list. List elements contain list-item elements, which further contain a list-item-label and a list-item-body.

- Graphic holds an image or vector graphic.

- Link defines a link. A link-end-locator defines the target of a link.

Associating Style Sheets with Documents

Style sheets can be associated with an XML document by using a processing instruction whose target is xml-stylesheet. This processing instruction follows the behavior of the HTML 4.0 LINK element <LINK REL="stylesheet">.

The xml-stylesheet processing instruction is parsed in the same way as a start tag, with the exception that entities other than predefined entities must not be referenced.

The following grammar is given by using the same notation as the grammar in the XML recommendation. Symbols in the grammar that are not defined here are defined in the XML recommendation.

The semantics of the pseudo-attributes are exactly as with <LINK REL="stylesheet"> in HTML 4.0, with the exception of the alternate pseudo-attribute. If alternate="yes" is specified, then the processing instruction has the semantics of <LINK REL="alternate stylesheet"> instead of <LINK REL="stylesheet">.

Because the value of the href attribute is a URI reference, it might be a relative URI and might contain a fragment identifier. In particular, the URI reference might contain only a fragment identifier. Such a URI reference is a reference to a part of the document containing the xml-stylesheet processing instruction. The consequence is that the xml-stylesheet processing instruction enables style sheets to be embedded in the same document as the xml-stylesheet processing instruction.

In some cases, style sheets might be linked with an XML document by means external to the document—for example, earlier versions of HTTP-enabled style sheets to be associated with XML documents by means of the Link header. Any links to style sheets that are specified externally to the document are considered to occur before the links specified by the xml-stylesheet processing instructions. This situation is the same as in HTML 4.0.

Here are some examples from HTML 4.0 with the corresponding processing instruction:

```
<LINK href="mystyle.css" rel="style sheet" type="text/css">
<?xml-stylesheet href="mystyle.css" type="text/css"?>

<LINK href="mystyle.css" title="Compact" rel="stylesheet"
type="text/css">

<?xml-stylesheet href="mystyle.css" title="Compact" type="text/css"?>

<LINK href="mystyle.css" title="Medium" rel="alternate stylesheet"
type="text/css">

<?xml-stylesheet alternate="yes" href="mystyle.css" title="Medium"
type="text/css"?>
```

Multiple xml-stylesheet processing instructions are also allowed with exactly the same semantics as with LINK REL="stylesheet". For example,

```
<LINK rel="alternate stylesheet" title="compact" href="small-base.css"
type="text/css">
<LINK rel="alternate stylesheet" title="compact" href="small-extras.css"
type="text/css">
<LINK rel="alternate stylesheet" title="big print" href="bigprint.css"
type="text/css">
<LINK rel="stylesheet" href="common.css" type="text/css">
```

would be equivalent to

```
<?xml-stylesheet alternate="yes" title="compact" href="small-base.css"
type="text/css"?>
<?xml-stylesheet alternate="yes" title="compact" href="small-extras.css"
type="text/css"?>
<?xml-stylesheet alternate="yes" title="big print" href="bigprint.css"
type="text/css"?>
<?xml-stylesheet href="common.css" type="text/css"?>
```

An XML style sheet declaration is used to associate an XML document with a CSS or XSLT style sheet. The syntax used is identical except for the value of the type attribute, which will be either text/css or text/xsl depending on which flavor of style sheet is used.

Here are the two variations side-by-side in order to illustrate the different values of the type attribute:

```
<?xml-stylesheet type="text/xsl" href="glossary.xsl"?>
<?xml-stylesheet type="text/css" href="glossary.css"?>
```

The correct placement of the style sheet declaration is within a document's prolog (after the XML declaration and before the root element):

```
<?xml version="1.0"?>
<?xml-stylesheet type="text/xsl" href="glossarytable.xsl"?>
<glossary>É</glossary>
```

Device Independence and Styling

The rendering semantics of much of the XSL vocabulary are device independent, so we can use one set of constructs regardless of the rendering medium. It is the rendering agent's responsibility to interpret these constructs accordingly. In this way, the XSL semantics can be interpreted for print, display, aural, or other presentations. There are, indeed, some specialized semantics that we can use to influence rendering on particular media, although these are just icing on the cake.

Web designers quite commonly feel that they have to create a special version of their documents for each user agent in which it will be viewed (for example, one for Netscape and another for Microsoft). If you perform this task in HTML, applying the formatting semantics built in to the browsers (not the language, actually—there is no specification anywhere

Table 8.1 CSS Media Types

MEDIA TYPE DESCRIPTOR	DESCRIPTION
all	The style is suitable for all devices.
aural	The style is intended for speech synthesizers. In CSS-2, there are a handful of properties related to aural style sheets.
braille	The style is intended for braille tactile feedback devices.
embossed	The style is intended for paginated braille printers.
handheld	The style is intended for handheld devices.
print	The style is intended for paginated media (like the printed page) or when representing the printed page on a screen (such as a print preview mode).
projection	The style is intended for projectors and printing to film slides and transparencies.
screen	The style is intended for color computer screens.
tty	The style is intended for devices using a fixed-pitch character grid, such as teletypes.
tv	The style is intended for television-type devices.

for how a <H1> should look), you will make it impossible to use the data for other purposes as well as very hard for people who have different display requirements (for example, mobile users but also people who cannot see the screen and who are forced to use screen readers).

Each of these devices is categorized as belonging to a certain media type. Media types include things like screen for computer monitors, print for printed paper, and aural for speech synthesizers.

So far, we have used two media types: screen and print. The CSS Level 2 specification identifies a handful of other media types and qualifies this list as not being considered definitive (see Table 8.1). With the explosions of Internet appliances, there are certain to be an increasing number of new media types.

As shown in the table, CSS Level 2 has 10 media types that represent target devices for XHTML content. The names of these media types are called media type descriptors. The media type descriptors are used as values for several case-sensitive attributes described as follows and must be in lower case.

Not every style sheet property is appropriate for every target device. The volume property, for example, refers to what is known as the median volume of a waveform. This property is clearly related to aural media types (in other words, sound) and not to visually oriented media types.

In fact, it turns out that there are relationships between the different media types. These relationships are called media groups, and the W3C identifies four of these media groups:

- Continuous or paginated media
- Visual, aural, or tactile media
- Grid or bitmap media
- Interactive or static media

Each media type is a member of one or more of these media groups. For example, the screen media type is a member of the continuous, visual, bitmap, interactive, and static media groups.

Continuous or paginated media refers to the surface on which content is rendered. If the surface can always extend to hold all of the content, the media is considered continuous. If the surface has a limited size and additional surfaces must be created to hold all of the content, the media are said to be paginated. Computer screens are continuous, and printed pages are paginated. We will talk about paginated media later in this chapter.

Visual, aural, or tactile media refers to how the information is presented to the user:

1. If the user must use his or her eyes to consume the content, then the media is said to be visual.
2. If the user must use his or her ears to consume the content, then the media is said to be aural.
3. If the user must use the sense of touch to consume the content, then the media is said to be tactile.

Computer screens are visual; voice browsers and screen readers are aural; and Braille printers are tactile.

Grid or bitmap media refers to how the visual or tactile information is rendered. If the information is rendered in a predefined grid layout (where every character has the same amount of space), then the media

Table 8.2 The Relationship between Media Types and Groups

Media Types		Media Groups	
CONTINUOUS OR PAGINATED	**VISUAL, AURAL, OR TACTILE**	**GRID OR BITMAP**	**INTERACTIVE OR STATIC**
aural continuous	aural	neither	both
braille continuous	tactile	grid	both
embossed paginated	tactile	grid	both
handheld both	visual	both	both
print paginated	visual	bitmap	static
projection paginated	visual	bitmap	static
screen continuous	visual	bitmap	both
tty continuous	visual	grid	both
tv both	visual, aural	bitmap	both

is said to be grid-based. If the information is rendered pixel by pixel (every character uses whatever space it needs), then the media is said to be bitmap-based. Teletypes are grid-based, and computer screens are bitmap-based.

Interactive or static media refers to whether the user can interact with the content. As would be expected, when the user can interact with the content, the media is said to be interactive. When the user cannot interact with the content, the media is said to be static. Computer screens are said to be interactive, and printed pages are said to be static.

Table 8.2 summarizes the relationships between media types and media groups.

Each CSS property is only valid for one or more media groups. When you are tailoring a presentation to a particular media type, you need to identify the appropriate media group and determine whether you can control the desired property for that media group.

You associate a style sheet with a document by embedding it or linking it to the document. There are four different mechanisms for specifying dependencies between style sheets and media types:

- The style element for embedding CSS
- The link element for external CSS
- @media rules
- @import rules

Actually, there is a fifth mechanism, which is why we raise the question about device independency in this book. You can transform the document to an appropriate presentation by using XSLT. This action might, in cases where the display allows it, mean only inserting a link to a different style sheet in the document. But it might also mean filtering out content.

As with all methods, it has its advantages and disadvantages. If you do it in the server, it will mean that the document that is transmitted over the connection from the server (or a proxy) to the client will be much smaller, because you only have to include a link to a style sheet (and that might already be cached on the client). Smaller means faster, which means less waiting time for the user (which means less frustration and more satisfaction with what he or she receives from you).

You can use XSLT style sheets to transform XML documents to HTML, which is specifically formatted for a certain browser type. For example, if a Netscape Navigator 4 browser requests a document, I detect the browser and the version and attach the style sheet for that particular browser. Because I have style sheets for Navigator 3 and 4, Internet Explorer 3, 4, and 5, and a generic one for other browsers, this situation results in a half dozen XSLT documents. I have several different types of documents, however (that is, documents of differing structures), so the propagation of style sheets grows exponentially.

This situation becomes a problem when you need to change something, like adding a new element type for a particular class of XML documents. Because your XSLT style sheets rely on the structure of your documents, a simple change such as this one could affect24 or more style sheets. That is far too fragile for my taste. Generating style sheets dynamically solves this problem. That is, because a program can now generate my style sheets, all I have to do is modify a few lines of code and I am done.

The disadvantage is that it is no longer a general document but is specifically adapted to the service on which it will be presented. Butbecause it can be assumed (given the stateless nature of HTTP) that it will only be used once anyway, that is fine. (HTTP does not have a memory of what the client does, so every time you make a request, you essentially have a fresh start in your relationship with the server.)

The beauty of it, however, is that by using XSLT, it is possible to not only provide for a fixed set of presentations, but also to actually create a chain of style sheets that enable you to create the appropriate document based on the input from the client.

First, let's assume that we have three documents. The first is the source document that you are requesting by either clicking a link or typing the URI http://www.historybuff.org/Napoleon in your browser. The second is the style sheet. You have created four different style sheets for each of the CSS media types (as you understand, this method can be extended to an infinite amount of styles, but then they would be hard to fit into a book). The third is a parameterization of the request that is created by using CC/PP.

CSS style sheets contain formatting rules, called statements, that consist of a selector to designate which elements the rule applies to and a declaration specifying which formatting properties should be applied.

A CSS selector identifies the element to which the declaration applies.

The declaration consists of a formatting property (such as text-weight) and a value (such as bold).

Here is an example of a CSS statement:

```
title          {font-weight:  bold}
  |                 |          |
selector        property     value
```

It is common for multiple style declarations to be grouped and applied to the same selector. Semi-colons are used between each declaration, and curly braces surround the completed set.

```
title           {font-weight:  bold;
           font-style:  normal;
           font-family:  helvetica
              }
```

A comma-separated list can be used to group selectors in order to enable declarations or groups of declarations to apply to multiple element types.

```
title, subtitle, name       {font-weight: bold}
```

Because the style sheet does not have to be included in the document but can be linked from it, you do not have to create the style sheet in the XSLT transformation sheet. It is sufficient if you include a link to it. So, to link to somestyle.css, I write my XSL code to look like the following:

```
<!-- Root template -->
<xsl:template match="/">
    <HTML>
     <HEAD>
...
        <!-- Import CSS Styles -->
        <LINK REL="STYLESHEET" TYPE="text/css" href="somestyle.css">
</xsl:template>
```

Mobile Presentation

If you have an XHTML document and want to present it on a mobile phone, there are several things you can do. If the phone is a WAP phone (which most mobile phones sold in western Europe are now), you can chop it into cards in a WML deck. The advantage is that it is relatively sparse, and if you also use the WMLscript language (which is a very lightweight language but correspondingly sparse in functionality), you can include some interactive features in your document. If you have a WAP 2.0 mobile phone, you will instead use XHTML with WML elements inserted into the text. Or, if the mobile phone supports CSS, you can use the paged media property of CSS to chunk the document up into presentation units. Because it turns out that mobile users have a different way of accessing the Web and have different reasons for doing it, you cannot take a document and transform it willy-nilly. You actually have to think about how you transform your document and especially what you put into it.

Now, let's look at a simple application: the winning lottery numbers in the state lottery. This application is typical, where everybody wants to know if they are the winner and they really care about only the highest wins. We might also make it possible to show the result file on a mobile phone.

The state lottery mainframes generate an intermediary format for transformation onto the Web and other display formats. This document is in an intentional intermediary format for demonstration purposes (actually, I have borrowed it from the XSLT specification). A transformation sheet can be used to create an XHTML file as well as a WML file.

The DTD for this file is very simple:

```
<!ELEMENT doc (section*)>
<!ELEMENT section (title,(para|note)*)>
<!ELEMENT title (#PCDATA|emph)*>
<!ELEMENT para (#PCDATA|emph)*>
<!ELEMENT note (#PCDATA|emph)*>
<!ELEMENT emph (#PCDATA|emph)*>
```

The following document is an XML document that follows that DTD:

```
<?xml version='1.0'?>
<?xml:stylesheet type="text/xsl" href="wap-style.xsl"?>
<!DOCTYPE doc SYSTEM "results.dtd">
          <doc>
          <section>
          <title>State Lottery Numbers</title>
          <para><emph>Draw of June 4, 2000</emph></para>
          <para><emph>Grand Prize Winner</emph></para>
          <para>2389104765</para>
          <note>Prize money is paid out at the central lottery office
only. Unless collected before June 4, 2001, the money defaults back to
the treasury </note>
          </section>
          <section>
          <title>Junior Grand Prize</title>
          <para>3490215876</para>
          <note>Prize money is paid out at the central lottery office
<emph>only</emph>. Unless collected before June 4, 2001, the money
defaults back to the treasury. </note>
          </section>
          </doc>
```

This file is relatively easy to divide in two cards or to display on a Web page. It is not independent of the presentation formats, however. It often helps to use several tools in parallel to design the XML source and the WML and HTML presentations in parallel. In a larger application with more presentation formats, this setup would become unsustainable. Then, the method of marking up the objects separately and the use of transformation sheets to generate separate presentations would make more sense. The transformation sheet for transforming the previous file to XHTML would look like the following example:

```
<?xml version='1.0'?>
<xsl:stylesheet
        xmlns:xsl="http://www.w3.org/1999/XSL/Transform"
        xmlns="http://www.w3.org/1999/xhtml">
<xsl:strip-space elements="results"/>

<xsl:template match="results">
 <html>
   <head>
     <title>
       <xsl:value-of select="title"/>
     </title>
   </head>
   <body>
     <xsl:apply-templates/>
   </body>
 </html>
</xsl:template>

<xsl:template match="title">
  <h1>
    <xsl:apply-templates/>
  </h1>
</xsl:template>

<xsl:template match="para">
  <p>
    <xsl:apply-templates/>
  </p>
</xsl:template>

<xsl:template match="note">
  <p class="note">
    NOTE:
    <xsl:apply-templates/>
  </p>
</xsl:template>

<xsl:template match="emph">
  <em>
    <xsl:apply-templates/>
  </em>
</xsl:template>

</xsl:stylesheet>
```

The XHTML page would look like the following:

```
<!DOCTYPE html PUBLIC "-//W3C//DTD XHTML Basic 1.0//EN"
"http://www.w3.org/TR/xhtml-basic/xhtml-basic10.dtd">
<head>
<title>State Lottery Numbers</title>
</head>
<body>
<h1> State Lottery Numbers</h1>
<h2> Draw of June 4, 2000</h2>
<h3>Grand Prize</h3>
<p>2389104765</p>
<h3>Junior Grand Prize</h3>
<p>This is the <em>other grand prize</em> winner</p>
<p>3490215876</p>
<p class="note">
<em>NOTE: </em>Prize money is paid out at the central lottery office
only</p>
<p class="note">
<em>NOTE: </em>Unless collected before June 4, 2001, the money defaults
back to the treasury</p>
</body>
</html>
```

This example looks okay on a regular HTML browser (nothing fancy), as shown in Figure 8.1.

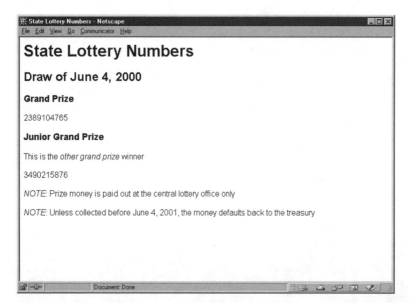

Figure 8.1 The page is without frills when displayed on an HTML browser.

That code worked for XHTML, but the same file can be transformed into WML by using the following transformation sheet:

```
<?xml version='1.0'?>
<xsl:stylesheet
        xmlns:xsl="http://www.w3.org/1999/XSL/Transform"
        result-ns="">
<xsl:strip-space elements="results section"/>
<xsl:output method="xml" indent="yes"/>

<xsl:template match="results">
 <wml>
<xsl:apply-templates/>
</wml>
</xsl:template>

<xsl:template match="section">
  <card>
     <p>
    <xsl:apply-templates/>
     </p>
  </card>
</xsl:template>

<xsl:template match="section/title">
  <strong>
    <xsl:apply-templates/>
  </strong>
<br/>
</xsl:template>

<xsl:template match="para">
<em>
    <xsl:apply-templates/>
</em>
<br/>
</xsl:template>

<xsl:template match="note">
<em>NOTE: </em>
    <xsl:apply-templates/>
  <br/>
</xsl:template>

<xsl:template match="emph">
  <em>
    <xsl:apply-templates/>
  </em>
</xsl:template>

</xsl:stylesheet>
```

The transformation sheet would produce the following WML deck as a result:

```
<?xml version="1.0"?>
<!DOCTYPE wml PUBLIC "-//WAPFORUM//DTD WML 1.1//EN"
                    "http://www.wapforum.org/DTD/wml_1.1.xml">


<!-- WapIDE SDK WML Application Sun Jan 02 21:29:54 Singapore Standard
Time 2000 -->
<wml>
    <card>
        <p>
          <strong>State Lottery Numbers</strong>
        <br/>
          <em>Draw of June 4, 2000</em>
        <br/>
          <em>Grand Prize Winner</em>
        <br/>
          2389104765
        <br/>
          <strong>NOTE:</strong>Prize money is paid out at the central
lottery office <em>only</em>. Unless collected before June 4, 2001, the
money defaults back to the treasury.
        <br/>
        </p>
    </card>
    <card>
        <p>
          <strong>Junior Grand Prize</strong>
        <br/>
          3490215876
        <br/>
          <strong>NOTE:</strong>Prize money is paid out at the central
lottery office <em>only</em>. Unless collected before June 4, 2001, the
money defaults back to the treasury.
        <br/>
        </p>
    </card>
</wml>
```

On the screen of the mobile telephone, the WML result would look like Figure 8.2.

Now, as you see, the user has to scroll through the page on his or her mobile. While scrolling might work, it would be far better if you could have divided the document into three cards. The division has to be prepared in some way in the original document, and you have to insert attributes on the elements that can be used to section the file into cards.

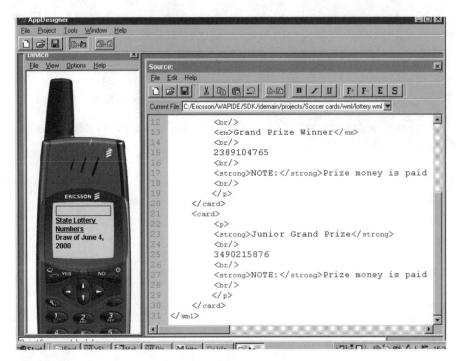

Figure 8.2 The lottery page simply converted to WML means that you have to scroll through the page.

In practice, these requirements mean that you have to be aware of the output format into which the document will be transformed when you design the canonical format.

User interaction is where the object analysis is involved. Look at the objects and think about how the user would interact with them. Here, the interaction method would be browsing, and the user interaction would be to flip between the cards. According to the WML specification, we are supposed to put one user interaction on each card. The document in the preceding example could be transformed into either one or two WML cards (one winning number on each). Or, you might need three cards if you want to put the legal stuff at the end.

In any case, you must have something for the transformation sheet to transform into WML cards—either something akin to the <DIV> elements in an HTML file or attributes on the elements. Whichever one you choose, the transformation sheet has to contain hooks for them and elements to insert. But I think that you understand how to insert elements now.

This chapter shows that to create multiple presentations from the same source file, you have to work directly with the objects the file consists of; otherwise, you will have to insert one set of formatting hints for each new presentation you want to create. Working directly with the XML file where the information is marked up as objects and generating the content by using XSLT enables you to create both WML and HTML.

Formatting Advice

There are a few pieces of non-technical advice that you might find useful when creating documents.

First, *focus on your audience.* Knowing audience specifics is critical to determining whether a particular style is an appropriate choice—especially if you are going to filter out some content.

Then, *determine the project's scope.* How many documents comprise the site? If it is only 10, style sheets can certainly be a helpful option. What if it is 100, 1,000, or 10,000 or more? External style sheets are the single most powerful way to update, change, and add style to all linked documents instantaneously. A single style sheet controlling many documents is the best example I have found of style living up to its promise. Using a master style sheet for the site enables us to make certain changes instantaneously to thousands of documents.

Third, *select the markup.* Depending upon what your site content covers, you might choose to use style, forgo it altogether, or use it combined with transitional HTML 4.0 or XHTML 1.0 elements to accomplish your goals. In some cases, you might be using CSS to apply presentation rules to XML documents. Transitional HTML 4.0 and XHTML 1.0 documents are natural and easy mates with CSS. With XHTML and other XML applications, you might wish to use CSS or examine other style sheet options, such as XSL/XSLT.

Finally, *pinpoint your presentation needs.* Before you dive headlong into working with style sheets, assess the extent of presentation styles that are necessary to accomplish your design. If it is a matter of using CSS to manage type versus the positioning of objects on a page, you will likely find that the typographic style options are better supported for wide audiences and therefore are a rational choice in many instances. If, however, your goal is to use style for positioning, you must revisit step 1 in order to ensure that your audience will be able to support it adequately.

Special Characters

The current definition of what a character is and what characters are allowed in an XML (XML, XSLT, XHTML, and so on) document can be found in a W3C document that defines the character model for XML languages. Specifically, the characters come from the Universal Character Set defined by ISO/IEC 10646. It is a 16-bit character code standard that is intended to provide character codes for, in principle, all of the world's written languages.

Unicode is a character repertoire, not a font encoding. If your keyboard is Latin1 or Latin2 or Japanese shift-jis, you can type that character data straight into an XML file as long as the XML declaration specifies the right encoding. As long as the characters in the encoding you use are in the Unicode tables somewhere, it will be all right. (Although, a given XML system is not forced to understand any encoding other than UTF-8 and UTF-16.) You do not need to add anything to the DTD in order to use Unicode.

A character repertoire is the set of named "things" by which I choose to name the characters I talk about—that is, a semantic interpretation that will differ across the world's languages. Each nation has its own character repertoire; for example: A, alpha, and the Cyrillic A are three different Unicode characters but normally have the same glyph or visual appearance. Actually, Unicode is more than just the character repertoire; it is an encoded character set (in other words, it assigns numbers), but it is not a character encoding in the sense of Latin-1 or Windows-ANSI.

Unicode is expressly (some would say religiously) not about glyph forms. So, two things that are different but look the same, such as A and the Greek capital alpha, have different slots, but things that look different but mean the same (like any number of fancy ampersand characters) all have the same slot.

Context-sensitive reading of character data is what Unicode was built to avoid. A Russian user hits an A on his or her keyboard, and whatever local encoding he uses, if Unicode is used, it arrives on your machine with that character unambiguously marked as a Cyrillic letter. Whether or not your system can show you that is another matter.

Note that if I receive an XML file with Latin2-encoded data, I cannot look at that file with a normal command-line tool—but any XML system will read it in and then the internal parsed tree displaying it will not have any indication of the original encoding. (For this reason, files tend to go in as XSL in Latin1 and come out UTF-8.)

There is a Unicode editor that is still beta testing (4/00), but it looks complete. It has a full character map; hence, you can paste those oddities that you cannot pronounce, never mind recognize. You can convert to XML entity references in hex or decimal, as well.

ASCII was originally defined as a 7-bit code, which used the extra bit in each byte for error control. Therefore, there were $2^7 = 128$ different codes available. This situation was fine for the English-speaking world (and I am sure that other languages had a local equivalent of ASCII). To accommodate other languages that had a relatively short alphabet, a kludge was made via the different forms of encoding. This kludge was that any byte that began with a zero was deemed U.S. ASCII, but if the first bit was a one, then the document should signal what all characters in the range 128–255 meant by declaring an ISO encoding.

To avoid this messiness, Unicode was developed. This code was, in its most basic form, meant to be a form of encoding by giving two bytes to each character; therefore, it could potentially support 65,536 different letters.

Because U.S. ASCII was the most common encoding used in the world, it was given the same character numbers of 0 to 127, so letters in the English alphabet are encoded as 00000000 0xxxxxxx. The problem with this system, however, was finding a means of keeping backward compatibility. If I open a text file encoded in Unicode in Notepad on Windows 95, I see h e l l o w o r l d. Even worse, Unix systems use 00000000 as a special character to indicate the end of strings of characters.

Thus, another kludge was devised to accommodate the problem whereby a variable number of bytes could be used to store a character. If a byte begins with a 0, it is taken to be a single byte referring to a single character in the original U.S. ASCII character set of 0 to 127. The two remaining problems needing to be sorted are how to signal to the computer the number of bytes used to encode a character and how to show where a character starts (remember that now there is no correspondence between bytes and characters).

To solve the first problem, it was decided that the number of leading ones indicated how many bytes were used to encode the character; thus, 110 indicates that two bytes are used, 1110 means three bytes, 11110 means four bytes, and so on.

To solve the second problem, it was decided that the first two bits in any byte that were part of the encoding of a single character should be 10. This system gives the following patterns:

```
One byte      0xxxxxxx          7 bits available for encoding
2 bytes       110xxxxx 10xxxxxx  11 bits available for encoding
3 bytes       1110xxxx 10xxxxxx 10xxxxxx 16 bits available for
encoding
```

This system is what UTF-8 is. The only problem with its adoption is that it means that most western languages need two bytes to encode letters, whereas they can get by with using one with other encodings, and Asian languages need three but by using straight Unicode (or other local encodings), they could get away with two.

This situation is transparent to XML/XSLT processing, which works in terms of characters (which are not the same as bytes). (The first lesson of i18n: do not assume one character equals one byte anymore.) It affects XSL as follows, however. If you want to change 1 into a letter, you can do it with translate( ) as long as the letter you want to translate is a single Unicode character. If the accented letter does not exist as a preformed Unicode character and is encoded in Unicode as a base letter followed by a combining accent, then you cannot use translate( ) and must use the slower named template approach to search and replace substrings.

The Unicode standard parallels ISO/IEC 10646, and its character charts for the U-00000000 through U-0000FFFD range are available at the Unicode site.

In order to select any non-ASCII (greater than decimal 127) character, find the Unicode number corresponding to the character required.

For example, the character left-angle bracket (<) has the code #3c, and the character for the Japanese Yen sign (¥) has code #a5.

Remember that some characters are special to XML; hence, if you do not want your document content to be interpreted as markup, then you must treat the following characters in the same way as foreign characters:

```
The Ampersand sign: &
The Left angle bracket sign: <
```

Enter the character into your XML source or XSL style sheet (for literals). This input can either be as an entity within either of the DTD's parts (internal or external) or as a character entity reference (decimal or hexadecimal) in context.

Example 1: Within the XML DTD

```
<!DOCTYPE document  SYSTEM "document.dtd" [
<!ENTITY nbsp " ">
]>
```

Now, I can use this coding within my XML document by referring to it through the entity:

```
<para>Item:    And its content </para>
```

Note that the # indicates that the value is decimal. With the addition of an x after the hash symbol, it would be interpreted as hexadecimal. At the URI given, all of the character numbers are in hexadecimal; hence, we will need the hash sign and x.

Example 2: Within the XSLT stylesheet

```
<!DOCTYPE xsl:stylesheet [
<!ENTITY nbsp " ">
]>
```

Example 3: In context

```
<xsl:text>   </xsl:text>
```

If the character you want will not display on the browsers you are targeting, it might be necessary to use an image. Remember to add an alt text to describe the image. With style sheets, you have a very high degree of control over the presentation, however, so you probably do not have to resort to presenting text as images. To do so just shows that you have not read up enough.

The problem might occur, however, if you have to display text in languages such as Urdu, and with the wide variety of old browsers out there, it is the only practical approach. On the other hand, if you are only displaying the stuff in locations where you have control over the client configuration, you can do much better.

If you are a Japanese supplier publishing Japanese language information to Japanese consumers, then you can be reasonably sure that your target audience will have installed a browser that can handle Japanese text. You might get a problem if you are using the shift-JIS formatting, however, because there are different versions of shift-JIS. All of the mobile operators in Japan have agreed to support XHTML in the future, and because XHTML is an XML version, the problem will disappear.

Most modern systems in western Europe and North America (with the exception of the Macintosh) tend to use the ISO 8859/1 character set. This situation is not the case for the remainder of the world, though. The best solution is for the sending system to package the file as XML and to specify what its encoding is. For exactitude, Windows boxes use Windows ANSI, which is more or less the same character set as Latin-1 but in a different order. You can reset the character set both for display and on the keyboard in Windows.

Do not be tempted to use keyboard characters for other than the basic character set. They might display well on your system, but there is no guarantee that by the time it has reached someone else's browser it will be readable. On Windows, for example, do not use the ALT-0123 method of getting the character you want unless you let the XML parser know what encoding you are going to use and the parser understands that encoding.

In XML, if you specify

```
<?xml version="1.0" encoding="iso-8859-1"?>
```

then you are saying that the file uses the character encoding Latin-1. Therefore, the parser (if it understands that encoding) will translate all incoming characters to Unicode character data. So, it is just as safe to use Latin1 as ASCII or UTF-8. Every XML file unambiguously declares what encoding it uses. XSLT, when it gets the input tree (and the parsed style sheet) from the XML parser, does not see what was in the original file; instead, it just sees the Unicode e-acute character whether it was entered in Latin-1 or in the Windows code page, or { or é, respectively.

If you want to use this method, just make sure that your XML document begins with

```
<?xml version="1.0" encoding="8859-1"?>
```

Otherwise, XSLT will assume that you have a UTF-8 document and will blow up on the accented characters.

If the Unicode combining character is used, however, and the input file has e' (where ' is really the combining acute character), then while any Unicode-aware renderer is supposed to make this character into an e acute for rendering, to an XML engine it is two characters, e and acute. (See the later section concerning multi-byte characters.)

The important thing is not how you enter the character, but rather matching the encoding of the file that you enter it into with your entry method. This situation depends on the version of Windows that you are using and probably on the text editor, as well. Simple text files in Windows, in western Europe, and in North America are typically in ISO 8859-1 code (Microsoft calls it ANSI code, but Microsoft is wrong), regardless of the keyboard you use. If you use a Macintosh, it is probably MacRoman, which no one else understands. If in doubt, stick to ASCII characters and use character entity references for anything else.

Within an XML file, specify the encoding that you want when declaring the file to be XML by using the encoding attribute

```
<?xml version="1.0" encoding="utf-8" ?>
```

This coding states that the document character set is UTF-8.

UTF-8 is essentially a way of compressing Unicode so that on average, it takes up much less than 16 bits per character. It also has the property that characters in the ASCII set are given their ASCII code value, so a file that consists predominantly of ASCII characters is easily readable and can often be processed by software that is designed to handle ASCII. But accented letters do not look the same in UTF-8 and ISO 8859-1, so software designed for ISO 8859-1 (such as Windows Notepad) will not correctly display a UTF-8 file containing such characters. Conversely, characters that are entered from a system using 8859-1 will not be handled correctly within an XML world, which uses UTF-8.

If you want the XSLT transformation sheet to produce XML, you should use the XML xsl:output encoding

```
<xsl:output type="text" encoding="utf-8"/>
```

The encoding attribute specifies the preferred character encoding that the XSLT processor should use to encode sequences of characters as sequences of bytes. Note the use of the word *preferred*. It is not a requirement to do any such conversion. utf-8 is a good choice if you are unsure.

The default XML encoding is UTF-8, and in UTF-8, position 160 is encoded as two bytes. If you look at the file on a terminal using Latin1 or ISO 8859-1, then you see the two bytes as two random characters, but a utf-8 terminal or a browser that understands utf-8 (which is most of the current versions of the main browsers) should do the right thing and show it as a non-breaking space. If you output , you are outputting the single Unicode character 160 (even if it is two bytes in utf-8).

If you output , then you are outputting the six characters 'ampersand' n b s p ;.

Note that you cannot use character references (in other words, the & syntax) in XML names (elements or attributes), so if you want your XML to have French element names, you have to use character data, not {. Hence, <element{> is neither well-formed nor valid XML.

In UTF-8, ASCII characters get one byte. The next 1,664 Unicode characters (including the whole Latin-1 set) get two bytes, and all others get three. Most texts in languages that use the extended Latin, Greek, Cyrillic, Hebrew, Armenian, and Arabic alphabets require at most two bytes; the other scripts (mostly from Asia) require three.

These should be treated the same as the Latin-1 characters. You either use a character set like UTF-8 that can handle them, or you enter them as character references such as Ξ Ξ.

The idea here is that there are two ways to write characters such as é (e with an acute accent). You can use either a single precomposed character, the same way that Latin-1 does it, or you can use a base character, which is a plain e followed by the character COMBINING ACUTE ACCENT (́).

The base and combining characters are two separate characters for processing purposes but are combined into a single glyph when displayed.

The Web standard is to use the precomposed form when possible. If you want "f with an acute accent," however, you will find that there is no such precomposed character in Unicode, so you need a plain "f" followed by ́.

Netscape 4.0 has a bug: it will not understand references to XML entities unless the character set is set to UTF-8.

Note that XML (including XSLT) and HTML 4.0 have exactly the same rules about these things. The only differences are that most HTML browsers do not support the hexadecimal form Ξ, so you must write Ξ instead, and that HTML defines a bunch of names for useful characters (whereas XML makes you define them yourself or else import them from Latin 1 Specials Symbols).

Here is a canned recipe for importing them all, to be placed at the top of an XSLT script:

```
<!DOCTYPE xsl:stylesheet SYSTEM [
  <!ENTITY xhtml-lat1 SYSTEM
     "http://www.w3.org/TR/xhtml1/DTD/xhtml-lat1.ent">
  <!ENTITY xhtml-special SYSTEM
     "http://www.w3.org/TR/xhtml1/DTD/xhtml-special.ent">
  <!ENTITY xhtml-symbol SYSTEM
     "http://www.w3.org/TR/xhtml1/DTD/xhtml-symbol.ent">
  &xhtml-lat1;
  &xhtml-special;
  &xhtml-symbol;
  ]>
```

Not all XSLT implementations are guaranteed to process these external parameter entities (depending on the underlying XML parser that is used in the XSLT software), in which case uses such as é will generate low-level parser errors.

Index